"At a time where so much of the world is ... Madigan provides a vision and guide for a ... Australia's broken 'business as usual' for how we deliver housing. An essential read for architects, planners, and developers alike, and anyone who thinks 'housing' could do better in supporting a future where we all thrive."

Brugh O'Brien, *Principal: Future of Home, The Australian Centre for Social Innovation*

"This book is both a grand vision for a future of housing and practical guide for how to achieve it. There are maps of global potential for transforming single family neighborhoods alongside ideas for how to manage suburban infill essentials such as laundry and garbage. It is an invaluable combination of speculative pragmatism and prosaic invention with tangible relevance for the suburbs of the US and Canada – a key reference for researchers and practitioners alike."

Michael Piper, *University of Toronto*

"More affordable, more diverse, and more delightful housing? Seems like everybody is after it and we need it more than ever, but the inertia of established systems discourages change. This book takes a suite of practical and highly effective design ideas and runs them through a rigorous process addressing financial opportunities, regulations, and community attitudes; showing how to move towards 'win–win' scenarios that deliver more dwellings and retain the character of the cities and suburbs we love. A timely and valuable contribution to the housing debate."

Nigel Bertram, *Professor of Architecture, Monash University, and Director, NMBW Architecture Studio*

"*Bluefield Housing* reminds us that our suburbs are not immutable, but ever-changing and malleable. It shows us why they can – and should be – altered and added to. This is design research at its best – useful, transferable, propositional – advocating a compelling alternative to planning metrics. Madigan's incisive work ranges from acute observation and analysis to lucid propositions showing the latent capacity of suburban form to accommodate more – more trees, open space, connections, diversity, people: more good stuff."

Jennie Officer, *Senior Lecturer, School of Design, University of Western Australia, and Director, Officer Woods Architects*

"In the face of dynamic global demographics we urgently need imaginative, land-efficient, habitat-protective, cost-effective housing solutions. Madigan's concept of 'Bluefield Housing' is an exciting proposition and, in truth, common sense."

Naomi Cleaver, *Designer, Author, and TV Presenter*

Bluefield Housing as Alternative Infill for the Suburbs

Suburbanised cities share a common dilemma: how to transition to more densely populated and socially connected urban systems while retaining low-rise character, avoiding gentrification, and opening neighbourhoods to more diverse housing choices. *Bluefield Housing* offers a new land definition and co-located infill model addressing these concerns, through describing and deploying the types of ad-hoc modifications that have been undertaken in the suburbs for decades. Extending green-, brown-, and greyfield definitions, it provides a necessary middle ground between the 'do nothing' attitude of suburban preservation and the 'do everything' approach of knock-down-rebuild regeneration.

An adjunct to 'missing middle' and subdivision densification models, with a focus on co-locating homes on small lots, *Bluefield Housing* presents a unified design approach to suburban infill: retrofitting original houses, retaining and enhancing landscape and urban tree canopies, and delivering additional homes as low-rise additions and backyard homes suited to the increasingly complex make-up of our households.

Extensively illustrated by the author with engaging architectural design studies, Damian Madigan describes how existing quirks of suburban housing can prompt new forms of infill, explains why a new suburban densification model is not only necessary but can be made desirable for varied stakeholders, and charts a path towards the types of statutory and market triggers required to make bluefield housing achievable. Using Australian housing as an example but addressing universal concerns around neighbourhood character, demographic needs, housing diversity, dwelling flexibility, and landscape amenity, *Bluefield Housing* offers innovative suburban infill ideas for policy makers, planners, architects, researchers and students of housing and design studies, and for those with a stake in the future of the suburbs.

Damian Madigan is a registered architect and Senior Lecturer in Architecture at the University of South Australia. A Fellow of the Australian Institute of Architects and a member of the South Australian State Government's Design Review Panel, he undertakes housing research through design, working collaboratively with academics, industry, and government to create suburban infill housing typologies that better suit changing demographics. As an individual and collaborator, his housing propositions have won design competition awards, shortlistings, and commendations from the City of Los Angeles, the New South Wales State Government, the City of Sydney, Architecture Australia, and the Guangzhou International Award for Urban Innovation.

Bluefield Housing as Alternative Infill for the Suburbs

Damian Madigan

Illustrated by Damian Madigan

NEW YORK AND LONDON

Designed cover image: Damian Madigan

First published 2024
by Routledge
605 Third Avenue, New York, NY 10158

and by Routledge
4 Park Square, Milton Park, Abingdon, Oxon, OX14 4RN

Routledge is an imprint of the Taylor & Francis Group, an informa business

© 2024 Damian Madigan

The right of Damian Madigan to be identified as author of this work has been asserted in accordance with sections 77 and 78 of the Copyright, Designs and Patents Act 1988.

The Open Access version of this book, available at www.taylorfrancis.com, has been made available under a Creative Commons Attribution-Non Commercial-No Derivatives (CC-BY-NC-ND) 4.0 license.

Trademark notice: Product or corporate names may be trademarks or registered trademarks, and are used only for identification and explanation without intent to infringe.

Library of Congress Cataloging-in-Publication Data
Names: Madigan, Damian, author.
Title: Bluefield housing as alternative infill for the suburbs / Damian Madigan.
Description: Abingdon, Oxon : Routledge, 2024. | Includes bibliographical references and index.
Identifiers: LCCN 2023024385 (print) | LCCN 2023024386 (ebook) | ISBN 9781032276908 (hardback) | ISBN 9781032276915 (paperback) | ISBN 9781003293736 (ebook)
Subjects: LCSH: City planning. | Suburbs. | Housing development. | Infill housing.
Classification: LCC NA9053.S82 M33 2024 (print) | LCC NA9053.S82 (ebook) | DDC 307.1/216–dc23/eng/20230804
LC record available at https://lccn.loc.gov/2023024385
LC ebook record available at https://lccn.loc.gov/2023024386

ISBN: 9781032276908 (hbk)
ISBN: 9781032276915 (pbk)
ISBN: 9781003293736 (ebk)

DOI: 10.4324/9781003293736

Typeset in Helvetica Neue
by Newgen Publishing UK

Printed and bound in Great Britain by
TJ Books Limited, Padstow, Cornwall

For Deborah, Daisy, and Maggie, whose kindness and patience make everything possible, and whose love and humour make it so much fun.

Contents

Acknowledgements	*xi*
How to use this book	*xiii*
Introducing Bluefield Housing	1

Part 1

1	Being 'suburban'	17
2	An appetite for new forms of suburban living	29
3	On character and 'fitting in'	42
4	Suburban anomalies and operations: catalogues of infill opportunities	60

Part 2

5	From green to blue: a new definition for suburban infill	81
6	The seven principles of bluefield housing	91
7	Lot-level design tactics	104
8	Design for liveability and sustainability	117

Part 3

9	From top-down to bottom-up: a deployable model	133
10	Single allotments	146
11	Double allotments	170
12	Multiple allotments	197

Part 4

13	A new normal: leveraging established conditions	211
14	Carrots and sticks: incentivising bluefield housing	217
15	Financing, operating, and selling bluefield housing	228
16	Zoning laws: enabling bluefield housing	245

Part 5

17	The value of the diagram and studies in rooms	255
18	Backgrounding design studies: a 'designerly' way of seeing	269
19	Generative design studies for bluefield housing	286
20	Housing for whom? Lessons from the Town Hall floor	300
	Index	*310*

Acknowledgements

Bluefield Housing began life as a deceptively simple research question at the core of my 'Alternative Infill' PhD studies at the School of Art Design and Architecture at Monash University in Melbourne: could stipulated 'no go' low-rise character neighbourhoods support medium-density infill while delivering some of the much-needed housing diversity that many of these older neighbourhoods lacked? This challenge was a case of swimming against the political tide at first, and still is in some jurisdictions, but through the course of the PhD and expanded design research projects since, what I now call the 'bluefield housing' approach has become much more mainstream. Many people have helped along the way.

At Monash University I am deeply grateful to Professor Shane Murray and Professor Nigel Bertram, my supervisors, and to Professor Diego Ramírez-Lovering and Associate Professor Ari Seligmann. Together they helped shape my practice in design research. At Monash I met Dr Alysia Bennett, who I've been fortunate to collaborate with ever since. Beyond her consistently wise counsel and support, I thank Alysia for her astute framing of a development scorecard in our LA Low-Rise Design Challenge entry, which is presented in Chapter 14.

Susan Davies from Sharing With Friends kindly allowed me to summarise and share SwF's Resident Agreement in Chapter 15. Thanks also to Andrew Mitchell at Planning and Land Use Services in the South Australian State Government for his support of the model, and for his advice and leadership around the bluefield zoning principles described in Chapter 16.

Over the years of this work, I have been continually supported by senior management and colleagues at the University of South Australia and humbled by the efforts of our architecture students who tested my early thinking in design studios so enthusiastically and imaginatively. I am so proud of the students you were and of the next generation of leaders you have become. Thank you to Dr Julie Collins at the UniSA Architecture Museum, who kindly reviewed the manuscript and offered encouragement and feedback.

Acknowledgements

I have been privileged over recent years to bring the bluefield model out of research and into practice through partnering with state and local governments in South Australia. To a person, everyone involved has shown a passion for bringing about positive change for their suburbs, while working with genuine compassion for the concerns of existing residents and the aspirations of new residents. I am grateful to the following groups for their support, deep knowledge, and proactivity: South Australian State Planning Commission; SA Planning and Land Use Services team; SA Office of the Registrar-General; Office for Design and Architecture SA; the City of Unley; the City of Burnside; Town of Walkerville; the City of Prospect; and the City of Campbelltown.

At Routledge, my thanks to Senior Editor Kate Schell for supporting the idea of this book and taking it forward, and to Editorial Assistants Megha Patel and Hannah Studd for their wonderful support during the writing, illustration, and pre-production processes. Thanks also to Kelly Winter, Project Manager at Newgen Publishing UK, for her fantastic work during the production stages of the book.

Beyond this, my love and appreciation go to my ever supportive and loving parents, Colleen and Haydn Madigan, and to my siblings and their families.

And as always, as with everything, my love, awe, and thanks go to my family: Deborah, Daisy, and Maggie. Without your love, support, patience, and generosity, there would be no work of which to write.

How to use this book

There is a deliberate and necessary simplicity to aspects of the work presented here. Given the complex social, racial, gendered, historical, and political backgrounds of much of suburbia, coupled with the geographic, climatic, and physical variances of housing and its environments, attempting to create a one-size-fits-all neighbourhood housing model is impossible and of little utility. Instead, this book offers an insight into some of the general issues in play in westernised suburbia. It uses design thinking to suggest ways that neighbourhoods seen as immune from change might allow new housing in, whilst increasing the diversity of existing housing choices. When much of the housing debate centres around the choice between apartments or single-family homes, Bluefield Housing offers a middle ground between the two, and a new approach to backyard infill. To work, it requires the reader to adapt the thinking to local contexts and politics.

The bluefield housing model was initially developed for Adelaide in South Australia, a nineteenth century planned colonial city with an abundance of character masonry cottages that have been adapted and extended over their lives. While these houses are common across many cities and towns in Australia, of course other housing forms exist. And while they *may* resemble some older housing in other countries, they are not presented here as being broadly representative. As such, it is necessary to engage with the work understanding that its core principles require tailoring to local conditions. For many readers the book's overarching methods of thinking about older neighbourhood housing, their lots, and their adaptation will be more ubiquitous and deployable than the actual housing types and designs themselves.

The model works well where the established housing displays common traits that enable them to be read as a repeated housing system. Where a neighbourhood has developed in a less-structured manner, one can nonetheless look for commonalities. These may not be found in the organisation of the floor plans or a repetition of styles but are most likely to be seen in other aspects of suburbia such as consistent setbacks, side clearances, building heights, and access points. To enable translation across different neighbourhoods, the design examples in this book are presented somewhat generically where possible. With tailoring, the reader can take the concepts and apply them to local conditions, adapting the tools as necessary. It may be that only one or two design tactics can be deployed in a certain neighbourhood, but these may be the key manoeuvres that generate additional dwellings and help fill a neighbourhood's evolving needs. Along with local housing types and lot sizes, topography will have to be factored into the reader's own explorations, particularly where lots slope from front-to-back or back-to-front and from one lot to another, where multi-lot designs will be particularly affected.

Given the heavy emphasis on design thinking and design demonstration in this book, it is important to address the aesthetics of the housing presented. The reader will see a common design language employed, most notably in rectilinear plan forms and steeply pitched gabled roofs. The underlying logic is simple: rectangles are spatially efficient on the lot and in the house itself, while gabled roofs enable varied internal spaces and options for additional accommodation or storage. These building forms also deliberately and simplistically respond to a common visual language of many westernised suburbs, helping to shift debate away from the look and feel of the new housing insertions and towards conversations around the general housing intensification strategy. However, this is not to say that there is not room within the system for the designer's nuance and much more idiosyncratic housing designs. Likewise, there is room for a builder's response in the absence of a recognised design process. What is important is for the reader to be able to distinguish between bluefield housing as an organising strategy and bluefield housing as individual built outcomes. The designs presented in this book are therefore just one architect's way of demonstrating the bluefield potential.

Density measures defined

The way density is defined varies across geographic locations and individual developments. In its simplest forms, there are two different types of density:

1. **Gross density**: where all spatial aspects required to make a new residential development are included in the land calculation, including non-residential elements such as parks, facilities, and streets.
2. **Net density**: where only the size of the individual residential allotment is used as the area calculation (in some cities this is called 'lot density').

In this book, dwelling densities are stated as net rather than gross, as this provides an easier mechanism by which to understand the housing numbers being provided, and a more exact understanding of how much space is allocated to a dwelling on average. Dwelling densities are calculated by simply dividing the total area of the lot by the number of dwellings accommodated, providing an average site allocation per dwelling. One hectare (10,000m^2 or ~107,640 sq ft) and one acre (43,560 sq ft or ~4,050m^2) are each divided by this average site area figure to determine the number of dwellings created per hectare or acre for the design example shown. These figures are described as dw/ha and dw/acre in the designs.

Achieving medium density is the primary goal of the bluefield housing model and this is defined for this book as anything between 34 and 67 dw/ha (14 to 27 dw/acre). However, as is described in the liveability studies of Part 2 and design studies of Part 3, when housing is seen as flexible and adaptable, dwelling numbers can be dialled up or down without necessarily adding or taking away building elements, demonstrating that density figures can be abstract concepts affected by use, not building numbers. The key to understanding the desirability or otherwise of medium density housing for the occupants and for the greater neighbourhood is therefore a nuanced reading of the underlying design logic and outcomes being presented for consideration. This requires thinking around the density of *people* per given area. This is a far more elusive measure of housing intensification, as a large house may have only one resident, while a small house may have many. In the design studies of this book, floor plans are furnished to enable the reader to study how many people might be accommodated in each scheme.

Existing similar models

Many readers will see a resemblance in the work to existing densification models that have already passed into law in their jurisdictions and offer higher densities and housing numbers than those shown in this book. Examples include 4-for-2 yields by allowing secondary suites to be added to duplexes and 3-for-1 intensifications via additions of a secondary suite plus a laneway house. In 2023, the Canadian city of Victoria in British Columbia passed its Missing Middle Bylaw Amendments to allow 6- or even 12-for-1 developments through the addition of multi-dwelling buildings in established single-family home neighbourhoods.[1]

The bluefield model is something of an amalgam of existing forms; part ADU, part secondary suite, and part backyard home. But it differentiates itself by incorporating adaptive reuse, establishing a flat hierarchy of homes, flexing up and down in dwelling numbers where possible, and emphasising living independence coupled with shared landscape. Importantly it is not a metrically driven model based on lot size, relying instead on a design-led approach to suitability within the neighbourhood. A key component is that existing housing is reworked and integrated into the development in a whole-of-site housing proposition where landscape is an inherent part of the development proposal and where local character is harnessed.

How to use this book

In coalescing existing infill models, bluefield housing champions low-rise density increases for neighbourhoods where it is oftentimes resisted.

	land division	unit	ADU	junior ADU	second suite	Bluefield Housing
design-led rather than metrics-led	✗	✗	✗	✗	✗	✓
no minimum lot size requirement	✗	✗	O	O	O	✓
no subdivision; retained lot size	✗	✗	✓	✓	✓	✓
holistic all-of-site design	✗	✓	✗	?	✗	✓
suburban garden setting	?	✗	✓	✓	✓	✓
landscape retention	✗	✗	?	?	✓	✓
landscape mandate	O	O	O	O	O	✓
character retention focus	✗	✗	O	O	✓	✓
adaptive reuse focus	✗	✗	✗	?	✓	✓
flat housing hierarchy	?	?	✗	✗	✗	✓
strategic sharing; social emphasis	✗	?	?	?	?	✓
reinstate to single home	✗	✗	✓	✓	✓	✓
sell or rent individual homes	✓	✓	O	O	O	✓

O jurisdiction-dependent   ? developer-dependent

0.1
A bluefield housing ready reckoner.

Ultimately, Bluefield Housing encourages the reader to use its arguments and strategies to explore and then demonstrate how an established neighbourhood can accommodate appropriate change with only minor tweaks to the underlying system. Some may use the model to lobby for densification where it is currently resisted, while others may use it as a means of minimising the impact of larger scale intensification. As such, bluefield housing is neither a so-called YIMBY (yes-in-my-backyard) nor NIMBY (no-in-my-backyard) model. Rather, it is a way of recognising that housing is elastic and can be changed, and that the suburbs can help accommodate new densities and housing forms with low impact, but high effect.

Note

1   "Missing Middle Housing Initiative," City of Victoria, last modified 3 February 2023, https://engage.victoria.ca/missing-middle-housing/.

Introducing Bluefield Housing

What's *really* stopping us?

As apartments, manor houses, accessory dwelling units, laneway housing, and secondary suites continue to play their part in increasing suburban housing supply, they do so entwined in the debate around neighbourhood fit. Meanwhile, many low-rise neighbourhoods remain exempt from densification increases on the assumption that the detached single-family home should remain the prevailing form. Such neighbourhoods may allow minor infill if it can work within the format of the detached home, or better yet, if it can be done without being noticed at all, but meaningful change in housing supply will remain limited. Within this mix of housing action and inaction, bluefield housing is offered as a supplement to existing medium density 'missing middle' strategies, which are discussed in Chapter 1 (Figure 0.2). Where missing middle housing may struggle to find traction in some older neighbourhoods, bluefield housing emphasises the retention and retrofitting of existing suburban housing and landscape because – in the first instance – this retention just makes sense. In simple terms, the bluefield housing model is a natural re-purposing of the established methods of altering and adding to the single-family house form, but for the supply of additional dwellings.

Bluefield housing is therefore not concerned with densification-by-stealth or in trying to masquerade additional housing in a palatable single-family house form, but in a demonstration of existing neighbourhood capacity. This difference is

DOI: 10.4324/9781003293736-1
This chapter has been made available under a CC-BY-NC-ND license.

subtle, but significant, and exists in a simple design intelligence: rather than configuring new multiple housing in a form that looks and feels compatible with the single detached house, bluefield housing instead simply turns to that existing neighbourhood built form and illustrates the types of additional housing it can already support. It works out from the existing housing rather than into it, with a natural neighbourhood fit being a by-product of the process rather than its starting point.

As such, where infill arguments consistently speak of how to make new forms 'fit' with the old, the bluefield perspective shifts this densification discussion away from *how* an established neighbourhood can support new housing, to identifying that *it already can*. The housing numbers achieved will not match those of higher density apartment buildings, but it can see a doubling or tripling of housing on lots that may otherwise be excluded from density increases. This requires a nuanced local understanding and identification of existing neighbourhood conditions, which in turn speaks to the very concerns of neighbourhood preservationists. And while this can be seen and potentially used as a weaponising of localised NIMBYist (not-in-my-backyard) sentiments against density increases, the bluefield model is simpler and less political than that. In re-presenting the neighbourhood to residents and policy makers, the bluefield approach asks a densification question for which a preservationist argument might be difficult to sustain: "if we can work within the prevailing pattern of the neighbourhood to create additional housing, what's *really* stopping us?".

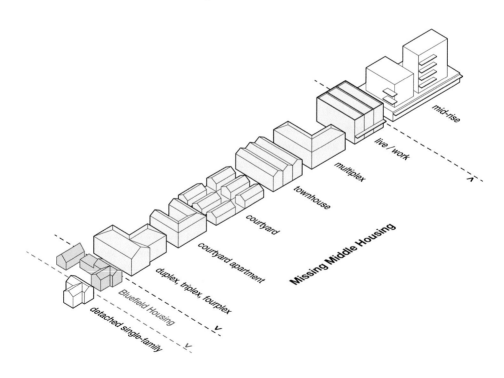

0.2
Bluefield housing as it sits on a housing spectrum, somewhere between a single-family home and a unit development (after Opticos Design's Missing Middle diagram).

Alternative infill for the suburbs

'Alternative' can be perceived as a negative term; a substitute for 'odd', 'fringe', or simply 'different'. But to offer an alternative is to simply offer choice – something new and innovative that takes the best parts of what we already have and makes them better. To offer an alternative is to also not replace: after all, an alternative offering relies on the presence of an original for its own existence. It is with this understanding that this book offers the bluefield housing model within the established single-family housing system, rather than in place of it. At its core, bluefield housing is a co-location infill model that mimics the prevailing pattern of housing development in a neighbourhood. This mimicry is not a tool for hiding additional housing, but one for leveraging the enormous capacity of many suburban allotments to support more than a single house.

Co-located housing is defined here as the strategic addition of one or more dwellings to an existing house on a single allotment where the site is not subdivided, the houses are not fenced off from each other, and the major outdoor space is shared to provide a degree of community amongst its residents. Where possible, the housing is arranged around existing mature landscape and where it is not, the houses are located such that deep root soil zones can be achieved for the planting of medium to large trees. In a co-location development, dwellings are usually self-contained, however, facilities such as laundries and clothes drying areas may be shared to free space from within and around each dwelling. Higher degrees of sharing can also be achieved by providing the type of 'common house' seen in traditional cohousing developments. A common house usually provides a kitchen, dining, and living space large enough for the residents to use together when desired. A common laundry, bathroom, and guest bedroom can also be incorporated. Where a common house is provided, individual dwellings may remain fully self-contained or be reduced to private bedrooms and bathrooms. The provision and location of facilities such as off-street car parking and rubbish bin storage may be segregated or shared and are provided in relation to the development's needs, and the local neighbourhood context.[1]

Using a design-led approach, the bluefield co-location method looks to the existing context of streetscape, landscape, house sizes, building forms, and site coverages to determine the capacity for a lot to support additional houses, even if the prevailing minimum lot size of the zone dictates otherwise. In short, for a lot that cannot be legally subdivided due to its size or zoning rules, the bluefield model allows the chance for it to be considered for additional housing through carefully designed co-location with the existing house on the property. This requires that the proponent demonstrates liveability, amenity, and neighbourhood fit. A bluefield redevelopment can be achieved by successfully retaining the existing house, re-configuring it to provide small footprint living, and co-locating one or more new dwellings in any combination of:

- a division of the existing house in to separate dwellings under the one roof;
- an extension to the existing dwelling; or
- as a detached backyard home.

Smaller lots might only accommodate one of the three strategies, while larger lots will be able to use all three in combination. These conditions are demonstrated in the design studies of Part 3. The appropriate neighbourhood fit is determined by the prevailing scale and site coverage patterns, and by the ability for the designer to demonstrate internal and external amenity coupled with functionality.

A single shared yard space, designed and integrated with the housing, binds the individual dwellings into a coherent whole. Whilst sharing the yard space is necessary for all bluefield developments, sharing facilities such as laundries or additional living spaces is at the discretion of residents and resolved at the point of approvals and permits being issued.

Providing certain qualitative measures can be achieved and adhered to, such as the retention of mature landscape or the creation of new deep root soil zones, there is no limitation on what size a lot can be to qualify for a bluefield redevelopment. Likewise, there is no limitation on the size or configuration of an individual bluefield house, although in the effort to design at a sensitive low-rise scale that maximises landscape amenity, a bluefield house will inevitably be compact. Sited as they are in established suburbs where real estate values are likely to be strong, bluefield housing may not ever be 'affordable' by definition, nor be provided as below-market rent, unless created and managed by a not-for-profit housing provider.[2] However, being sized as a mid-point between a stand-alone house and an Accessory Dwelling Unit (ADU), they will add a more affordable offering to the mix than a full single-family home, potentially creating gateway houses for people wanting to live in a particular neighbourhood, and inward mobility options for residents who already do.

Because bluefield housing is about tweaking the existing alterations and additions development models of the single-family home, it has the potential to introduce smaller and more affordable housing options in the absence of a speculative market housing developer. Homeowners can develop the model with a 'light touch' level of assistance from domestic construction companies, while larger developments could be undertaken by community housing providers, housing associations, or small scale ethical or socially responsible developers. The model offers the potential to sit in a suburban development 'sweet spot' between two- to four-bedroom profit-driven market housing at one end of the spectrum, and private ADU development undertaken by homeowners at the other, enabling small-scale residential builders to undertake the work within their existing skillsets and capacity.

A successful bluefield housing development will ultimately distinguish itself not by being demonstrably bigger than its neighbours, nor by hiding itself away behind a 'main' house, but by demonstrating that socially-connected homes can sit comfortably on a single allotment alongside single-family housing as a positive contribution to the evolving neighbourhood.

What this points to is the potential for a hybrid model that sits between single-family zoning on one end of the development spectrum, and intense densification at the other. Offered as a logical extension of the business-as-usual alterations and additions development model of the suburbs, it is a replacement of neither model, but their adjunct. Thought of in this way, this Bluefield Housing book is a conversation starter.

Both / And

This is a book that invites discussion. It sits within the ongoing debate of how to marshal our suburbs through change, with homes that are a necessary social fit for our changing household structures, and a complementary physical fit within changing suburban landscapes. It presents a way of thinking about infill housing that is not a replacement of the existing models nor of single-family homes, but an add-on to them.

It has become increasingly clear in recent years that the suburbs will have to play their part in supporting an increase in housing supply, affordability, and choice. No longer can suburbia be left in its twentieth century spread-out form while new housing finds its place solely on cities' fringes or within dense urban centres. But that is not to say that low scale single family homes, old or new, are to be vilified as something that needs wholesale replacement or stopping. They have served cities well for generations and in many circumstances will continue to do so. For a lot of people, they remain the perfect fit. However, as much as the suburbs are often guarded against wholesale change, they nevertheless find themselves being encroached upon from outside, as city centres spread, and from within, as opportunities are taken to demolish detached homes and replace them with apartments, townhouses, and semi-detached triplexes and duplexes. This can naturally change the established character of a place, leading to anxieties around whether new housing forms should be allowed to integrate with the old, and if so, how.

Discussions around these tensions invariably result when wholesale change is being considered. In its simplest terms, physical neighbourhood change is seeing one house after another being replaced by two or more less-recognised housing forms. Varied suburban foundations are being lost in the transaction: from familiar-looking houses, streetscape, scale, trees, setbacks, sunlight, and cultural memory to on-street car parking spaces. Change is evidenced in the pragmatic as much as it is in the ontological. There is a delicate balance to be struck when attempting to deliver necessary new housing in an area that has been working well for decades. Of course, the issue of intensifying housing in and around suburbia is much more complex than this. Suburbs can be replete with social, political, economic, and racial issues that run deep, while new housing forms can be offered with an intelligence around social, equitable, financial, spatial, material, and environmental issues that we did not possess in such abundance when many suburbs were first formed. Adjudications of whether change is appropriate will most often be made on a site-by-site or neighbourhood-by-neighbourhood basis.

This book does not pretend to solve the NIMBY and YIMBY (yes-in-my-backyard) tensions of the densification debate. Rather, it opens the opportunity for a YIMBY discussion to be had in places where neighbourhood change is opposed, by acknowledging that suburbs exist on a continuum of constant change and have done so since their inception, and that blanket NIMBYism is therefore founded on a flawed 'do nothing' principle. Suburban change is seen in its most widespread form as individual customisation, where owners have tailored and extended the single-family home to their own tastes and needs, particularly when taking over an existing home as new owners. Now, as demographic pressures mount, this change through personalisation is being joined by change through densification, and the suburbs will continue to see change over coming decades as housing numbers increase to meet needs. Meanwhile, individual homes will continue to be customised, and a variety of suburban intensification strategies is needed that can operate within that evolutionary behaviour.

ADUs are one established means of introducing increased housing numbers into the existing suburban mix. These small backyard homes are accepted as infill because of their ability to occupy excess backyard space inoffensively and without affecting the physical or functional operation of the existing home. They are a sensible and usually sensitive means of increasing density but there is a limit to how broadly they are accepted in some jurisdictions – even those with a long history of earlier coach houses and mews houses. The successful passage of ADUs into legislation is often accompanied by restrictions on their size, the relationship of the occupant to the owner of the 'main' house, and their ability (or not) to be rented out in the general market. However, the larger debate around new suburban housing invariably relates to the physical and social effects on the suburbs of knock-down-rebuild (KDR) development: the removal of something old and its replacement with something new and potentially foreign. Unlike the ADU, in the KDR development model it is an 'either / or' decision of retaining the existing single-family home or introducing some new residential form.

'Bluefield housing', as a land definition and an accompanying housing model, offers instead a 'both / and' approach. It looks to how existing housing can be retained, adapted, and extended to increase residential densities and housing choices: it is both the retention of what people value of the suburbs *and* the addition of new housing that operates within the established mix. It retrofits a house to convert it to multiple dwellings and although this is nothing new, it generally only currently occurs through anomalies in the statutory system,[3] or where a one-off proposal is able to achieve approval in the absence of any wholesale zoning that actively encourages such a model *en masse*. Bluefield housing takes its cues from what people are already doing with their homes. It is a process of recognising the existing patterns of alterations and extensions to single-family homes and systematising this as a form of alternative suburban densification through the processes of retrofitting and co-location. It is not about building more to get more, but about reconfiguring the suburban pattern we already have.

Co-location, shared landscape, flat hierarchy

The bluefield model takes a whole-of-site approach that co-locates the new housing with the old without establishing a hierarchy between the housing units. Whereas ADUs are subordinate 'accessories' to a 'main' house – a naming convention which instantly renders them as something 'other' – a bluefield approach simply creates housing. Regardless of whether the new dwelling is created by adapting all or part of an existing house, made through an extension to it, or created as a detached backyard home, no single dwelling in a bluefield development is viewed as a 'main' or 'secondary' dwelling. The attraction to living in one bluefield house over any other on the same site should ultimately be determined by individual preference based on what the home offers and its configuration on the site, rather than through any sense of which of the offerings might be considered the 'main' house.

This flat hierarchy is achieved in the first instance by simply not subdividing the allotment. Rather than reading a site as an area calculation that can be divided into predetermined minimum allotments, the site is instead considered holistically from boundary to boundary. If one or more additional dwellings can be created, this is done in the first instance by a tailored design study, rather than via some predetermined metric calculation of amenable minimum lot size. Given that minimum lot size stipulations are no promise of achieving housing success, there is no logic in assuming that additional housing created below such thresholds are any guarantee of failure. The key is a carefully considered design solution that co-locates the housing around single high quality shared landscape rather than carving out smaller private open spaces.

Designing for the entire site, and in the absence of familiar zoning tools such as minimum allotment size, requires each bluefield proposal to be achieved through first principles. Using the design tactics outlined in Part 2 and demonstrated in Part 3, the onus will be on the proponent of a bluefield development to demonstrate the appropriateness of the proposal. On face value, this may seem untenable if the model is to achieve any penetration into the established processes of housing supply. However, as UCLA cityLAB's *Backyard Homes & Local Concerns* study found, resident attitudes to the acceptable size and nature of proposed backyard homes often relate directly to the idiosyncrasies of an individual allotment, its existing house, and its street configuration.[4] It is bluefield housing's specific allotment-level design strategy that enables the model to scale, as it theoretically allows the site of any single-family home to be considered for a bluefield intensification based on that site's characteristics, the underlying pattern of development in the neighbourhood, and the demonstrated fit of the design proposal.[5] While the model may not offer the speed of a fast-track checkbox approvals system, its ability to be applied on a vast suburban scale makes it agile and highly scalable.

Why 'bluefield': extending the 'colour' field nomenclature

'Bluefield housing' is a descriptor that strategically extends the three predominant suburban land and housing forms, each of which is described in more detail in Chapter 5:

1. **Greenfield housing**: where undeveloped land (most often on a city's fringes) is developed for housing for the first time, extending suburbia.
2. **Brownfield housing**: where redundant non-residential land is converted to residential use, often at a medium- to high-density scale.
3. **Greyfield housing**: where ageing housing stock is demolished and replaced with new medium-density housing on subdivided or consolidated allotments.[6]

By comparison, bluefield housing is none of these, as it specifically targets low-rise and low-density suburbs that infill zoning policy traditionally ignores. Operating through an alterations and additions model as opposed to traditional knock-down-rebuild, it is an adjunct to these three established models that responds to specific neighbourhood pressures that have emerged in recent years. These shifts have seen increased pressure on previously considered 'no go' suburbs to receive infill housing and, having established a new model as one means of achieving this, it becomes necessary for an additional definition that extends the 'colour-field' nomenclature.

Adding bluefield to the mix is not about demonising the existing green-, brown-, and greyfield models, nor lionising the bluefield model as some sort of suburban housing saviour. Rather, it is about recognising that established suburbs are no longer immune from change and there is both the need and room for a defined addition to the existing mix.

Why blue? Whilst other colours could be used, blue has been selected for its association with calmness, stability, and tradition – traits that can be attributed to many older suburban neighbourhoods – and for its ability to represent the perceived fixedness of established suburbs. The concept of 'tradition' here is politically unaligned, and its association with 'blue' should not be conflated with political leanings. In many parts of the world, including Australia, the UK, and Canada, blue is used in politics by conservative parties and can thereby be linked to notions of traditional political or social values. In the US these political colours are inverted, with red associated with conservatism and blue with liberalism. The blue in 'bluefield' does not, therefore, relate to politics. However, the colour can be used to evoke notions of 'blue chip' suburbs, where high financial and emotional values are often in play. This is particularly the case in neighbourhoods that have seen strong increases in property values over prolonged periods, have traditionally resisted systematic change, and are particularly susceptible to gentrification and exclusion. This recognition is important, given how many suburbs are experiencing gentrification through exclusionary policies that deny new housing forms in traditionally single-family neighbourhoods.

Establishing a new label will inevitably draw comparisons with existing terms or use of the bluefield naming convention. In the data management and software fields, 'bluefield' relates to data conversion practices that are a hybrid of new 'greenfield' installations and technologies and 'brownfield' data conversion activities. Bluefield is therefore not a new term. It also already exists as a place name in several locations. 'Bluefield housing' as described in this book as a new land definition and associated infill housing model, should therefore not be confused with any housing associations from places sharing the same name, such as those in the US and Nicaragua. Similarly, 'bluefield' in the context of this work should not be confused with 'blue spaces', a term used to describe urban places adjacent to or incorporating water,[7] or with 'blue zones', which describes places associated with human longevity.

A housing model for older people?

'Bluefield' also deserves clarifying in relation to older people. As many societies age, they do so with increasing numbers of their older people living outside of institutionalised or organised aged care systems, which were never designed for the sizes of ageing cohorts we currently see. Australia is currently experiencing a phenomenon where the number of older people receiving government-provided home care packages is increasing. These are financial support services to assist older residents living at home, ranging in scale from home cleaning and showering assistance, up to higher needs support that includes nursing and allied medical assistance within the home. At the same time, and despite the country having an ageing population, the number of people living in aged care facilities remains stable, suggesting that an increasing number of older people are either avoiding or delaying a move from independent living to supported accommodation.[8]

While the bluefield housing model lends itself well to downsizing and ageing-in-place, it has not been established as a model explicitly for these purposes. The blue in 'bluefield' is not a reference to older people, and this merits emphasising. 'Blue rinse' or 'blue hair' is a stereotype of older people (often pejorative) via a reference to the hair colouring system sometimes used to mask the yellowing of grey hair. In the UK and Australia, 'blue rinse brigade' has traditionally been used as a label for cohorts of older people, particularly in relation to perceived conservative political affiliations. Bluefield housing has not been developed as housing specifically for older people and its name should not be conflated with any stereotyped use of the colour.

However, given the bluefield housing model is one aimed at providing smaller footprint homes in the suburbs, it is an obvious fit for downsizers and older people who wish to age well in their community. This was demonstrated in the Cohousing for Ageing Well design research project which tested the model across four single allotments of varying sizes, as presented in Chapter 10.[9] In that project, as in this book, the people being helped to 'age well' or simply live well in the suburbs are not defined by their age, but by their ambitions. They are those who wish to age-in-place in familiar surroundings and with increased confidence and wellbeing. They are those who wish to live independently for as long as they can and to do so in connection with others. These others might be relatives, friends, or new connections who are coming together with a shared set of goals for the type of smaller-footprint suburban housing to which they would like to transition.

On sharing

This raises the concept of sharing one's living arrangements with others. This can be challenging for people of any age, particularly where someone does not have a cultural background where community or multigenerational living is common. 'Co-location' is the term used in this book to describe the sharing model of bluefield housing. It is specific enough to suggest that some degree of sharing among residents is required, but loose enough for the extent of that sharing to be flexible. As such, the degree of sharing in each bluefield project will be determined by those creating each housing scheme.

Two factors are key here. The first is that the co-location model put forward in the bluefield system is for those who wish to take advantage of a shared-site model in a suburban setting, meaning they are predisposed to wanting to share with others to some degree. The second is that many people are not only happy to share, but to do so with others who are not necessarily the same as themselves. When Bridge et al surveyed lower income older Australian residents, asking them to comment on their attitudes to sharing, only 27% felt that it was important to share with those of similar religious, gender, or other characteristics.[10] In order to inform the design work for the Cohousing for Ageing Well project, a co-design workshop was undertaken with residents who had previously never considered a co-location model. Participants stated that a good social mix of residents would be key to successfully transitioning from a single-family home to a co-location model, but that did not automatically mean having to share with people who were like themselves. Some people liked the idea of sharing with others who would be different to themselves, with a co-location model potentially providing the opportunity to broaden their established connections and experiences. Some of the participants would only consider sharing with immediate or extended family while others stated that they would never want to share with family. Depending on the individual and their lived experiences, the idea of sharing facilities such as a washing machine or a washing line could be anything from a non-issue to a deal-breaker.[11]

In simple terms, then, there is no one-size-fits all approach to a co-location model and to the degrees of sharing across the development. This is true of the extent of facilities to be shared, and to the make-up of the occupants doing the sharing. This is not a new understanding, having been well tested and communicated by the cohousing movement since the 1970s. What is important is that the sharing profile of each bluefield scheme is established at its outset and that residents are given agency over determining the guidelines and rules for how the housing development will operate. These decisions need to be clearly understood, communicated, and protected by a well organised 'committee of residents', with rights and obligations enshrined in a 'residents' agreement', which is discussed in Chapter 15.

A unified design approach

Bluefield housing is about infill for the traditionally homogenous, gentrified suburbs, but the methods can be deployed elsewhere. Its intention is to respond to local and nuanced prevailing suburban conditions and at the same time act as an armature for infill housing that can be deployed elsewhere. It is what Dana Cuff and Roger Sherman might label a 'radical increment': a solution to a design problem that can spread in search of systemic change.[12]

This relies on a unified design approach, whereby demographics, design, suburban understanding, policy, and communication work holistically. Organised in five parts, this book positions the role of design and design communication at the head of a research process, describing existing suburban conditions alongside the potential reconfigured conditions achieved by the new bluefield model. This is to complement traditional modes of housing strategy leadership, which is often undertaken through metric data-driven approaches to housing needs.

Part 1 explores the types of suburban traits that can be common across jurisdictions, while acknowledging that neighbourhoods within suburbs and suburbs within cities display idiosyncratic nuances. Using Australia as an example, it discusses the concept of housing character as both an architectural and behavioural concept, and the types of physical and demographic changes that can occur in neighbourhood housing over time. It explores the search for amenable and effective low-rise infill solutions across various housing forms, highlighting the fact that although the morphology and scale of cities varies, local concerns and ambitions are oftentimes shared.

Part 2 introduces and describes 'bluefield housing' as both a land definition and as an infill housing model. Responding to Part 1, wherein the prevailing suburban conditions are discussed, it explains why the suburbs need an extension of the existing greenfield, brownfield, and greyfield land definitions. It then outlines the seven key principles of a corresponding bluefield housing model, concluding with site and building design tactics that can help to couple increased suburban density and diversity with dwelling and landscape amenity.

Part 3 provides illustrated design examples of the bluefield housing model. These are presented as anonymised allotments applicable across cities and thereby deployable as a general framework. The model is discussed as a lot-scale bottom-up approach to infill, offering a counterpoint to traditional top-down city-wide densification strategies. Demonstrated across single, double, and multiple allotments, the case studies illustrate approaches to increasing housing supply and diversity whilst addressing issues of adaptive reuse, neighbourhood character, streetscape amenity, and community-building.

Part 4 outlines the types of considerations necessary to systematise bluefield housing, describing the issues to be resolved in transitioning it into the established business-as-usual residential construction market. It discusses the model as a natural extension to the established housing market, the benefits of strategic staging of development over time, the incentivising of uptake, and the zoning, financing, and land titling considerations necessary for bluefield housing to be mainstreamed.

Part 5 is primarily for architecture and urban planning practitioners, researchers, and students. With a particular focus on diagramming and drawing, it offers six design research exercises as a way of exploring the underlying structures of housing and the suburbs more deeply. Read in conjunction with the case studies of Part 3, it provides a means by which to see the morphology of a suburban block and its potential for infill with new eyes. Scenario planning is discussed as an essential tool to use in concert with graphic presentation, to shift housing innovation from the abstract to the relatable. The book closes with lessons learnt from presenting the bluefield model to lay, industry, and government audiences over the course of several years, offering advice on how (and how not) to engage audiences with new housing ideas.

Notes

1   This definition of co-located housing was first written for the Future Living Code Amendment to the South Australian State Planning and Design Code, as discussed in Chapter 16.
2   Housing affordability is a relative term and is defined in different ways. A common measure for affordable housing is one where housing costs, including running costs, constitute no more than 30% of the household's before-tax income.
3   The Library Cottages project in Healdsburg, California, is a notable example of a non-conforming 3-for-1 intensification of an existing property: an original house plus two ADUs. Retention and renovation of the project was allowed without a zoning change only due to the established non-conforming status: Daniel Parolek and Arthur C Nelson, *Missing Middle Housing: Thinking Big and Building Small to Respond to Today's Housing Crisis*. Washington, District of Columbia: Island Press, 2020, 185–191.
4   Vinit Mukhija, Dana Cuff, and Kimberly Serrano, *Backyard Homes & Local Concerns: How Can These Concerns Be Better Addressed?* Los Angeles: cityLAB – UCLA Department of Architecture + Urban Design, 2014, 82.
5   'Fit' is used here in its broadest terms. Depending on the application, this may refer to any combination of social, morphological, or affordability fit.

Introducing Bluefield Housing

6 'Greyfields' is often used to describe a predominance of asphalt and in relation to vacant or under-performing shopping malls. 'Greyfield housing' is referenced here as a discrete use of the term in relation to suburban housing regeneration, as explained in Chapter 5.

7 BlueHealth is a pan-European research group studying the links between blue spaces, climate, and health: https://bluehealth2020.eu/

8 Australian Government Productivity Commission, *Report on Government Services 2022*, Australian Government (Canberra, 2022), www.pc.gov.au/research/ongoing/report-on-government-services/2022.

9 Damian Madigan, *Cohousing for Ageing Well: Design Report*, University of South Australia (Adelaide, 2020).

10 Catherine Bridge et al., *Age-specific Housing and Care for Low to Moderate Income Older People*, AHURI Final Report No. 174, Australian Housing and Urban Research Institute Limited (Melbourne, 2011), 44, www.ahuri.edu.au/research/final-reports/174.

11 Madigan, *Cohousing for Ageing Well: Design Report*, 12.

12 Dana Cuff and Roger Sherman, *Fast-forward Urbanism: Rethinking Architecture's Engagement with the City*. New York: Princeton Architectural Press, 2011, 25.

Part 1

1   Being 'suburban'

A necessary generalism

In many suburban circumstances, the politics of race, wealth, and equity will continue to loom large, particularly in neighbourhoods that were established for the white middle-class. Even in cities that are outwardly diverse, that diversity can be clumped into non-diverse suburban groupings where everything from average income to life expectancy lessens across neighbourhoods.[1] In other places, the suburban divide is physical, with public infrastructure creating barriers too big for a pedestrian to cross, essentially locking people into their own neighbourhoods while excluding them from others.[2] Where many middle-class suburbs were created to escape the grit and proximity of the city and to separate work from home life, working-class suburbs often had forms of industry embedded, with residents drawn to these neighbourhoods for employment rather than lifestyle. Some scholars have argued that the working-class have therefore never truly been suburbanites, although as suburbs have aged, such distinctions have not always been maintained, with some neighbourhoods presenting a range of class and racial diversity. Similarly, physical idiosyncrasies are evident across the layout of suburban housing, with some working-class suburbs showing irregular setbacks, indicating a degree of informal development. This is in opposition to master-planned middle-class suburbs with predetermined setbacks that have arranged the housing in predictable rows.[3]

A design-led response to suburban infill housing such as the bluefield model cannot, then, expect to address deep suburban politics that underlie and

DOI: 10.4324/9781003293736-3

This chapter has been made available under a CC-BY-NC-ND license.

continue to affect the social and physical structure of a suburb; it can only operate on a morphological level of physical neighbourhood fit while attempting to offer smaller and more affordable housing options. In some suburbs it may help to address inequity; in others it may actually drive gentrification by increasing the value of what would otherwise have been a cheaper single-family home. Ultimately, its aim is to merely provide an additional suburban infill housing model that can add to the existing low-rise mix in what can be a difficult to define 'suburbia' which is often incorrectly stereotyped as homogenous.[4]

As such, the bluefield housing model is necessarily a generalism; it will range from being directly deployable in some suburban circumstances to being irrelevant in others. Adopters will inevitably need to tailor it to the local physical, political, social, and financial conditions of their own neighbourhoods.

A hit with the public

Leveraging the pattern of suburban change, bluefield housing relies on rather than critiques suburbia. Writing of the American suburbs at the end of the twentieth century, Peter Lang argued against the mistreatment suburbia had traditionally received at the hands of critics. For Lang, such criticism could be likened to that of a popular film that was "panned by the critics, but a hit with the public".[5] The success of the suburbs could be evidenced in the volume of people who continue to rush to them, and in the passion with which the suburbs have continually been protected from change. More than 20 years on, preservation tensions continue to play out, as urbanists arguing against single-family zoning face off against protectionists wishing to maintain the suburban status quo. Ultimately, attempting to understand and influence a denser future for the suburbs requires acknowledging what has made them so attractive to so many for so long.

The earliest suburbs in many post-Industrial Revolution cities were the first escapes away from the grime, intensity, and stress of town to a cleaner, more spacious, and calmer way of life. Early suburbs were where residents could achieve the 'best of town and country': living in a garden setting while making the short commute into town for work. There remains of course an irony in this logic, as the suburbs replace the countryside with the very towns from which suburbanites retreat.[6] However, this underpinning 'town and country' logic survives today when the spaciousness of a new suburban development is advertised adjacent to its proximity to major centres. Where being just a penny-fare tram ride away from town was an initial incentive to suburbanise, particularly for the working-class, minutes-by-car is the contemporary measure; the early rationale of the suburbs as convenient oases remains the same today.

For the generations of people who have been able to afford and access them, the suburbs have for the most part continued to provide the benefits held in the initial promise, creating a dedicated space for a home life quarantined from work.

And when space has been one of the most enduring and successful features of suburbia, new, unfamiliar, and denser forms of development are easy to see as threats. To simply say that the suburbs no longer work is to ignore the fact that in many respects the suburbs are doing just fine. Put simply, many suburbs continue to work very well for the vast populations they already house.

Suburban DNA: houses as building blocks

At the heart of suburbia is the ability to personalise the home through both decoration and construction. For renters, this can be that elusive capacity to tailor one's home when that property is owned by someone else. When permission is required from a homeowner to hang a picture hook, there is little agency for a renter to shape their home for themselves. For many others, however, most obviously owner-occupiers, a house presents a stage on which personalisation can play out. This is true even of volume housing, where builders offer the opportunity for their clients to tweak standard designs at little to no extra cost.

Building can be seen as a social act, the process of which is rooted in the subtleties of local culture and is fluid over time. It is also seen as a systematic process led variously by the access (or lack thereof) to finance, materials, labour, and land. There are complex relationships that exist not only at the physical level of building production, where construction techniques and procurement methods operate together to affect settlement patterns, but also in socio-cultural terms. In the latter, large variances can occur in the manner with which settlements are established, ranging from a building's patron being one person gathering and arranging material to create a building, to a collection of invested people including owners, architects, builders, developers, financiers, and statutory authorities. These relationships also vary with scale, as development grows from the single building towards villages, towns, and cities, each with their own sub-groupings. When viewed over time, the culture of building as an activity can be seen as reflective of the social and political culture that has informed and enabled it.[7]

When it comes to the building of housing and the suburbs they collectively form, oftentimes those responsible for its creation are not those who end up living in it. Much of many cities' housing is developed speculatively by small scale developers, lived in for several years by an initial owner, and then purchased by new and subsequent households. Whether rented out or owner-occupied, the majority of suburban housing is privately owned by the middle-class, who have a financial interest in maintaining the suburban status quo whilst realising ever-increasing property values.[8] Inasmuch as houses are homes in which to live, in many countries they are the seats of individual wealth. Dominated by private ownership, the suburbs are the spaces of wealth-accumulation and the single biggest means of banking for individual futures. When housing is seen as a personal investment in the first instance and a home in the second, this creates a dilemma for those facing a lifetime or near-lifetime of rent, as house prices rise faster than wages. The COVID-19 pandemic has added to housing investment and heightened affordability pressures for renters and homeowners alike, created by a desire for larger work-from-home spaces, an accumulation of savings during lockdown, and historically low interest rates from governments attempting to take the pressure off household finances.[9] With existing issues of class, race, gender, age, and affordability already putting many in crisis, the pandemic has added an unwlecome layer of pressure to our housing.[10]

Yet the suburbs continue to change over, fuelled by a DIY capacity that provides an avenue for individual expression, and supported by the spacious suburban conditions of single houses set on individual lots. These personalisations range from simple lifestyle adjuncts to large renovations and additions that render the original house unrecognisable.[11] In addition, a 'flipping' culture, brought into heightened awareness by a seemingly endless supply of reality television shows, has mainstreamed the image of the suburban house as a malleable and nimble profit-making device where 'before and after' comparisons are made relative to finances as much as they are to inward liveability and outward neighbourhood contribution.

Landscape: the collateral damage of knock-down-rebuild

Inasmuch as suburban change can be seen in a gradual accretion of construction activity that builds up around the single house, it is also witnessed in more stark contrast by knock-down-rebuild, or KDR redevelopment. The effects are most obvious in the cases of so-called 'minor infill': sites where the demolition of an existing house yields ten or less additional dwellings, but most commonly only one or two.[12] Yet, the negative effects of KDR can also be felt when an older single house is demolished and replaced with only a single but usually larger replacement dwelling. Beyond the more obvious considerations of a loss of (or shift in) built neighbourhood character, is the impact of KDR at a site level, where the values of newness and lifestyle often trump all other considerations. The push to new patterns of living is often so strong that it can outweigh any perceived benefits of the retention of open landscape. This can be seen in the move of contemporary dwelling away from small cottages and starter homes on large lots towards larger houses on smaller lots and with less yard space. In the desire to demolish the suburban home for contemporary needs, mature trees and space for soft ground cover are regularly the collateral damage.

Inasmuch as KDR development has a negative effect on the landscape character of an older suburb, eroding the leafiness that is so desirable in many suburban settings, there are significant micro-climatic effects that loss of backyard habitat presents. This is particularly evident when backyards are read not as smaller single entities sitting adjacent to each other, but as large, connected landscapes and ecosystems across allotments.[13] As mature landscape is lost from incremental single-lot KDR development across a neighbourhood, it has a cumulative effect of breaking established tree corridors, with the corollary consequence of an increase in roof space and hard ground surfaces contributing to higher heat loads and greater water run-off. As houses grow, the ability for yards to mitigate heat build-up and return rainfall to the water table is significantly diminished. And it is not the case that mature landscape lost from private land can simply be offset by local authorities planting more trees elsewhere, as they often lack the budget, resources, and public land needed to keep up with the pace of loss. Even if some form of break-even tree canopy planting could be achieved across public space inside the suburbs, it would not work to resolve the loss of landscape character and cooling effects at the scale of the suburban street.

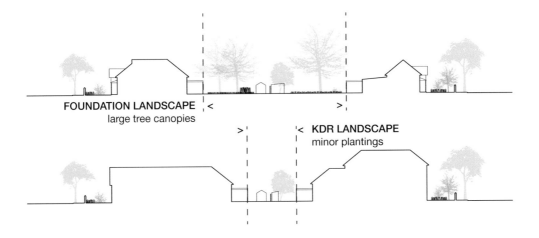

1.1
Over time, single allotments in the suburbs have enabled large areas of soft ground and tree cover to work together as landscape and wildlife corridors, minimising heat build-up from roofs and hard ground surfaces, and maintaining healthy water tables. Incremental KDR development disrupts this.

Contextualising suburban change

Within this setting of neighbourhood change and loss of landscape, suburbanised cities face a well-understood, broad, and pressing social dilemma: populations are increasing, communities are ageing, housing construction rates are lagging, and at the same time household structures are changing, with a move towards smaller households of more complex variety. This can be seen in a comparison between the average household sizes today with those at the start of the 1960s, 15 years after the end of World War II when the oldest of the Baby Boomers were in their early- to mid-teens. Households today are around 24% smaller in Australia, New Zealand, and the UK than they were in 1960–1961. In the US and Canada, the figure is around 30%. But the real change is seen in the proportion of one-person households, which over the same time have more than doubled in Australia and New Zealand, and increased by 2.5 times in the UK, the US, and Canada.

This raises the question of where and how these increasing cohorts of the community are to be housed. These rates of demographic change are so great and so suggestive of continuing trends, that they underline the fact that the suburbs

Household Size 1960-61 vs today
(the average number of people per dwelling)
data sources: national population censuses

One-person Households 1960-61 vs today
(as a percentage of all households)
data sources: national population censuses

1.2 and 1.3
Since the start of the 1960s, the average number of people per dwelling has declined in Australia and New Zealand, the UK, and in the US and Canada, while the number of people living alone has more than doubled.

cannot be excluded from forming part of a city's strategy for housing supply and choice. Despite long-term trends in household sizes shrinking, new suburban houses are largely still being supplied in a family model of multiple bedrooms, bathrooms, and living spaces. Significantly, these repeated housing models are creating entire suburbs lacking in housing choice, and this is not a new phenomenon.[14] Across both new and established suburbs, internal mobility can be limited, with residents having few options to downsize or upsize their housing whilst remaining in the suburb of their choosing.

Similarly, a homogeneity of housing types provides limited choice for both existing and potential new residents of a suburb while creating unaffordable price points that become largely consistent across a suburb. Those outside a particular suburb can struggle to purchase into the area while existing residents can face prohibitive change-over costs when looking to move to something nearby that better suits their current and future needs, assuming that a choice of housing model is available in the first instance. In Australia, this phenomenon can be seen in the increasingly common redevelopment model whereby a single house is sold for land value only and replaced with two duplexes. At completion, each of the two new dwellings is often more valuable than the original house they have replaced, while offering equivalent accommodation despite occupying only half of the lot. The process yields one additional house for the neighbourhood, but no additional affordability or choice, while significantly diminishing the landscape and contributing to urban heat island (UHI) effects. This is further discussed in the context of 'greyfield' suburbs in Chapter 5.

What is clear is that in many westernised suburban cities, suburbs are changing while demographics evolve and housing pressures mount. An increase in population growth despite falling fertility rates is resulting in ageing populations, with the cohorts of the population aged over 65 and 80 each growing significantly since 1960.

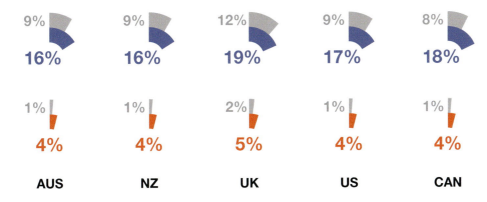

1.4
Populations are getting older, with marked increases in the proportion of people aged 65+ and 80+ since 1960.

The result is a rise in smaller households, with a general decrease in the proportion of couples with children, but increases in couples without children, one parent families and those living alone. Put simply, more houses are needed to accommodate the same number of people as in the past and these houses need to be of a far greater variety. Significantly, the need for more housing that suits smaller households can be seen in highly populated cities as much as it can in smaller cities, as any city facing a shortage of housing numbers and choice can only increase its supply off its own base load of existing housing stock. The dilemma is relative and any city facing a necessary percentage increase in housing stock must not only find the space for these new homes, but the capacity within industry to deliver them in well-serviced locations. In a best-case scenario, all suburbs and neighbourhoods would be considered for their potential to contribute to the shift.

As such, it simply makes sense for us to consider how our suburban houses and suburbs might adapt over time to meet increasing social and environmental demands: more houses of a far greater variety and interconnected in a socially and environmentally sustainable manner.

The search for amenable low-rise densification models

Apartment buildings deliver a quick injection of housing supply. At their best, they bring together a mix of residents who can take advantage of generous communal spaces and facilities coupled with well-considered private interiors that offer good levels of function, amenity, light, and ventilation. At their worst, apartments are mean developments driven by maximum unit yield. In these circumstances they can operate as unwelcoming places, with limited or undesirable shared facilities and poorly designed dwelling layouts compromised by the need to access too many dwellings off a single corridor. This often results in complex circulation systems leading to apartments with limited exposure to the building's facade. Furthermore, in the absence of an overriding affordability or diversity driver for the project, apartment developers in some jurisdictions can choose to pay a fee in lieu of providing a mandated percentage of units as affordable housing. In these circumstances, the fee becomes a simple cost of development, recouped by the profits made from selling the entire development at market rates. But both good and bad apartments share a common challenge: how to deliver the minimum number of dwellings to ensure financial and social viability, while finding a comfortable urban fit as the new entrant to the neighbourhood.

The morphological price to pay for the housing efficiency of apartment buildings is height and mass, particularly where the site cannot accommodate significant setbacks from the street and neighbours. Podium bases allow the first few levels of an apartment building to occupy the maximum possible footprint before the main tower of apartments steps back to reduce bulk. This manoeuvre plays a role in helping to diminish overall visual impact while reducing overshadowing of neighbours, but it can only do so much to help a large building appear smaller. In low scale neighbourhoods where allotment size presents a challenge, the amount of step-back that can be achieved in a tower is lessened, meaning many mid-sized neighbourhood apartment buildings rise straight up in the shape of the allotment and with minimum setbacks from the boundaries.

The tensions between medium- and high-density apartments and low-rise neighbours plays out across cities, where a common challenge is found around how to both increase housing densities and retain building compatibility with the low scale of the suburbs. The most identifiable approach to bridging the gap is Daniel Parolek's 'Missing Middle' phraseology,[15] which describes housing on a spectrum from mid-rise apartment buildings at one end, to the single-family home at the other. The clarity and accessibility of missing middle thinking, as diagrammed in the Introduction, allows density opportunities to be explored in a manner that feels familiar, as densities can be dialled up and down relative to the prevailing neighbourhood character and the housing model being deployed.

The influence of the Missing Middle model, both directly and indirectly, is evident across several international design competitions with a shared rhetoric around urban and suburban fit. In Australia, the 2017 New South Wales Government's Missing Middle Open Ideas Design Competition sought design propositions that tested the state's Draft Medium Density Housing Code.[16] Schemes were called for across the three missing middle low-rise housing categories earmarked for complying development pathways: 2-for-1 dual occupancies (or duplexes), 3-for-1 terrace housing, and 4-for-1 manor houses. The overarching narrative of the competition was to work within a desirable low-rise medium density form defined as two or more dwellings with a combined height of no more than 10m (32'8"), and a resulting net density of 25 to 45 dw/ha (10 to 18 dw/acre). Together, these metrics forced schemes to deal with common suburban housing issues across the greater Sydney metropolitan area: the provision of a range of smaller housing choices, density gains within a contextually fitting suburban scale, and reduced site coverages that forced entrants to design the connections between landscape and home.

In its 2019 Alternative Housing Ideas Challenge,[17] the City of Sydney would explore similar issues of contextual fit for inner-suburban housing, but with an increased focus on affordability and housing access. Winning schemes were funded to explore how existing zoning frameworks in Sydney could be reshaped to open new housing opportunities.

Brisbane's 2017 Density and Diversity Done Well Competition[18] proposed a refreshingly simple challenge for entrants: to explore missing middle typologies while 'being a good neighbour'. Neighbourliness here meant providing opportunities for both privacy and for coming together as a community. A competition across an expanded territory of an entire suburban block of 20 lots, entrants had the choice to demolish, re-use, or otherwise integrate the existing housing. Working to achieve housing outcomes at a medium scale not generally seen across Queensland, entrants were to address suburban, sustainability, and community needs whilst having the flexibility to determine their own building setbacks, open space provisions, and car parking requirements.

In Canada, the 2019 Edmonton Missing Middle Infill Design Competition[19] was endorsed by the community of Spring Avenue, whose description of their neighbourhood formed the introduction to the competition brief. Written as a letter to potential entrants, the community described their neighbourhood as a mix of smaller homes with community-minded street presences, significant street trees and open space, community and retail offerings that support a well-functioning suburb, and a general sense of suburban living that can be heard in the sounds of gardening, home maintenance, and daily domestic life. Competition entrants were invited to create a winning medium-density design that would be welcomed by residents into this mix, providing it could demonstrate housing innovation that complemented rather than competed with the prevailing pattern of the neighbourhood. Importantly, schemes that supported greater diversity of cultural, economic, age, and ability backgrounds were particularly welcomed.

The Edmonton competition continued investigations that began in a 2016 Infill Design Competition, which looked for low-density infill on an imagined site. This 2019 version scaled the model for the provision of a medium-density development across five adjacent lots owned by the City of Edmonton, with the winning team being given the option to purchase the site, demolish the four existing post-war single-family homes, and construct their competition proposal. Repeating the narrative of other competitions, entrants were required to provide housing schemes that achieved medium-density multi-unit housing that addressed the established neighbourhood context, design innovation, financial viability, constructability, liveability across various household structures, age-friendly design, access for different abilities, and environmental, social, and financial sustainability.

In the UK, where housing affordability and quality issues can be particularly acute, especially in London, the cross-government Home of 2030 competition launched in 2020 to seek better health and wellbeing outcomes.[20] Whist not specifically a competition for the suburbs, entrants were asked to address familiar themes: age friendly and inclusive living, low environmental impact, healthy living, and deliverability and scalability. Density targets and housing aspirations also sat in familiar territory: medium-density housing of between 30 to 70 dw/ha (12 to 28 dw/acre) that encouraged social interaction, strong connections to outdoor space, dwelling flexibility, and accessibility for varied demographics.

In 2021 the LA Low-Rise Design Challenge,[21] organised by the Los Angeles Mayor's Office, invited architects and landscape architects globally to propose low-rise multi-unit housing schemes that demonstrated sustainability and high levels of amenity in LA suburbs. It further had overlays requiring entrants to demonstrate new strategies for housing affordability and ownership in the city, along with design excellence, the mitigation of racial and environmental injustice, and models for suburban living post-COVID. Community-engagement listening sessions were used to guide the development of the competition, with recordings of these provided to entrants as briefing material. These sessions highlighted the criticality of the suburbs in supporting housing that is socially, environmentally, and financially sustainable. Entries were called across four suburban intensification strategies: 4-for-1 fourplexes on a single lot, 3-for-1 increases via rear yard subdivision, 4-for-1 adaptive reuse of an existing large home, and 10-for-2 designs for two amalgamated lots on a street corner.

Displaying degrees of housing requests, from open-ended ambitions to highly scripted contextual approaches, these global calls for housing innovation demonstrate a collective commitment across cities to the search for socially diverse housing models that can find their place within the existing spectrum of housing forms. Although differing in scales and in the nuances of their housing issues, cities and towns are seeking similar housing outcomes of increased densities at a low-rise scale that is responsive to local urban, suburban, and social conditions. The bluefield model has found its own measure of success here, with its principles of adaptive reuse, landscape retention, and smaller-footprint homes responding directly to these shared low-rise ambitions.[22] In doing so, the model responds to a growing appetite for more communal ways of living. Not a new concept, these social ambitions are described in Chapter 2.

Notes

1 Jan Nijman, "American Suburbs Radically Changed Over the Decades – and So Have Their Politics," The Conversation Media Group Ltd, last modified 29 October 2020, https://theconversation.com/american-suburbs-radically-changed-over-the-decades-and-so-have-their-politics-147731.

2 The United States' US$1.2T Bipartisan Infrastructure Law (Infrastructure Investment and Jobs Act) was passed in November 2021, containing US$1bn (down from an initial $20bn proposal) for its 'Reconnecting Communities' pilot program, established as the 'first step' in attempting to transform physically divisive 1950s and 1960s highways into connective and socially responsible infrastructure: The White House, *Building a Better America: A Guidebook to the Bipartisan Infrastructure Law* (Washington, District of Columbia: The White House, 2022).

3 Becky M Nicolaides and Andrew Wiese, "The Other Suburbanites: Class, Racial, and Ethnic Deiversity in Early Suburbia," in *The Suburb Reader*, ed. Becky M Nicolaides and Andrew Wiese, New York: Routledge, 2016.

4 Jan Nijman, ed., *The Life of North Amercian Suburbs*. Toronto: University of Toronto Press, 2020, 3.

5 Peter Lang, "The Occulted Suburb," in *Suburban Discipline*, ed. Peter Lang and Tam Miller, New York: Princeton Architectural Press, 1997, 5.

6 Elizabeth Warburton, *The Paddocks Beneath: A History of Burnside from the Beginning*. Burnside, South Australia: Corporation of the City of Burnside, 1981.

7 Howard Davis, *The Culture of Building*. New York: Oxford University Press, 2006.

8 Jenny Schuetz, *Fixer-Upper: How to Repair America's Broken Housing Systems*. Washington, DC: Brookings Institution Press, 2022.

9 Valentina Romei and Chris Giles, "Pandemic Fuels Broadest Global House Price Boom in Two Decades," *The Australian Financial Review* (Sydney), 2 August 2021, www.afr.com/property/residential/pandemic-fuels-broadest-global-house-price-boom-in-two-decades-20210802-p58f19.

10 Dallas Rogers and Emma R Power, "The Global Pandemic is Accelerating Housing Crises," *International Journal of Housing Policy* 21, no. 3 (2021): 315–320, https://doi.org/10.1080/19491247.2021.1957564.

11 Leon Van Schaik and Nigel Bertram, *Suburbia Reimagined: Ageing and Increasing Populations in the Low-Rise City*. New York: Routledge, 2019.

12 'Minor infill' is a common form of density increases in Australian suburbs. The numerical definition provided here is that used by the South Australian State Government in its scenario planning: South Australian Department of Planning Transport and Infrastructure, *Housing and Employment Land Supply Program*. Adelaide: Government of South Australia, 2012.

13 Tony Hall, *The Life and Death of the Australian Backyard*. Melbourne, Victoria: CSIRO Publishing, 2010.

14 Jane-Frances Kelly et al., *Tomorrow's Suburbs*. Melbourne: Grattan Institute, 2012.

15 Daniel Parolek and Arthur C Nelson, *Missing Middle Housing: Thinking Big and Building Small to Respond to Today's Housing Crisis*. Washington, DC: Island Press, 2020.

16 "New South Wales Missing Middle Design Competition," Government Architect New South Wales, accessed 25 February 2022, www.governmentarchitect.nsw.gov.au/projects/missing-middle-design-competition.

17 "City of Sydney Alternative Housing Ideas Challenge," City of Sydney, last modified 8 May 2019, https://news.cityofsydney.nsw.gov.au/articles/5-minutes-with-our-alternative-housing-ideas-challenge-registrar.

18 "Qeensland Density and Diversity Done Well Competition," Office of the Queensland Government Architect, last modified 29 November 2019, www.epw.qld.gov.au/about/initiatives/density-diversity-competition.

19 "Edmonton 'Missing Middle' Design Competition," City of Edmonton, accessed 25 February 2022, www.edmonton.ca/programs_services/recognition_awards/infill-design-competition.

20 "Home of 2030," Royal Institute of British Architects, accessed 25 February 2022, www.ribac ompetitions.com/homeof2030/.
21 "Low Rise: Housing Ideas for Los Angeles," Los Angeles Mayor's Office, accessed 25 February 2022, https://lowrise.la/.
22 Using the bluefield housing design principles of Chapter 6, 'Established Manors' won the Manor House category of the NSW Missing Middle Design Competition. 'Fourflex', a collaboration with Alysia Bennett, received an Honourable Mention in the Fourplex category of the LA Low Rise Design Challenge, and 'The Rightsize Service', a collaboration with Alysia Bennett and Dana Cuff, was one of the seven winners of the City of Sydney Alternative Housing Ideas Challenge.

2 An appetite for new forms of suburban living

Domestic independence / domestic sharing

Living in a traditional westernised suburban setting has generally meant occupying a house offering space, separation, and autonomy from other residents. In contemporary suburbs, a certain detachment from neighbours is heightened when access to and from the home is via a garage connected directly to the inside of the house. The convenience of door-to-door travel has seen a shift in the suburban front yard. No longer a threshold for incidental conversations between neighbours as they come and go, front yards are in many places a purely decorative set-back from the street, with the automated garage panel becoming the *de facto* front door for many suburban dwellers. Such modern convenience has been a natural progression of the suburbs as they look to accommodate increasing levels of size, comfort, and ease. The graduation as a young adult from growing up in the suburbs with one's parents to establishing one's own home in the same but often improved mould, has been a predetermined rite of passage for many. This transition to suburban independence, captured as the great housing 'dream' associated with the achievement of personal and financial autonomy, often results in ever-increasing standards of living from one generation to the next. And as the search for improved standards of living grows, so too does the suburban house. While in the UK, research suggests that average house sizes have declined each decade since the 1970s,[1] Australia, the US, and Canada are seeing house sizes increase despite household numbers falling. Such growth has added to the complex network of housing affordability issues.

DOI: 10.4324/9781003293736-4
This chapter has been made available under a CC-BY-NC-ND license.

In many parts of the western world the housing dream has become increasingly out of reach, with so-called 'generation rent' facing the difficulty of achieving homeownership in increasingly unaffordable housing markets.

Meanwhile, for many people living in the suburbs, the autonomy of the home has often masked a social isolation that exists within it. Loneliness in the suburbs has generally been understood to exist for decades, from young women giving up their jobs upon marriage to become 'housewives' who spend hours alone at home, to older residents whose worlds shrink over time as their ability to be independently mobile diminishes, and as family and friends move on or pass away. Yet although the number of one-person households has clearly increased in recent decades, as identified in Chapter 1, living alone should not automatically be correlated with living with loneliness.[2] One pre-pandemic study from the US comparing the loneliness levels of baby boomers (those born between 1948 and 1965) with those of the previous generation (1920 to 1947), found no evidence to suggest that loneliness levels are significantly higher now than they were for previous generations, or that loneliness levels had increased in the ten years preceding the study.[3]

However, domestic independence is not always the norm, with degrees of sharing to be found across both related and non-related household members. Shared housing arrangements can be undertaken for social, financial, and cultural reasons. In simple terms, sharing exists for multiple overlapping reasons, and it is nothing new. For millennia, courtyard housing has repeatedly been deployed across cultures to not only protect against weather extremes and create local microclimates, but for its ability to respond to cultural and familial needs. Forming an enclosing perimeter of dwellings between which open space is created and contained, courtyard housing has allowed strategic staging over time as households grow. Importantly, it has allowed familial relationships to operate across households but within a coherent whole, where independence and sharing work cooperatively.

While it is easy to romanticise the courtyard as a housing ideal where residents are provided with the best of private and communal lives, the reality is that many courtyard models resulted from strict social hierarchies and a combined financial and spatial necessity to share single outdoor spaces and facilities. Courtyard living for many has often been by necessity, not choice. Nevertheless, the capacity of the courtyard model to enable and encourage aspects of community living remains an important typology in suburbanised cities, with so-called 'courtyard homes' forming part of the suburban vernacular and coalescing communities through the act of sharing a site.

Multigenerational living

By comparison with traditional courtyard models where multigenerational living is key, the westernised post-war enthusiasm of low density living on individual lots saw many suburbanites shy away from cohabiting with other generations of their families. When land and fuel were cheap, generations could spread across houses, either in the same or nearby neighbourhoods, or across different towns and cities. But as housing pressures have mounted in the twenty-first century it has become increasingly common to see stories of multigenerational living playing out in the suburbs.

In Australia, research has shown that the fastest growing cohort of people at risk of experiencing homelessnes are single women over the age of 55, with the cohort aged 45 to 54 also at an increasing risk. In the past, older people have traditionally experienced high rates of homeownership and subsequent housing security. However, as living expenses and housing costs have risen, older people renting in the private sector as a single person or single parent have been exposed to increasing housing affordability stress, particularly in the absence of meaningful personal savings. And when older single women lose their private rental properties, they can find it difficult to secure another lease. Older couples can also fear precarious housing scenarios when facing the reality of one partner dying, for as a couple becomes single, government allowances will reduce while rent continues to rise.[4] In these circumstances, the ability for an older person to share their living arrangements with younger generations can be the difference between experiencing or avoiding housing precarity. And it is not always the case that sharing is within a familial setting, or that living across generations is an effect of the young always assisting the old.

Stories of proactive sharing

As public awareness of housing stress grows, an increasing catalogue of online news articles regularly brings otherwise hidden stories of multigenerational and shared living to prominence. Collectively, these show the types of proactive measures people are taking to remove theselves from precarious housing situations, or to simply take advantage of the benefits shared living arrangements can provide. A few of these stories are aggregated here.

Joan, 94, and Yve, 52, were previously unknown to each other before undertaking a homeshare arrangement in Sydney.[5] In a scenario each describes as a win–win, Yve rents a room in Joan's home. This provides a passive income for Joan and rental security for Yve, who was otherwise facing the difficulty of finding an affordable rental property as a single person in one of Australia's most expensive cities. Beyond the companionship achieved in the homesharing relationship, Yve's ability to undertake some of the household chores helps Joan remain in her home, while the rental arrangement mitigates Yve's housing vulnerability. Match-making and vetting of this mutually-beneficial arrangement is undertaken by a specialist not-for-profit homecare agency, providing security and surety for both women. Similarly, in the US, Los Angeles' ADU Accelerator Program matches homeowners wishing to rent their ADUs to older residents in a mutually-beneficial brokerage.[6] Institutional brokerage is discussed further in Chapter 14.

For Louise, 39, the choice of a house for her family factored in the potential need to accommodate an additional family member at some point in the future – an increasing reality in Australia, where people aged 65+ represent the fastest growing cohort of people who move in with relatives.[7] When Louise's 70-year-old mother Janine hurriedly left her husband after the breakdown of the relationship – a phonomenon known as the 'grey divorce' – she faced a shortage of emergency accommodation and the inability to afford a rental property on her own. Moving in with Louise and her family was seen as Janine's only option and required adapting for all parties. For Janine, this meant learning to resist the parenting of her grandchildren; for Louise, it required becoming comfortable with a relinquishing of privacy as her mother was brought into the family's daily life. For each, the sharing has been socially advantageous, with the children the beneficiaries of two generations of care and learning.

A similar story is told by single mother Kate, 35, whose parents Ian and Irene, both in their 60s, moved in with their daughter and her two primary-school-aged children.[8] The household shares a familial as well as fiscal arrangement. Ian and Irene run an online business from the home and do not pay rent. In exchange, the pair act as carers for the children during out-of-school hours, and prepare the meals. This allows Kate to maintain full-time employment, while the benefits of sharing are seen by everyone in stronger relationships, reduced living costs, inbuilt childcare, and the ability for the children to undertake extra-curricular activities supported by their grandparents. A further benefit is seen in Ian having taken on a male role-model position with Kate's children, who would otherwise not have an adult male in the family. To maintain necessary distance, Ian and Irene give Kate space with her children in the hour before school each morning, while the house is large enough for the generations to retreat to separate areas when needed.

In a regional community north of Sydney, three couples in their 70s – friends for nearly 40 years – transitioned from holidaying together during their working lives to living in a share house in retirement.[9] Having trialled the model in Sydney first to gauge its desirability and feasilibity, the six pooled their finances to purchase a block of land in the country where they could construct a share house and retire with a level of financial freedom none of them could envisage if they retired independently in the city. Making the move to a new community together made it easier for each couple to settle into their new surroundings and made it safe and encouraging for the more introverted members of the group to embrace community life in their newfound retirement. Beyond this safety in numbers, the group cites communication as the key to making their community of six functional, while the sharing of housework, cooking, and bills makes it managable. Underpinning the success of their model is a collective sense that any share house mistakes made in their youth – selfishness coupled with a failure to make a positive contribution to the household – have been rectified with maturity.

Equipped with an older person's understanding of the dynamics of a functioning household, the best aspects of share housing from their youth can be enjoyed again.

Cohousing and pocket neighbourhoods

Deliberative sharing models such as these are by no means a new concept, with the first cohousing development undertaken in 1972 by 27 families outside Copenhagen. Kathryn McCamant and Charles Durrett, architects who introduced the concept of cohousing to the US in the 1990s, describe it as a contemporary approach to a new idea; a logical extension to the traditional notion of the village. Where a village develops organically over time along with a set of social rules, cohousing develops strategically and deliberately, defining its rules through consensus.[10] Often mistaken for a commune, cohousing has become a mainstream housing form. From 2016 to 2022 the UK Government offered The Community Housing Fund aimed at creating a national network of technical, regulatory, and financial services to support those wishing to undertake a cohousing development.[11]

Usually consisting of between 20 to 30 homes arranged across a large site of often agglomerated allotments, cohousing developments usually work off a common structure:

- the houses are privately owned, with residents owning a share of common areas, as per a multi-unit development;
- houses are self-contained, with their own kitchen, dining space, living space, and bedroom(s);
- houses often have a front porch or some form of outward-facing design to encourage engagement among residents;
- a common house – usually incorporated, but not mandatory – provides a large kitchen, dining area, and a living space(s) for residents to share a meal when they choose, to undertake hobbies, to socialise, and to hold meetings;
- a common laundry and drying areas can be included, freeing space in the individual houses;
- a guest room in the common house can be booked by residents for when family, friends, or a carer come to stay, further freeing space in the individual houses;
- shared amenities such as barbecues or even a swimming pool can be incorporated;
- tools and equipment can be shared, negating the need for each household to own and store its own; and
- car parking is consolidated such that residents must walk through the facility and past residences, further encouraging interaction and providing passive surveillance as a check on the welfare of neighbours.

An appetite for new forms of suburban living

Importantly, cohousing developments are designed *with* the residents rather than *for* them. Created to provide a neighbourhood within the neighbourhood, the system functions well for singles, couples, families, and multigenerational households as much as it does when designed specifically for older people, where there is a particularly good fit between the ambitions of cohousing and the needs for older residents to stay connected as they age.[12]

Cohousing commonly operates on large development sites, where at least 20 dwellings are required for development feasibility and for the creation of a diverse community, and where a maximum of around 30 dwellings is preferred for manageability and the achievement of consensus. A scaled-down version is the 'pocket neighbourhood', developed as a concept by American architect Ross Chapin.[13] Recognising that cohousing developments often arrange their housing into smaller sub-groupings, Chapin developed the pocket neighbourhood concept on a reduced scale of around eight to 12 individual houses. Four is seen as the minimum viable number of dwellings to foster community, while a cap of between 12 and 16 limits the loss of connectedness seen in larger multi-unit developments.

In a pocket neighbourhood, small homes are clustered around a central shared common at a scale that is smaller than a cohousing development, but much larger than a single lot. This common space, visible from each house, operates between the public scale of a street or park and the private realm of the personal yard. Owned and maintained by the group, the common is a space in which formal and informal contact between neighbours can occur. To ease the transition from public to private space, landscaping is layered between the common and the individual house, with gates and fences provided if desired. Like traditional cohousing, pocket neighbourhoods look to create front porches that encourage incidental contact amongst neighbours, while cars are clustered on the periphery of the development. Pocket neighbourhood developments will almost always include a shared toolshed for the common, and in larger forms may include a common house akin to that seen in cohousing.

Similarly, the bluefield housing model operates on a spectrum of sharing but at a much smaller scale than either cohousing or pocket neighbourhoods, as demonstrated in Part 3. Where sites are very small, or where the residents prefer greater autonomy and privacy, only the lot and its garden will be shared. In some schemes, facilities such as laundries can be shared to maximise space in the individual dwellings. Where space allows and residents wish to amplify the shared living experience, a full common house model can be incorporated, likening the bluefield model to a what might be described as 'cohousing lite'. Cohousing lite is a concept described in Sheffield University's Designing With Downsizers research project, whereby some of the key concepts and advantages of traditional cohousing developments are integrated into an otherwise normative residential development to enhance resident wellbeing.[14]

Intentional communities

The desire for improved wellbeing through a sharing or partial sharing of living arrangements can be seen in the popularity of intentional communities. A variety of factors can influence a collective's decision to actively create a shared living environment, but two common traits often drive the decision: the ability of pooled resources to reduce individual costs and increase affordability; and a general belief that the sense of community established in the model will be a positive outcome, despite the compromises to autonomy that may be required.

Women's Property Initiatives is a not-for-profit housing provider to women and women-led households, established in direct response to the housing vulnerabilities faced by many women disadvantaged by gender disparity. In an outer suburb of Melbourne, WPI's Older Women's Housing Project by Studio Bright provides four connected dwellings on a typical suburban lot of around 830m^2 (8,930 sq ft), arranged as two one-bedroom and two two-bedroom homes in a scalable model.[15] Each dwelling is designed with an L-shaped plan, with the four arranged in two back-to-back configurations. This creates two double carports which convert to shared social spaces that augment four private courtyards (Figure 2.1). In redeveloping the site with a 4-for-1 yield, small socially-connected homes are created as long-term affordable rentals.

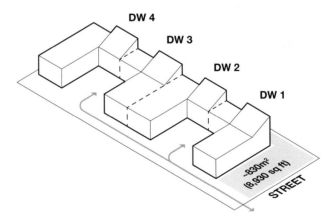

2.1
The design parti of Studio Bright's Older Women's Housing Project for WPI: a four-for-one deliberative development on a single-family home lot.

The idea of the Narara Ecovillage was initially conceived as a community support mechanism for two recently widowed women.[16] At the time of writing, this has grown to a community of over 100 people across 50 dwellings. The ages of residents range from a newborn to a person in her 80s, with older women making up most of the cohort. Entirely self-funded and self-initiated, the village adopts elements of cohousing through providing a common house, common laundries, and additional toilets. This keeps the individual residences small, where desired, supporting the sustainability ethos of the development. Within the whole, there are layers of additional sharing, with one group of women collectively buying an allotment to build a share house together.

In a similar mould, Sharing With Friends is a Queensland-based not-for-profit organisation looking to create small-footprint shared living models for the more than 120 women on its waiting list.[17] Starting as a group of five friends wishing to build a house together in their retirement, the organisation has evolved to become a public benevolent institution working to develop suburban-scale cohousing developments coupling independence with community sharing at times of the residents' choosing. The model, designed by Deicke Richards, sees five single-room studio apartments plus a common house on an 800m^2 (8,610 sq ft) single-family home lot. The organisation acts as a facilitator, holding workshops to help individual groups of potential residents design the way their cohousing community will operate. The challenge for the group is in navigating zoning controls, with Deicke Richards' pilot project testing the statutory control mechanisms that currently block such development on suburban sites in Queensland (Figure 2.2).

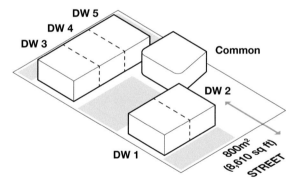

2.2
The design parti of Deicke Richards' Sharing With Friends project: a five-for-one cohousing development on a single-family home lot.

In Perth, Western Australia, Ecoburbia is a suburban residential community and micro-farm founded on sustainability and community principles.[18] A converted two-storey 1970s house on a traditional quarter-acre (1,000m^2) corner block provides accommodation for around eight people, while the yard houses goats, chickens, beehives, and fruit and vegetable production. Herb gardens at the front of the property are offered for passers-by to pick, and all organic matter created onsite is reused, as is that of neighbours who bring their own organic waste for reuse. Water is harvested and recycled through underground rainwater collection tanks, a bore, and an onsite greywater recycling system. Community engagement is undertaken on site through sustainability workshops run for and with neighbours.

The previous property owners had prepared the house for sale assuming new owners would subdivide the block, as had been done with other properties in the neighbourhood. This meant that the rear yard of 223m^2 (2,400 sq ft) had been fully cleared as a new housing lot prior to sale, and Ecoburbia's sustainable micro-farm has therefore been created in this space from the ground-up. The development's density principle is simple: to house the same number of people that would have been accommodated had a second house been built in the subdivided backyard, but to do so in only one house that fosters a sense of community while leaving the backyard space for a sustainable shared garden. Shared facilities in the cohousing model enable private living quarters to remain small.

Beyond a commitment to providing an alternative form of infill housing focussing on community and sustainability, Ecoburbia is a residential business model for the owners, who retain financial control of the development. This is a point of difference from many other forms of shared housing models. Whereas cohousing is formed of individual owners each taking a share in common facilities, and community housing models are owned by associations who rent to tenants, the Ecoburbia property was purchased by a couple who live in the development and derive income from the other residents through affordable rent, which in turn allows the financing of daily operations and housing costs.

Backyard homes

Where a sharing model such as Ecoburbia presents little, if any, discernible physical change to suburban living, it can present a challenge to traditional ways of thinking about how we live in the suburbs, particularly in respect to individual privacy and autonomy. For decades, the most widely accepted and understood minimally invasive method of housing additional people in the suburbs has been the Accessory Dwelling Unit, or ADU, also referred to (among other names) as the granny flat, garden suite, in-law apartment, laneway house, and when associated with a dwelling located over a garage or parking space, Fonzie flat, coach house, or carriage house. Taking its lead from research by UCLA's cityLAB, this book uses the more simple and useful term 'backyard home', where possible.[19] This nomenclature removes any predetermination of who the housing is for and how it may be formed and opens the possibility that backyard dwellings can be more than an 'accessory' to a 'main' house, as discussed in the Introduction.

Backyard homes are generally considered to provide social, financial, and environmental benefits due to their ability to harness existing land, particularly in neighbourhoods that are well connected to existing infrastructure and services. Socially, they can encourage connectivity between residents, particularly when the households are related, which for many people is where sharing shifts from a fringe concept to something more normative. Financially, they can provide housing choices for people otherwise locked-out of a particular neighbourhood while generating income for homeowners, particularly if the costs of developing the backyard home can be amortised over several years. Environmentally, they help keep a city compact, providing housing where it can be easily serviced, and helping to reduce urban sprawl.

Social and financial advantages can be found in backyard homes across several factors, as identified by cityLAB's research:

- in comparison to large housing developments that can raise resident concerns, housing increases can be achieved by spreading the supply load across larger territories and at a smaller scale;
- the sharing economy of backyard homes works across ages: older homeowners can help provide starter homes for younger generations, while younger homeowners can help create ageing-in-place opportunities for older generations;
- sharing can be a personal gain for the property owner through the ability to house an on-site carer, or to help pay down a mortgage, or to supplement income;
- as a housing supply model, affordability is found not through government subsidies, but through land supply being removed from the development equation; and
- when the residents of backyard homes are related or otherwise known to the owners, rent can be negotiated at levels acceptable to each party, rather than being set by the market via those who are able to pay the highest price.[20]

In Canada and the US, an appetite for increased production of backyard homes is particularly notable. Yet despite the advantages of backyard homes, and the history of people creating them informally for generations, the successful introduction of backyard homes policy has been mixed. In some jurisdictions the debate on whether to introduce policy to encourage backyard homes is highly contested, with local resident groups often mobilising to stop the successful passage of ADU bills. In other places the provision of additional housing, either in the form of backyard homes or as additional units within existing houses, is encouraged and supported through the approvals process.

The City of Vancouver was an early advocate for backyard homes as we see them today, making a significant move towards encouraging laneway houses with its 2008 EcoDensity initiative. This allowed an existing detached home to add a laneway house even if it already contained a secondary suite – a small home created within the footprint of the existing house. This 3-for-1 zoning was applied to all low-density single-family home neighbourhoods, effectively ruling out a lot being restricted solely to single-family home usage.[21] In 2009, 95% of single-family home suburbs in Vancouver were rezoned to allow such intensification, and today, duplexes can each have one secondary suite incorporated, allowing up to four dwellings per lot. One recent study of the take-up of backyard homes in Vancouver found that rather than simply adding a new unit to an old house, over two-thirds had been built as part of the construction of a new house. This suggests that backyard homes in Vancouver are being thought of by property owners not just as suburban infill adjuncts, but as part of a holistic household strategy. The same study found that the addition of a laneway house in Vancouver increases neighbouring values, but that this increase is commensurate with the value added by a standard renovation that does not include the addition of a second dwelling. This added value lessens in wealthier neighbourhoods, where fewer laneway houses are built and where the addition of a second dwelling does little to affect inherently high prices.[22]

In California, the model is not only permitted under a series of legislative measures but championed by the Los Angeles Department of Building and Safety's Standard Plan Program of over 50 pre-approved backyard home designs from licenced architects. Applicants pay a fee to the architect to use the design, which is checked by the LADBS against site-specific conditions before granting final approval.[23] In Chicago, a 1957 ban on backyard homes has been lifted, acknowledging the city's history of carriage houses dating back to an era where living quarters were provided above stables. The Additional Dwelling Units (ADU) Ordinance allows extra dwellings in basements, attics, and as backyard homes, while legalising existing units that were built without approval.[24]

In Washington State, House Bill 1660 was modified to loosen restrictions on what a backyard home can offer, as well as the way in which it can monetised. 2022 amendments to the Bill included the removal of additional parking space requirements if the property is located within 400m (a quarter-mile) of a major transit centre, the prohibition of resident groups being able to block backyard home developments in urban growth areas, and the removal of the requirement for an owner-occupier to reside onsite unless the backyard dwelling is used for short-term rentals. The Amendment also allowed two backyard homes to be created where specified minimum lot sizes were achieved and legalised the sale of the homes as separate entities.[25]

A similar relaxing of zoning controls in Toronto, recognised for its existing 'laneway suites' legislation, was enacted by the City of Toronto in 2022. Having taken advantage of its network of laneways to provide backyard home opportunities for several years, the city expanded the model to allow the construction of backyard homes on sites not abutting a rear lane. The relaxation of controls is part of the City's 'Expanding Housing Options in Neighbourhoods' initiative, with the backyard homes zoning changes forming part of a suite of Missing Middle strategies to increase housing numbers and improve housing choices.[26]

Collaborative housing goals

Together, the range of home and site sharing projects described here – while by no means exhaustive – demonstrate an established and growing appetite to look beyond normative suburban housing for solutions to socially sensitive infill opportunities. A range of sharing scenarios exist and not all collaborative housing engages in a fully cooperative model. The collaborative goals of residents are varied and cut across social, sustainable, and financial imperatives, as described by Sheila Foster and Christian Iaione:

> The goal of those living in collaborative housing spaces today is not just that of sharing common spaces or saving money, but also having a lower impact on the environment, building relationships and satisfying socialization needs, as well as gaining access to social services or creating collaborative economic activities. Additionally, some emerging forms of co-operative and co-managed housing reflect institutional, technological or design innovations that address social inequalities, greater ecological sensitivity, and the shortage of affordable housing.[27]

A shared infill housing model, whether by sharing a redistributed house, or common facilities, or simply an allotment and its garden, will never be desirable for everyone. However, it will be an attractive form of living for many people at various life stages. The key to the success of any shared model that finds its place in the traditional pattern of suburban housing is the degree to which the new modes can tap into the nuances of the old. This brings into play the concept of neighbourhood character and what it means to 'fit in' to an established context. The goes beyond size, look, and feel, and requires an understanding of suburban settlement patterns. This is discussed next in Chapter 3.

Notes

1 "What is the average house size in the UK?," LABC, last modified 29 August 2018, www.labc.co.uk/news/what-average-house-size-uk.
2 Esteban Ortiz-Ospina, "Is there a loneliness epidemic?," Our Wold In Data, last modified 11 December 2019, https://ourworldindata.org/loneliness-epidemic.
3 Louise C Hawkley et al., "Are U.S. Older Adults Getting Lonelier? Age, Period, and Cohort Differences," *Psychology and Aging* 34, no. 8 (2019): 1144–1157, https://doi.org/http://dx.doi.org/10.1037/pag0000365.
4 Debbie Faulkner and Laurence Lester, "Establishing the Number of Older Women at Risk of Homelessness," *Parity* 33, no. 9 (2020): 32–33.
5 Zoe Ferguson, "Aged Care: You don't have to end up alone or in a nursing home — there are alternatives," Australian Broadcasting Corporation, last modified 24 September 2018, www.abc.net.au/news/2018-09-24/aged-care-nursing-home-and-living-along-alternatives-available/10289758.
6 "LA ADU Accelerator Program," City of Los Angeles, accessed 30 March 2022, https://adu.lacity.org/.
7 Carol Rääbus, "How this family makes it work with three generations living together," Australian Broadcasting Corporation, last modified 9 April 2021, www.abc.net.au/everyday/more-parents-are-moving-in-with-adult-children/100024202.
8 Kellie Scott, "Multi-generational Living: When Mum and Dad move in," Australian Broadcasting Corporation, last modified 27 August 2019, www.abc.net.au/everyday/multigenerational-living-parents-moving-into-your-home/9935538.
9 Lisa Clarke, "The experience of retiring into a share house," Australian Broadcasting Corporation, last modified 4 February 2020, www.abc.net.au/everyday/the-experience-of-retiring-into-a-share-house/11076624.
10 Kathryn McCamant and Charles Durrett, *Creating Cohousing: Building Sustainable Communities*. Gabriola Island, British Columbia: New Society Publishers, 2011.
11 David Levitt and Jo McCafferty, *The Housing Design Handbook: A Guide to Good Practice, 2nd Edition*. London; New York: Routledge, 2018, 301–303.

12 Charles Durrett, *The Senior Cohousing Handbook: A Community Approach to Independent Living*. 2nd ed. Gabriola Island, Britsh Columbia: New Society Publishers, 2009.

13 Ross Chapin, *Pocket Neighborhoods: Creating Small-scale Community in a Large-scale World*. Newtown, Connecticut: Taunton Press, 2011.

14 Adam Park, Friederike Ziegler, and Sarah Wigglesworth, *Designing With Downsizers: The Next Generation of 'Downsizer Homes' for an Active Third Age*, University of Sheffield (Sheffield, England: University of Sheffield, 2016), https://dwell.group.shef.ac.uk/downsizing/.

15 Alexis Kalagas, "Humble, But Potent: WPI Older Women's Housing Project," *Architecture Australia* 111, no. 2 (2022): 62–68.

16 Maani Truu, "Could collaborative living provide an answer to the housing crisis and climate change? Some people think so," Australian Broadcasting Corporation, last modified 5 January 2022, www.abc.net.au/news/2022-01-05/collaborative-housing-could-be-an-answer-to-the-housing-crisis/100629994.

17 "Sharing With Friends," Older Women Co-housing Association, accessed 24 July 2021, www.sharingwithfriends.org/.

18 "Ecoburbia," Ecoburbia, accessed 5 January 2022, https://ecoburbia.com.au/.

19 Vinit Mukhija, Dana Cuff, and Kimberly Serrano, *Backyard Homes & Local Concerns: How Can These Concerns Be Better Addressed?* Los Angeles: cityLAB – UCLA Department of Architecture + Urban Design, 2014.

20 Dana Cuff, "The Architect's Lot: Backyard Homes Policy and Design," *Housing as Intervention: Architecture Towards Social Equity, Architectural Design (A.D.)* 88, no. 4 (July/August 2018): 62–69.

21 Brent Toderian, "Density Done Well" (Conference Presentation, Vancouver Urban Forum, Vancouver, 6 June 2012).

22 Thomas Davidoff, Andrey Pavlov, and Tsur Somerville, "Not In My Neighbour's Back Yard? Laneway Homes and Neighbours' Property Values," *Journal of Urban Economics* 128 (March 2022), 103405, https://doi.org/https://doi.org/10.1016/j.jue.2021.103405.

23 "ADU Standard Plan Program," Los Angeles Department of Building and Safety, accessed 10 March 2022, www.ladbs.org/adu/standard-plan-program.

24 "Additional Dwelling Units (ADU) Ordinance," City of Chicago, accessed 10 March 2022, www.chicago.gov/city/en/sites/additional-dwelling-units-ordinance/home.html.

25 "Washington State Legislature HB 1660 – 2021–22," Washington State Legislature, accessed 10 March 2022, https://app.leg.wa.gov/billsummary?BillNumber=1660&Initiative=false&Year=2021.

26 "Garden Suites," City of Toronto, accessed 10 March 2022, www.toronto.ca/city-government/planning-development/planning-studies-initiatives/garden-suites/.

27 Sheila R Foster and Christian Iaione, "Ostrom in the City: Design Principles and Practices for the Urban Commons," in *Routledge Handbook of the Study of the Commons*, ed. Blake Hudson, Jonathan Rosenbloom, and Dan Cole, Abingdon, Oxon: Routledge, 2019, 245.

3　On character and 'fitting in'

The rhetoric of strategic growth

In the effort to transition cities to more dense housing futures, agencies responsible for implementing and managing change seek to strike a balance between introducing new housing forms and retaining the best of the established suburban way of life. It is natural for cities to look for housing opportunities where numbers can be increased efficiently and with as little impact as possible on the existing fabric of the city. Greenfield, brownfield, and greyfield sites – discussed in Chapter 5 – are obvious contenders, where a city can unlock new residential land on its fringes, convert disused industrial sites to new residential use, or turn-over under-performing houses in ageing suburbs for new housing at higher densities. A more intense option is the transit-oriented development, or TOD, where large-scale mixed-use developments integrated with public transit hubs can house residents in medium to high density apartment buildings. A subgrouping of the TOD is the less intense transit corridor development, where apartments are housed on upper levels, while the ground floor offers commercial, retail, or hospitality offerings. They are ideally located on or near roads already well-serviced by public transport, and in theory can offer less space for on-site car parking, as residents forgo car ownership by taking advantage of the nearby public transportation. Transit corridor developments are well-suited to cities with established tram and train networks that can efficiently move people outside of the contested and unpredictable car-dominated road network. Being sited on or near main roads, their scale can theoretically be absorbed into existing urban

DOI: 10.4324/9781003293736-5

This chapter has been made available under a CC-BY-NC-ND license.

and semi-urban precincts with little concern over suburban fit. This prompts a common rhetoric that has emerged around transit corridors and activity centres as strategies for cities to meet their housing targets:

- the pattern of new housing development will shift from a reliance on developing cities' fringes to providing most of the new housing within existing city limits;
- growth will be achieved while creating a more compact city with greater interconnectivity; and
- the shift will occur without negatively impacting established neighbourhood character or underlying suburban patterns.

In short, new and strategic mixed-use TODs, activity centres, and transit corridors will do the heavy lifting of housing supply, allowing established neighbourhoods to remain 'largely unchanged'; the rhetoric of many city housing plans. They will be places that are vibrant, social, well-serviced, community-focussed, and people-centric, whilst being socially and environmentally sustainable. They will be networked, walkable places supported by well-connected public transportation systems.

One of the intrinsic difficulties with this policy framework, particularly in lower-scale, lower-density cities, is that the demarcation between intensification and non-intensification zones can establish tensions between the existing settlement patterns and the new. The urban and occupational nature of the proposed higher density mixed-use zones can be largely untested within a neighbourhood and must therefore be defined by aspirational goals rather than tangible built space that people can engage with and understand. Additionally, there are often assumptions that due to proximity alone, there will be negative relationships between these higher density, higher scale new forms and the established low scale precincts and neighbourhoods they adjoin.

Notwithstanding the nuances of local zoning controls, the transit-oriented density strategy is a relatively generic concept across cities, when not all cities are the same. Across locations, population projections and housing targets differ markedly, as do public transportation infrastructure and the attitudes to its use. In some smaller cities there may be little experience with, and few good examples of, higher density apartment living. In others the supply and take-up of public transportation may be poor, thereby forcing car dependence, or car parking may be convenient and inexpensive, creating a reluctance to reduce car usage. Attempting to apply a universal principle of transit-oriented urban housing in a city with little tradition of it or without the requisite public transport system in place, not only takes time for the model and related city systems to evolve to their full potential – it requires addressing the fear that adjacent low-rise neighbourhoods will lose their character and qualities.

In addition, zoning aimed at uplifting housing numbers in activity centres or along transit corridors does not automatically result in developer take-up in these targeted locations or the desired quarantining of the suburbs from densification. For up-zoning to work, the attractiveness of the zoning principles must match the prevailing business model of the housing suppliers. Developers will understandably be opportunistic. They will look to sites that best match the scale and nature of their prevailing business model and often these are found in smaller lots with buildings of a more modest scale; developments that do not provide the financial returns of big apartment developments on large land holdings, but also do not expose the developer to as much risk. In Australia, there have been relatively slow construction rates in transit corridors relative to the zoning opportunities, as many developers are better suited to smaller-scale apartment buildings.[1] As a result, many infill housing developments sit at an in-between scale that is large enough to be a significant size-jump when compared to adjacent low-rise neighbourhoods, but too small in unit numbers and corresponding budget for the types of architectural investment seen in large housing projects. This is most notable in the absence of basement construction that can house car parking, services, and waste, and in limited or absent common spaces and public realm design. The result has often been three- to six-storey apartment buildings elevated over ground level car parking with little site amenity for residents and poor streetscape interfaces (Figure 3.1).

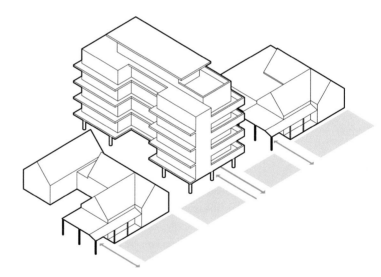

3.1
A challenge of physical and budgetary scale: multi-level apartment infill buildings with on-grade car parking, large site coverage, and poor street-level amenity for residents and neighbours.

Adjacencies between such medium-density developments and their single-family home neighbours are difficult to mitigate. Large cities with a graduation of scale from urban centres, through downtowns, and into inner suburbs can accommodate the scale of apartment buildings with relative ease. However, in smaller cities or those with a more direct reduction in scale from the city to the suburbs, the model can present a dilemma of proximity between urban zones and low-rise neighbourhoods.

Fear of the known

Pressures of density in the suburbs can also be felt from within. Resistance to infill development can be partially explained by the fact that many low-rise neighbourhoods do not have a deep history of medium density living. This can be an artefact of having a slower rate of growth compared with more urbanised cities, or with an inherent sense that suburbs formed to provide an escape from the city should always be places of large houses on big lots. Not-in-my-backyard-ism, or NIMBYism, is that element of resident concern associated with avoiding neighbourhood change or perpetuating the status quo. At its best, it can represent self-interests that mitigate some of the negative effects of poorly designed over-development, resulting in a common good related to a building's size and scale.[2] At its worst, NIMBYism can have racist[3] or other exclusionary ambitions.[4] In *Neighborhood of Fear*, Kyle Riismandel links the rise and perpetuation of American NIMBYism to a growing suburban vigilantism since the mid-1970s, perpetuated by the misconceptions that white suburbanites have been victimised through neighbourhood change and are susceptible to ever-increasing crime rates as the suburbs evolve. In moving out of the city and into the perceived orderliness of the suburbs, suburbanites of the 1950s and 1960s had given themselves the luxury of temporarily ignoring the realities of more proximate forms of city living, despite the suburbs themselves displaying their own shortcomings of equality and safety.[5]

While it is acknowledged that NIMBYism is a complex issue with deep-rooted social and political associations, 'NIMBY' in this book is a neutral rather than pejorative catch-all description related primarily to those who use physical change as their primary argument against suburban infill. It refers to those who suspect the introduction of infill housing means losing rather than gaining something positive for their neighbourhood. It also points to an attitude that new housing forms should happen 'somewhere else', and that neighbourhood change should be treated with suspicion; scepticism that can be well-founded on physical grounds in neighbourhoods with poor knock-down-rebuild development practices already in place (Figure 3.2).

It can be argued that what concerns residents as much as a fear of the unknown is a concern over the widespread escalation of the types of infill developments that have already been witnessed. Poor examples of infill are not always as obvious as the out-of-scale addition of multi-storey units. A far less blatant form of intensification is minor infill, as described in Chapter 1. An example is the hammerhead subdivision, where the back yard of the original house is sectioned-off for a new house, accessed via a driveway down the side of the original dwelling. This commonly results in two houses of equivalent size, a significant increase in site coverage, and a loss of landscape. Related models see the entire lot demolished to create a three-for-one intensification. An alternative approach sees the lot subdivided down the centre, with the original house replaced by duplexes running the length of the site (Figure 3.3).

On character and 'fitting in'

3.2
Examples of poor suburban infill practices are common and easy to weaponise against the introduction of new housing forms into established neighbourhoods.
Source: Google Earth

3.3
A neighbourhood block in Adelaide, South Australia, demonstrating the degrees of infill achieved via subdivision.
Source: Google Earth

In most subdivision cases, the intention is to create additional individualised houses in the image of the single-family home. This sees the land shrink while the housing remains large. At a neighbourhood scale the results are changed street conditions, altered house-to-lot proportions, loss of landscape, and significant increases in built space and hard ground surfaces. In a subdivision, individual privacy for each dwelling is commonly achieved by demarcating the new boundaries with internal 1.8m high (6') fences. This compresses the space, compartmentalising the housing on the lot, and shrinking views within the reduced sites. And as lot sizes reduce while the hard surfaces of roofs and paving increase, mature landscape and soft ground surfaces are removed: neighbourhood loss described in Chapter 1 as the 'collateral damage' of infill. In the push to create more houses in the suburban mould, the primacy of the large house on an individual lot often presents as a trump card that beats other housing sensibilities. In the absence of sophisticated low-rise infill models that think beyond land division and maximum site coverage, neighbourhood debate around increases in density in the suburbs faces the task of first having to move beyond a fear of the known before demonstrating that new models have learned to be better.

Nothing to see here . . .

Neighbourhoods often display a unique character that differentiates them from other places, even those within the same city. This can occur subtly, with different neighbourhoods generally presenting as similar but with minor spatial or stylistic idiosyncrasies, or more overtly, with distinct differences in street sizes and layouts, landscape attributes, housing sizes and types, aesthetic styles, land uses, and underlying settlement patterns. Post-war tract housing in the US, for example, differs markedly in form and suburban layout from inner-suburban US housing. The compact semi-detached bungalows of dense UK cities differ from the detached two-storey homes found in the regions. Even the detached Victorian-era housing of Canada differs from the Victorian housing found in Australia. Variances are found despite these suburban forms generally presenting as neatly arranged rows of houses with shared morphological traits. Common across all established suburbs, however, is a general suspicion of and resistance to change. Even when the pressing demographic and affordability needs identified in Chapter 1 are understood on an intellectual level, residents can be resistant to neighbourhood change on an emotional level. People are less likely to ask *why* changes to our housing need to occur, but rather *why here?*

This is a common challenge levelled at proponents of alternative forms of housing, with a supporting argument often running along the lines of "I moved to this neighbourhood because of the way it is now, not because of what you're trying to turn it into", or "this type of development simply doesn't fit here", or "why can't you do this type of thing somewhere else?", or simply "but things are different here". In essence, these sentiments attempt to halt neighbourhood change in its current form. In doing so, the argument ignores any change that has occurred since the inception of the neighbourhood, both physically and occupationally. In denying the history of a neighbourhood's innate transformation, opponents of change are effectively saying "there's nothing to see here!", even if doing so inadvertently.[6]

Conversely, hard-line YIMBY proponents risk advocating for housing increases without acknowledging local concerns. Attempts to negotiate the NIMBY–YIMBY divide result in useful terms like 'gentle density', generally defined as low-rise densification offering an alternative to larger scale apartment buildings, 'hidden density', which includes the backyard and laneway homes discussed in Chapter 2, and 'invisible density', secondary suites created within the footprint of an existing house.[7] These are all approaches to infill that successfully increase housing supply while minimising residents' concerns. This introduces new housing into the established mix with a form of camouflage that eases suburban tensions. However, any attempt to understand what residents *will* accept as new in their neighbourhoods should always prompt the question of what they already *have* accepted – not in the form of replacement dwellings or new 'accessories' to the mainstream housing – but through long-term and low-intensity incremental change over generations. Many protectionist arguments over the preservation of neighbourhood character fail to recognise that change has been occurring for decades, albeit as a slow burn. Acknowledging such transformation requires an understanding of character over time and beyond the outward look and feel of a place. It means turning the question back on the suburbs and its residents to challenge which version of a neighbourhood's history we are choosing to preserve.

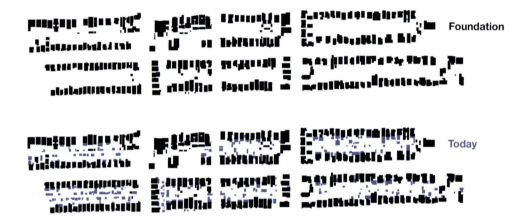

3.4
In their original settlement patterns (top), many suburbs presented small-footprint houses on large allotments, with the backyard space used for productive gardens. Over time (bottom), houses have grown through adaptation and extension, or have been replaced with dwellings much larger than the original housing forms.

Change in the suburbs occurs at two speeds. Up-zoning, where policies are enacted to immediately allow housing intensification, is overt and fast-acting. It can be the difference between a neighbourhood denying multi-storey development one day and allowing it the next, often with associated affordable housing targets linked to supply. But there is also a slow and evolutionary change that occurs in neighbourhoods: incremental adjustments to the individual house and its lot that are linked to changes in household structures, modifications to lifestyles, and evolving tastes over time. In many suburban circumstances these are fine-tunings of the single-family home that are often apparent in the outward appearance of suburban houses but are more elusive and perhaps less understood in the manner in which homes are now used. There have been large shifts in the way neighbourhood homes function over time and the way density has been witnessed in the suburbs; changes that can be conveniently ignored when opposing new housing forms. In acknowledging our histories of suburban change, we bring into the discussion the question of evolving neighbourhood character related not just to aesthetics, but to activity.

Unintentional monuments: the character of aesthetics

In 1903, when contemplating the more elusive aspects of what draws us to the old, Aloïs Riegl wrote of commemorative as opposed to purely artistic values.[8] He described monuments as works created either specifically to keep cultural memories alive for future generations ('intentional monuments'), or by accident, where later generations attribute meaning to a work that may never have been intended by its creator ('unintentional monuments'). I am substituting 'monuments' with 'buildings' in this argument, as was Riegl's intention,[9] and applying the thinking directly to suburban housing, where 'age value' and 'historical value' each come into play. For Riegl, age and historical values were not the same considerations when attributing meaning to an unintentional monument. Where historical value requires some formal understanding of the building's place and role in a historical context and will be of higher or lower significance to a person based on their ability to contextualise that history, age value is universal. Providing the age of the building is sufficiently identifiable from the new, everyone will appreciate its age value to some degree – as a value system available to all, age will always have the advantage over more obscure socio-cultural characteristics.

If one accepts established suburban houses as unintentional monuments – houses with humble beginnings that have generated contemporary reverence over time – then this may explain part of their attraction, or to be more direct, their character. Even in the absence of specific historical significance, their age value offers the opportunity for reminiscence. This can be real or perceived, and an experience potentially identifiable by and therefore attractive to anyone. Riegl argued however, that value could be evidenced beyond qualities of age and history; if this was not the case, all artistic works would eventually achieve a high level of value based on some level of longevity infamy, yet clearly it is entirely possible for a new work to be valued more highly than something older by any cultural, aesthetic, technical, or monetary measure. Beyond age and history, there are other aspects of value at play which Riegl identified as 'use value' and 'newness value'. Use value is the ability for a building to maintain its utility in current times. Without it, a building becomes locked in its era and worthy of protection and upkeep only for its own sake. When related to established suburban housing, use value is seen in robust construction that accepts alterations and additions, and in the general layout and size of the rooms; qualities that lend themselves to longevity coupled with adaptability.

Newness value, described by Riegl as age value's most 'formidable opponent', is inexorably linked to domestic adaptive reuse where character houses are concerned, as they are moulded to work with contemporary life: people might desire the appearance of older housing and neighbourhoods, but very few will decide to live in them in their original functional form. What is required, then, is a means by which to discuss how the values of use and newness compete with or complement the values of age and history.

Nostalgia

If the concept of age value is in play when deciding to retain or replace an older house, it is often actually the *idea* of age, or in another word 'nostalgia', that drives the decision. To put this in Riegl's terms, the idea of age value when applied to established neighbourhood housing is one that can be comfortably overlaid with the values of use and newness, coupled as a matched pair. In its simplest form, this is evidenced by reproductions, which attempt to replicate the established pattern of housing from another era so dutifully as to render it difficult to identify a new construction from a recently renovated old house. Such reproduction of style occurs in the absence of any attempt to recreate the programmatic pattern of the source material (Figure 3.5).

The same can be said of some character renovations even before changes in programmatic conditions are considered, where almost all architectural elements – timberwork, roof framing, roofing, rainwater goods, joinery, flooring, mortaring, and pointing – can be replaced, leaving only the original façade elements intact. In its most extreme form, such as that shown in the contemporary building project of Figure 3.6, the need to protect the street presence is so dominant that the face of the building becomes the only element retained as all else gets built anew behind it. The perceived neighbourhood character of the façade alone is so embedded that it can serve as the only element required to trigger memories of the past. Significantly, such limited retention of the outward face of the dwelling is enough to satisfy the statutory conditions of what is otherwise a fresh start after wholesale demolition of the house and garden. In the suburban character debate, age and newness values sometimes operate in an odd pairing.

Remembering the past: the character of activity

When considering an older neighbourhood, the natural inclination is to think of its heritage or character as immutable; something that seems to have always been there and is beyond question. But if the physical character of a place is coupled with the character of activity it accommodates, and both evolve in line with Riegl's values of age, history, use, and newness, then our contemporary understanding of a neighbourhood's character can only ever be temporal. The real question of how something new fits with the character of the old is not about how a thing looks *per se*, commonly referred to as 'fitting in', but how a true sense of context might be realised at an occupational level. The bluefield housing case studies presented in Part 3 are ultimately concerned with this

3.5
A contemporary reproduction of a Victorian-era villa: the street facade replicates the styling of early housing with far more deference than its corresponding program, albeit with the addition of a side garage that breaks the original character.

question – that is, experimenting with housing arrangements and new modes of occupation that ultimately affect subtle change in established neighbourhoods. Subtlety is deemed important not because suburban infill development is something to hide or have secreted into the suburbs by stealth for fear of push-back, but because subtlety is the manner with which the suburban home has slowly evolved and will continue to evolve over time.

A common criticism of infill work in older suburbs is that it is being undertaken in the wrong place; that there are suburbs where density increases do not matter as much, and where these other neighbourhoods' lack of aesthetic coherence or unrecognised histories mean that new forms of housing can be more easily absorbed into the existing housing mix. In most instances, the

3.6
Alterations and additions to a late nineteenth century villa where only the facade has been retained while all else, including the landscape, has been removed.

more architecturally consistent and intact the place, the more difficult it is to successfully argue for systemic change. This often results in debates around the sanctity of the neighbourhood's scale, with the single-family home serving as the yardstick. This position helps to resist anything dramatically bigger or more dense and can be weaponised against the introduction of anything smaller or more numerous. It requires the advocates for infill housing demonstrate how the new can be incorporated with the old in physical terms: usually by not being too big, too visible, or too 'different'. A more productive way of forming an argument around neighbourhood fit can be found by leaning into the history of a place and by discussing its potential future within the context of its past. Drawings and photographs of previous neighbourhood activity help enormously here, as they contextualise neighbourhood character as evolutionary and allow us to understand our new housing on the historical spectrum of a place.

An example for Australia can be found in the work of photographer Theo Bachmann, who captured candid domestic scenes in Adelaide from around 1890 to 1950. Photographing his own family and their friends, his familiarity with his subjects resulted in images of unfiltered domestic space and life. Presenting as un-staged and often intimate records of those around him, Bachmann's images enable an example reading of early suburban life in houses that remain in contemporary occupation today. Moments of domesticity are captured by images such as *Group … May 92*, where three figures sit at a table after dinner to eat fruit and cake while reading and sewing over sherry (Figure 3.7). Their dress, formal by contemporary standards, belies the relaxed atmosphere of the room which houses a cupboard, side table with books, and wall-mounted bookshelf. There is a proximity of every element in the photograph, evidenced by the placement of furniture, the items they house, and the three figures who are clearly undertaking complementary, yet singular activities at a small table in what appears to be a small room.

On character and 'fitting in'

3.7
Theo Bachmann,
Group: Father, Elise, Miss Appleton, taken May 92 at 10 o'clock pm . . ., 1892.
Courtesy of State Library of South Australia, B 71826/502.

Such domestic intimacy was common in early Australian housing, as tangibly described in words and drawings in 1860 by Joseph Elliott who migrated to Australia from England at the age of 17. He lived with his family in a four-roomed Adelaide row house, which he rented from the owner who lived in the other half. Here, less than 25 years after the colony was established, and located only 2km (1.2 miles) from the centre of town, is suburban housing developed in a compact duplex form and in a hybrid financial model of owner-occupation plus rental property. Hoping, by letter, to entice his mother to join his family in the new colony, Elliott detailed every item of furniture in every room of their home, going so far as to describe each piece of furniture and their use, while numbering drawers and itemising the pieces they held and for whom. This personal cataloguing provides detailed evidence of the multiple uses Victorian-era rooms served and the way almost all rooms were occupied in some form by each member of the family at different times of the day.

In a walk-through narrative that shares a resonance with Bachmann's photographic portraits of compact domestic life, Elliott describes and draws his family's multi-purpose sitting room (Figure 3.8). Reconfigured for different uses at different times of the day, it houses chairs for children and adults, a clothes cupboard for one of the children, a ride-on toy horse, a sofa that becomes a bed for a five-year-old child at night, a clothes basket, a pump organ, wall hung bookshelves, sewing boxes, boxes for papers, medicines and schoolbooks, and a dining table with extending side flaps added by Elliott for extra space when needed. These multiple items and activities occupied a room of only 3.2m x 3.5m (10½' x 11½'), with such proximate and flexible living common at the time the Adelaide suburbs were established. Poignantly, the Elliott's sitting room was also the place where their son Joseph died at just 20 months.[10]

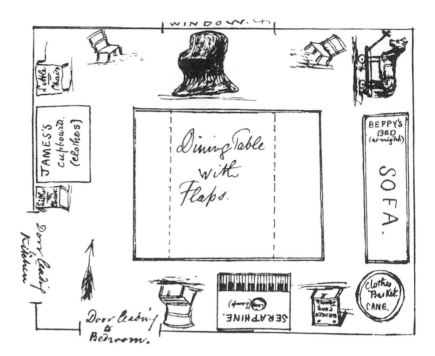

3.8
Joseph Elliott, sitting room sketch, 1860.
Source: State Library of South Australia, D 2759(L).

Elliott's further description and diagramming of the back yard (Figure 3.9) indicates that, like the rooms of the house, the yard served multiple uses of play and work, incorporating dedicated zones for productive gardening, chickens, wood and water storage, waste, and overflow storage from the house. Over 50 years later, Bachmann's *Group, 1912* (Figure 3.10) presents such a working backyard, which was common in early working-class suburbs where produce and chickens were accommodated for personal use, sale, and bartering.[11] Here, the ground has been left as dirt, a chicken pen occupies the back corner, and a rubbish or compost pile sits behind a makeshift enclosure formed of remnant chicken wire. An unlocked gate provides access outside the property, potentially to a neighbouring yard but most likely to the rear night cart lane where the outside toilet would have been emptied.

These summary examples of Elliott's letter and drawings, and of Bachmann's catalogue of photographs, are useful tools for understanding the development of early neighbourhood housing on a spectrum of time. They can never be universal, however. Each established neighbourhood has its own history; subtleties of development rooted in political, social, cultural, economic, and physical traits, and attempting to provide a coverall summary of neighbourhood change is as useful as it is dangerous. However, looking back to the historic uses of our neighbourhoods is a way of seeing more holistically what character means across the history of a place, rather than simply relative to our own current day version of it. In seeing historic housing photographs, we read the built character in expressed timberwork and stone, traditional verandahs, and profiled chimneys; the physical traits that help establish a neighbourhood pattern in a

On character and 'fitting in'

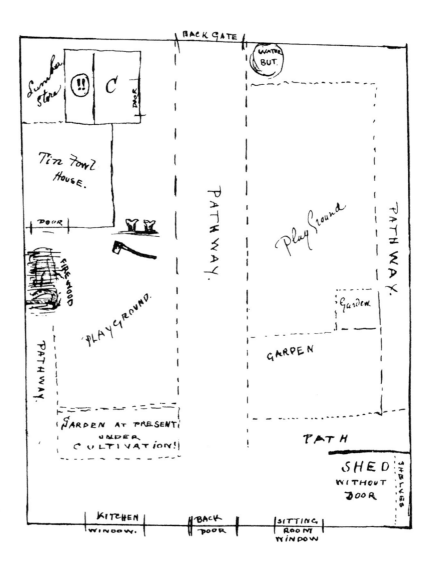

3.9
Joseph Elliott, back yard sketch, 1860. State Library of South Australia, D 2759(L).

particular location and draw people to occupying, renovating, and even reproducing old houses there. But in Theo Bachmann's more intimate catalogue we also witness intangible heritage in the spaces of backyard production, the multiple uses of spaces, and in more proximate ways of living – occupational understandings that are enhanced by Joseph Elliott's descriptions and drawings of early suburban life.

Further, these nuanced observations of early suburban living point to a dramatic spatial shift in the house, and our contemporary move away from the life of the street. Where in the past, visitors would be accepted only into a front parlour room – a formal space in which to receive guests and shield them from the day-to-day experiences of the household – contemporary renovations and extensions have flipped the private/public relationship. This is evidenced in the old rooms at the front of the lot often being given over to private bedrooms,

3.10
Theo Bachmann, *Group, 1912*.
Courtesy of State Library of South Australia, B 71826/24.

studies, and second living spaces, while visitors are welcomed to large open plan living areas at the rear of the house, and outside entertainment areas in the recreational backyard. People may be drawn to Victorian-era homes, but they do not wish to live as the Victorians lived.

Permission to change

Such observation of change is notable for two reasons. First, it is not a value judgement, but a simple statement of fact around the types of physical and occupational change that older neighbourhoods tend to have supported over time, even as they have remained places of predominantly single-family housing. Comparing the old with the new makes no claim over whether the contemporary use of the suburbs is better or worse; it simply acknowledges that it is different. Second, in comparing historic and contemporary uses, and in speaking of nostalgia, the observations make no suggestion on how new housing forms can or should operate on an aesthetic level. Rather, the comparative method simply argues that even old neighbourhoods that present as architecturally intact can undergo significant physical and operational change that its original inhabitants would find difficult to reconcile with their historic experience of the place. As such, in recognising the neighbourhood change that has occurred in the past, we give ourselves permission to strategically change that neighbourhood in the future. The alternative is complete preservation of a contemporary version of the place.

In allowing the suburbs to experience incremental change, we have protected the street aesthetic that helps sustain outward neighbourhood character while reshaping the inner workings of the house and outer operations of the yards to contemporary life. In advocating today for the retention of neighbourhood character we are drawn simultaneously to concepts of preservation and destruction. When we speak in opposition to more outward forms of neighbourhood change, such as the provision of new housing forms, we risk doing so in a blinkered manner that ignores the enormous change that has already occurred. New housing that looks familiar or is designed in a way that replicates historic styles, masks the types of slow incremental changes that have scratched away at the origins of our older neighbourhoods. While much of our new housing looks familiar to traditional forms, it often bears a decreasing performative resemblance when compared to homes of the past. Our new houses beg the question of how the original occupants of the suburbs would reconcile their experiences of neighbourhood life today with decreased household occupant numbers, increased housing sizes, the introduction of (or at least increase in) cars and car parking, the loss and reintroduction of productive gardens, and a fundamental shift in lifestyle away from the formalities of parlours and living rooms to the relaxed amenity of the modernist open plan.

Where a city has a demonstrated need to introduce dense housing forms adjacent to or within low density neighbourhoods, it also begs a spatial capacity question of why one would *not* consider the existing residential areas for inclusion in helping to achieve housing targets, albeit in a contextually appropriate and reduced form. Temporarily setting aside concerns over a perceived loss of neighbourhood character on the assumption that good design can mitigate resident anxieties, there is an argument to be made that on spatial capacity alone, existing low-rise residential areas might logically form part of a broader discussion of infill housing strategy. In any city facing issues of adjacency between new and more dense housing forms and established low-rise neighbours, a zoned demarcation of old and new is merely diagrammatic and thereby academic. This is particularly notable in the irony of single-family home neighbourhoods that readily approve dramatic scale shifts from the original houses to so-called 'McMansions' providing the small single-family home is only being replaced with a bigger version of itself.

In real terms, engaging with a city's transition to a denser form necessarily means engaging with its suburbs, even when they demonstrate heritage and character overlays or have not experienced strategic growth in the past outside of private residents simply making their houses bigger.

Unintended hubris and character shaping

In a democratic society with multiple layers of government, fierce localism can be a defining feature and the greatest inhibitor of change.[12] But to suggest that the suburbs should not form part of a city's strategy around housing needs and supply is to ignore the fact that established neighbourhoods are rarely physically or occupationally the same now as they were when they were first established. By extension, these suburbs will not be the same in the future as they are now.

On character and 'fitting in'

Believing that suburban change should happen 'elsewhere' and away from those suburbs with character overlays, fails to acknowledge that suburbs exist in a continuum in which the current day forms only one moment. It also suggests that our contemporary experience of a place is where we determine the developmental line in the sand should be drawn. Such a position sets our contemporary development pattern as the norm while implying that as current custodians, we are the ones best placed to determine a neighbourhood's future.

This can be described as hubris, as it is clearly understood that the first residents of an established neighbourhood are unlikely to recognise all its current day traits, even as an argument is made to preserve that neighbourhood's contemporary form from further development. I would argue that this hubris is, however, unintended; an inadvertent yet understandable sense that the status quo must be maintained, even in the presence of an altered way of suburban life. This sense of 'unintended hubris' is not universal, however. Much of contemporary heritage policy and practice centres on recognising and managing change in older neighbourhoods as opposed to ensuring outright preservation. In the context of this book, hubris can be applied to those who tacitly accept the types of change described in this chapter and the next (and by extension, the zoning policies that enable them), but will not entertain a broader discussion around strategic infill and density increases for established suburbs. This applies not only to NIMBY resident groups, but to policy makers attempting to preserve entire neighbourhoods with exclusively single-family zoning.

The Elliott family's 1860 sitting room, which formed one-quarter of their small, rented home, was at any given time a place to eat, sit, read, entertain, learn, play, mend, dress, sleep, and, as was common in Victorian times, be nursed through death. Elliott's narrative to his mother, espousing the virtues of his new life in Australia, speaks to the fact that the physical character of our housing and the character of our domestic activity operate at multiple scales, evolve over time, and are difficult to predict.

Character is evidenced, then, not just in how something looks or is styled and formed, but by the way a space is occupied and imbued with everyday activity.[13] Jeremy Till describes such architecture as 'moments of occupation' or 'Lo- Fi Architecture'.[14] Such flexibility of thought requires a shift away from the identification of character as a static visual entity towards one of elasticity where character is shaped over time and witnessed at multiple material and occupational scales. This is not to suggest that the concept of character shaping is a reformist activity, nor that there is something wrong with the established suburbs that needs to be fixed. Indeed, the success of the established suburbs is perhaps the largest impediment for discussing their change, as they support so well the types of rewritten single-family activity that occurs within them. Our houses allow – if not welcome – shifts in use and physical modifications in response to changing needs, domestic patterns, and tastes. They accommodate the evolving temptations of newness and use values in both material and occupational terms, and as a society we have formed mannerisms with which to change and add to them; identifiable patterns that have become part of suburban character.

The following chapter explores these tropes of modifications, which I call 'Commonly Accepted Anomalies'.

Notes

1 Peter Newton et al., *Greening the Greyfields: New Models for Regenerating the Middle Suburbs of Low-Density Cities*. Singapore: Palgrave Macmillan, 2022.
2 Meg Holden and Alex Jürgen Thumm, *Bringing the Neighbourhood into Infill – Report 1* (Vancouver: Small Housing BC and Simon Fraser University, 2016), www.smallhousingbc.org/reports/.
3 Karen Kubey, "Allies in Equity," *Housing as Intervention: Architecture Towards Social Equity, Architectural Design (A.D.)* 88, no. 4 (July/August 2018): 128–135.
4 Dana Cuff, *The Provisional City: Los Angeles Stories of Architecture and Urbanism*. Cambridge, MA: MIT Press, 2000.
5 Kyle Riismandel, *Neighborhood of Fear: The Suburban Crisis in American Culture, 1975–2001*. Baltimore, MD: Johns Hopkins University Press, 2020.
6 Tactics for how to engage with opposition arguments in a constructive and respectful manner are provided in Chapter 20.
7 Brent Toderian, "Density Done Well" (Conference Presentation, Vancouver Urban Forum, Vancouver, 6 June 2012).
8 Aloïs Riegl, "The Modern Cult of Monuments: Its Character and Its Origin," in *Oppositions Reader: Selected Readings from a Journal for Ideas and Criticism in Architecture, 1973–1984.*, ed. K. Michael Hays, New York: Princeton Architectural Press, 1998.
9 Alan Colquhoun, "Newness and 'Age-Value' in Aloïs Riegl," in *Modernity and the classical tradition: architectural essays, 1980–1987*, Cambridge, MA: MIT Press, 1989.
10 Joseph Elliott, *Our Home in Australia: A Description of Cottage Life in 1860*. Introduction and commentary by Stefan Pikusa. Sydney: Flannel Flower Press, 1984.
11 Working yards have long been seen in the suburbs. For Los Angeles, for example, see Becky M. Nicolaides and Andrew Wiese, "The Other Suburbanites: Class, Racial, and Ethnic Deiversity in Early Suburbia," in *The Suburb Reader*, ed. Becky M. Nicolaides and Andrew Wiese, New York: Routledge, 2016.
12 Jenny Schuetz, *Fixer-Upper: How to Repair America's Broken Housing Systems*. Washington, DC: Brookings Institution Press, 2022.
13 For a broader discussion of this, see for example, Margie Ruddick, "Tom's Garden," in *Architecture of the Everyday*, ed. Steven Harris and Deborah Berke, New York: Princeton Architectural Press, 1997.
14 Jeremy Till, *Architecture Depends*. Cambridge, MA: MIT Press, 2009.

4 Suburban anomalies and operations

Catalogues of infill opportunities

Suburban scaffolds

As enduring and static as they may seem at times, houses are adaptive. Even when not initially designed to be flexible, houses can be reshaped, as often occurs with new owners. Although modifying a house can be expensive and wasteful of resources in the absence of inbuilt flexibility tactics, modifications can be achieved in sedentary masonry structures as much as in lightweight timber framed construction. And while we tend to consider changes of neighbourhood character at the scale of the block, street, and house, the ways in which houses are massaged into new uses begins at the scale of the single room. Where external aesthetic 'make-overs' may be applied to the whole house, or at least to its front façade, occupational chages happen via a collection of rooms, either internally through modifications, or externally via additions. The potential for rooms to transform the way a house is occupied is explored in the Porous Rooms flexibility design study of Chapter 17.

At times, the addition of rooms can be so disruptive to prevailing suburban conditions as to generate a groundswell of opposition. The #StopThePop Campaign of the Chicago Bungalow Association[1] aims to steer homeowners of circa 1910–1930 bungalows away from large second-storey additions that change the mass of traditional housing, instead encouraging additions towards the rear of the house that are less visually dominant and retain more of the original street-facing building fabric. But in advocating for their preferred form of

DOI: 10.4324/9781003293736-6

This chapter has been made available under a CC-BY-NC-ND license.

Suburban anomalies and operations

remodelling, the organisation recognises the need to balance the type of small and cellular accommodation a traditional Chicago bungalow offers relative to contemporary desires for a more open and expansive plan. The association therefore offers a range of internal and external modification choices that recognise that housing from 100 years ago is unlikely to fit contemporary needs without being adapted; in arguing for preservation, a case can also be made for change.

Housing therfore acts as a scaffold for living; an armature in and around which change can be accommodated (Figure 4.1). In some cases modifications are informal, occurring without the necessary zoning or building approvals in place. Alongside kitchen and bathroom refits – forms of housing change that are expected due to the wear and tear these spaces experience – the most major change to housing is found internally, via:

- Room amalgamations, where two or more rooms are connected to form a single space, either through demolishing a non-load-bearing wall, or creating an opening via a lintel in a load-bearing wall.
- Room divisions, where a non-load-bearing wall is constructed to create an additional room.
- Attic conversions, where access to light and ventilation is provided by operable skylights and/or the addition of a dormer window.
- Basement conversions, where spaces previously used for storage and services are converted to sleeping, living, recreation, hobby, and work areas.

While habitable basements are uncommon in Australia and the UK, except in some older forms of housing, they are often found in cold weather climates such as Canada and parts of the northern US. Here, the need to dig footings below

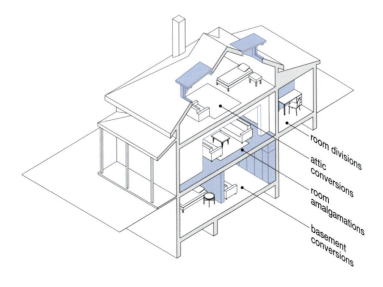

4.1
Internal modifications to houses are common, and often achieved informally, and without the requisite approvals in place.

frost lines to minimise cracking as ground water freezes and thaws, results in the excavation of deep trenches for external walls and internal load-bearing walls. The extra construction effort and expense necessary to do this makes it sensible to excavate the spaces between these deep footings to create full basements, which can accommodate so-called secondary suites. Providing space for dwellings within a dwelling, basements have traditionally encouraged a form of densification largely hidden within the suburbs.

Both large and small internal changes can be undertaken via a formal design process (through a direct construction process with a builder in the absence of an instigating design), or as an informal DIY home improvement project (often undertaken by the owners over time). In internal modifications we see the types of spatial agency a house can afford its owners, who work to tailor their living arrangements in a manner of their choosing.[2] In some instances, informal and once-illegal building practices can be retrospectively acknowledged and approved, with new zoning laws catching up with unofficial building practice. This is the case in Vancouver, where current legislation permitting secondary suites within the existing footprint of a house – most commonly found in basements – can be retrospectively applied to existing suites created illegally before the legislation came into place. A further mechanism exists for disused secondary suites to be deregistered, with the space returned to the main dwelling. This demonstrates the capicity for homes to expand as well as contract in response to changing needs. This ability for houses to flex is seen in even the most spatially restricted of housing, with Victorian-era terrace houses in London displaying the ability across generations to be versatile, either through division into smaller housing units or by opening rooms to each other to create larger spaces not found in the original cellular layouts.[3]

Commonly accepted anomalies

Where internal alterations to homes can provide significant amenity and usage upgrades, additions to the original footprint of a house are of course more recognisable and subject to higher scrutiny, particularly from neighbours. Yet there can be enormous physical change to houses that is broadly tolerated by local residents and authorities, even when the base housing displays heritage characteristics or is subject to neighbourhood character overlays. Given the enormous variety in housing types across cities and countries, any broad attempt to catalogue such change is difficult. However, early Australian housing is a useful example here, as it offers an easily-identifiable base housing unit that regularly accepts a series of common additions. And while the examples shown here will not always be directly translateable to other housing forms, the method of analysis is.

One of the most common forms of early Australian housing is the Victorian-era four- or six-roomed cottage, variously described by Robin Boyd as the

Suburban anomalies and operations

'bungalow'[4] and by Philip Cox et al as 'verandah vernacular'.[5] Boyd described the symmetrical cottage and its projected bay villa variant as two of his *Five Principal Plan Types* by which all Australian housing up to the mid-twentieth century could be described. An identifiable derivative of the eighteenth-century English cottage, its plan arrangement of a central hall flanked by rooms is seen in bungalows and cottages across Australia, the US, Canada, and the UK (Figure 4.2 and Figure 4.3).

Highly useful in their plan arrangements, many older houses such as these in Australia resist wholesale demolition due to their robust masonry construction and the ease with which their room structures continue to accommodate domestic life. They accept common forms of additions seen in Australian suburbs, and while these building anomalies may not be the same everywhere,

4.2
Floor plan of an Australian symmetrical cottage (left) and projected bay villa (right). A derivative of the English cottage and a layout common to many suburban housing forms. The room sizes shown are typical of smaller cottages and villas.

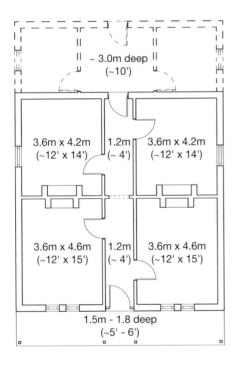
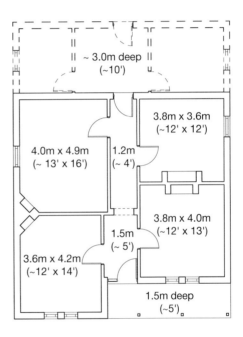

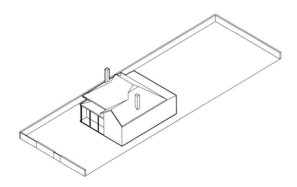

4.3
A cottage's foundation conditions.

63

a similar analytical approach can be taken by the reader and adapted to their local conditions. In some cases, the base housing stock may not be as identifiable and predictable as a cottage or bungalow and the anomalies may be more difficult to identify. However, commonly accepted anomalies can usually be found in a neighbourhood, and once identified an analysis of change can be undertaken and communicated.

A 1. Raised fences

In Australia, one of the most common and highly accepted anomalies is a solidification and vertical extension of fences (Figure 4.4). Even in the absence of other changes, side, rear, and even front fences have routinely grown over time as both privacy and the creation of space-enclosing perimeters have become increasingly favoured. In many instances, rendered masonry walls or high hedges provide little clue as to the activity behind the street boundary.

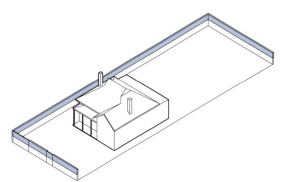

4.4
Anomaly 1: raised fences.

A 2. Extruded verandahs

An artefact of historic carriage lanes changing over from rear stable access path to a driveway for cars, verandahs are commonly extruded to read as a natural extension of the house-proper (Figure 4.5). Often extending back with a roof for the entire length of the house to accommodate two vehicles parked back-to-back, they are either left as an open carport or enclosed with a garage door.

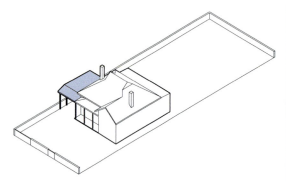

4.5
Anomaly 2: extruded verandahs.

Suburban anomalies and operations

A 3. Side pods

Having first moved from a washstand in the bedroom, or a room in a rear lean-to, into the house-proper, the bathroom has generated enormous change in early suburban housing. And as real estate fashions push for self-contained 'master suites', space to create an en suite bathroom can be difficult to come by. In cottages, these are commonly formed in two varieties. When internalised, one of the original rooms is serviced and adapted to suit its new function. However, when this space cannot be afforded, bathrooms are commonly realised as pods attached to the side of the house, most often in the narrow walkway gap down the side of the house (Figure 4.6). Commonly presenting to the street with a parapet or roof that sits under the eaves line of the house, current suburban tastes indicate that mimicking the materials of the house-proper is the default method for attempting to reduce the anomalous nature of the new addition. Although the most common reason for inserting new side additions is for bathrooms, other forms provide rooms with external doors, unlocking commercial or dual-key uses.

4.6
Anomaly 3: side pods.

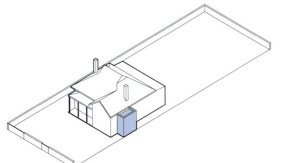

A 4. Rear additions

Exemplifying the most significant spatial change to the traditional four room house typology, rear extensions can include incursions into the roof space (Figure 4.7). Providing not only a major increase in the size of the house and a resultant reduction in yard space, but extensions also fundamentally alter the way cottages are now occupied. The front room parlour, which once gave life to the street-half of the house, has generally become a bedroom and reaccommodated in the new open plan kitchen, dining, and living space in the rear extension. Usually capped in height to two storeys, rear extensions often replace or absorb an original lean-to and are commonly seen obliquely from the street when looking down the driveway, although many visible examples behind the original roof are also seen.

It is increasingly rare, however, that these anomalies appear in isolation. In certain circumstances, there is even a logic to using one of the anomalies to support another. It is not uncommon for en suite pods, as an example, to be constructed

Suburban anomalies and operations

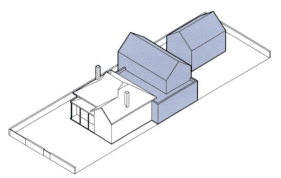

4.7
Anomaly 4: rear additions.

as part of an overall development staging strategy before the original bathroom is decommissioned to make way for a new rear addition. When viewed as an undeveloped and developed pair (Figure 4.8), what becomes evident is the retained legibility of the base house in both the foundation and modified forms. This is exemplified by Figure 4.9, where a temporary dimming of the base conditions allows the anomalies to be highlighted in a manner not otherwise readily seen. The use of materials and treatments that many preservationists would argue 'fit in' with the original house and its neighbours, can only do so much to mask the fact that the house has undergone significant change.

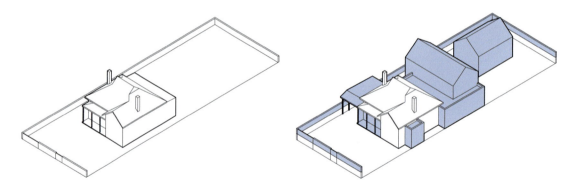

4.8
Foundation conditions and commonly accepted anomalies.

A 5. Front additions

The least common of the anomalies, diagrammed here as a simple verandah enclosure (Figure 4.10). In Australia, larger front additions were once routinely accepted, particularly as a means of transforming an older house from domestic to commercial use before notions of heritage protection came to prominence in the 1970s and 1980s. Unless a front yard addition can restore an otherwise irregular setback to the street, it now generally sits outside social and statutory norms for character houses and is neither encouraged nor supported by zoning laws. This denial of front additions belies the fact that many examples still exist, evidence perhaps that the utility of such additions still holds currency, albeit in opposition to what is now deemed to be normative adaptive reuse principles.

Suburban anomalies and operations

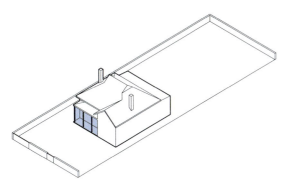

4.9
Commonly accepted anomalies.

4.10
Anomaly 5: front additions.

Together, these commonly accepted anomalies are so pervasive in Australia's older suburbs that their method of deployment is regularly adopted in new housing, such as that shown in Figure 4.11. So engrained is the character of the foundation cottage and the habitual pattern of its additions, that even when designed as new construction, en suite pods, verandah enclosures, and side garaging can present as additive elements to a base form. These habits of suburban construction are reminders of the persuasive power of the nostalgia of age value discussed in Chapter 3. In the effort to 'fit in', reproductions not only copy the original but imitate the ways the original has been added to in the intervening decades.

The individual tropes of suburban change will vary from city to city, but their identification can help us understand the occupational adaptations to the suburbs as much as they can the physical. Once identified as a collection of neighbourhood observations, commonly accepted anomalies are not just descriptive,

4.11
A contemporary reproduction cottage, following anomalous norms.

but instructional. And as much as they describe what is there, they also have the capacity to imply what might be. In essence, they give us permission to undertake suburban change. Extended to their logical conclusion, they can be leveraged into what I call 'suburban operations'.

Suburban operations

Suburban operations represent a set of simplified three-dimensional development tactics which together offer a sequence of arrangement possibilities. They are offered as a more universal way of thinking about a localised suburban system, where the complexities of working around and between existing houses are distilled to a series of spatial patterns that are communicated through generative diagrams. In describing siting and massing properties as a series of three-dimensional strategies, complex relationships between old and new are temporarily made simple, providing design cues for investigating new patterns of suburban living. These simplifications can then be overlaid with the much more nuanced tactics of detailed design studies, such as those demonstrated in Part 3.

Such a cartooning of design strategy is not unprecedented, with the operations following the work of Anthony Di Mari and Nora Yoo, whose cataloguing of spatial verbs seek to establish a simple set of architectural strategies that together form a unified design logic.[6]

The operations present a series of mapped possibilities that encourage new opportunities borne of a design logic, in what Di Mari and Yoo would describe as a 'system of options'. This is not to be confused with a form-based zoning code. Rather, the operations are a limited kit of parts presented without any aesthetic overlay or value judgement on whether they are architecturally appropriate for

Suburban anomalies and operations

a particular neighbourhood. They therefore speak to what may be *possible* in a neighbourhood, not what is *desirable* or even *acceptable*. As such, they work together with the commonly accepted anomalies as conversation starters – a catalogue of initial infill opportunities that allow broad conceptual thinking first, and nuanced design later. Depicting the existing house in white and the additive infill elements in blue (Figure 4.12), the operations are abstract enough that one can imagine future scenarios and opportunities without that future having been designed by the operations themselves. The existing house has a strategically undisclosed size, height, setback, and side separations, yet is rendered specific-enough to be read as an identifiable entity. By contrast, the massed additive elements are deliberately simple and suggest opportunity rather than declared architectural solution.

4.12
Base suburban conditions showing a house and the footprint of its neighbour (left), and a suburban operation (blue). The dashed line represents the boundary between the two properties.

The reader can therefore create their own suburban operations suited to local conditions. Solar orientation, shadow-casting, access to light and ventilation, and the interfaces between new elements and existing rooflines, walls, and windows, are all intricacies requiring project-specific decisions to be made. These issues will need to be resolved on a case-by-case basis, established by the physical nuances of the individual buildings and the functional design of their combined operation. As such, these smaller intricacies are excluded from the operations; crucial to resolve at a project level, but important to defer until overall strategic ambitions can be explored.

Presented as an assessment of tactical possibilities, the utility of the operations might be imagined in several ways, depending on their audience:

- For **local authorities**, they might form part of a descriptive pre-approval strategy or be taken through a nuanced local design study and developed into a form-based code, particularly in combination with some type of context-specific explanatory text and more detailed diagramming; they may form a means by which to describe formal morphologies that follow an established neighbourhood's pattern.
- For **architects**, they may become a useful design manual; an alternative way to quickly conceive and describe a project, or a means by which to discuss design precedent and lineage.
- For **developers**, they might be a tool with which to help establish arguments over the viability (or otherwise) of residential amalgamation; no longer only a size, form, and material exercise, but a means by which to discuss overarching site development strategies in simple terms.

- For **building owners**, they may represent a way of visualising suggestions for what might be possible; a more immediate means by which to reimagine how a particular house and site might evolve individually or in concert with its neighbour(s) to meet changing needs.

Broken down into identifiable components to be combined at the user's discretion, the suburban operations are arranged as follows. In each case, the additive elements are suggestive only and might be made smaller, bigger, shorter, or taller and might be conceived as fully attached to the existing house, partially attached, or detached. Whilst they are diagrammed notionally as single, double, or triple storey, with heights set to match the ridgeline of an existing house, that is not to say that a user might not form design propositions that break this datum in favour of an appropriate localised design response or better housing outcomes.

SO 1. Rear additions

A simple diagramming of current domestic alterations practice. Realised as either a single- or multiple-storey addition, this exercise might reinstate, replace, subsume, or extend the rear of a house (Figure 4.13). Tactically, these two operations reinforce the prevailing adaptive reuse behaviour evidenced in the suburbs, simultaneously acknowledging the success of current practice, and using it as a form of tacit infill approval or acceptance.

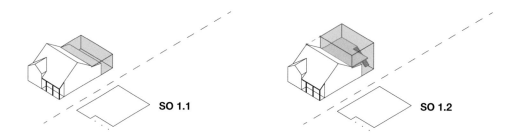

4.13
Suburban operation 1: rear additions.

SO 2. Side pods

An addition, grafted to the side of the existing house in a walkway zone. This is a way of thinking about side conditions that works across different walkway widths from 0.9 to 1.8m (3–5'), as shown in Figure 4.14 to Figure 4.17. For the purposes of the exercise, 1.8m or 6' has been set as an optimum width for a small room addition to provide meaningful utility or amenity. This allows a bathroom or other small self-contained space to be added to an existing room (Figure 4.14).

Where the walkway is narrowed to 1.5m (5'), the same type of room can be achieved, but this requires the formation of an opening in the house's external wall to gain the necessary additional space (Figure 4.15). The benefits of such openings are discussed in Chapter 8 in the context of 'finding space' in older homes, and in Chapter 17 in the Porous Rooms design exercise.

Suburban anomalies and operations

A walkway of 1.2m (4') can still offer an important gain in amenity by extending an existing space (Figure 4.16), whilst even a narrow 0.9m (3') walkway can offer substantial gains when put to utilitarian use as a kitchen (Figure 4.17 and Figure 4.18). Significantly, this thinking exploits the *en suite* pod anomaly identified in Figure 4.6 and in doing so, leverages what many established suburbs already support without argument.

SO 3. Side additions

More substantial in width than side pods in a walkway, these are additions in a wider carriage lane or driveway. Exploiting the common practice of building carports and garages where originally none existed, these might be realised as single storey at ground level, elevated, or multi storeyed (Figure 4.19). They prompt the question: if adding for cars, why not for people?

4.14
Suburban operation 2.4: side pods in a 1.8m or 6' wide walkway.

4.15
Suburban operation 2.3: side pods in a 1.5m or 5' wide walkway.

4.16
Suburban operation 2.2: side pods in a 1.2m or 4' wide walkway.

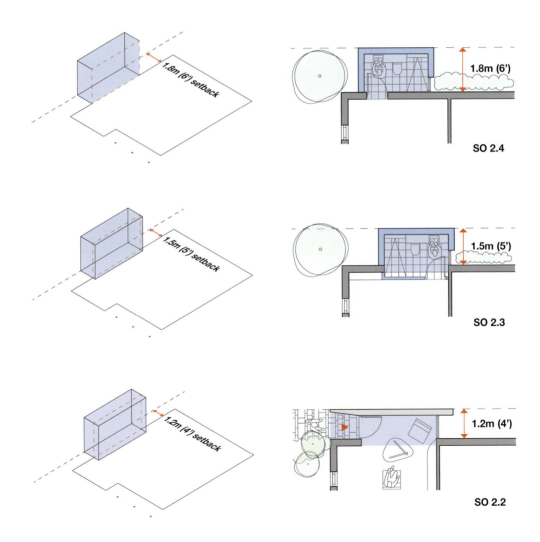

Suburban anomalies and operations

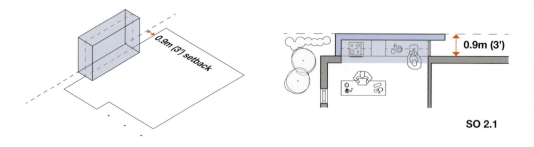

4.17 (above)
Suburban operation 2.1: side pods in a 0.9m or 3' wide walkway.

4.18 (right)
A kitchen pod created off the side of a front room in a walkway gap of only 1.2m (4'), becomes an important trigger for the creation of additional housing on the lot.

4.19
Suburban operation 3: side additions in a carriage lane or driveway.

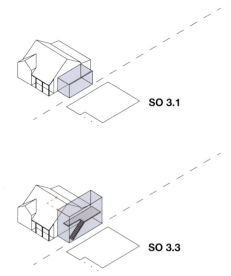

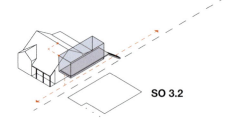

72

SO 4. Front additions

Additions at the front of the house for all or part of its width. This might be realised as an infill of a verandah, a wholesale addition to a projecting bay, or an extension across the entire width of an existing house (Figure 4.20). Worked across two adjacent sites, one might imagine an entirely new entity at the front of the lot. Although often a challenge to current thinking, particularly in neighbourhoods with character overlays, there is logic to the proposition, particularly where older houses are kept for their building value and ongoing utility rather than for any specific heritage, character, or cultural meaning.

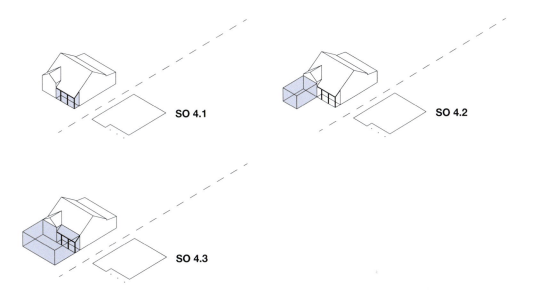

4.20
Suburban operation 4: front additions.

SO 5. Top additions

Relatively easy to achieve when the base building is of masonry construction and can support an upper level with little structural intervention, these are diagrammed in two forms. The first is in a manner which pushes the addition back, retaining the legibility of the original house from the street. The second is one that masks the form of the original house, creating a new two-storey form (Figure 4.21).

SO 6. Yard additions

Evidenced as fully detached infill elements in back yard spaces, commonly seen as ADUs, they are diagrammed here with accompanying notional landscape or yard space. Shown in single- and double-storey grounded forms in Figure 4.22, these may also be elevated off the ground plane. A three-storey form utilising a half-level basement is also diagrammed. In addition to mitigating potential

Suburban anomalies and operations

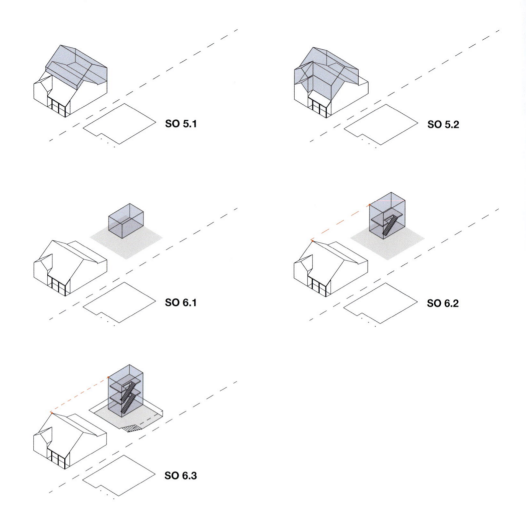

4.21
Suburban operation 5: top additions.

4.22
Suburban operation 6: yard additions.

height, mass and overshadowing effects, the accompanying sunken courtyard suggests potentially increased landscape amenity, achieved through manipulating the ground plane and demarcating a dedicated and curated outdoor space. Illustrated as small-footprint objects, yard additions can either be located between and amongst mature landscape elements or made larger where space and context allow. Shown as discrete elements to reflect their potential for use as additional dwellings or new non-residential uses, they may be imagined as attached to each other or to the existing housing, or both.

SO 7. Side additions (double allotments)

Matching the single allotment side additions, these infill elements take advantage of the extra space afforded new work when adjacent sites are made one (Figure 4.23). Diagrammed as an adjacent driveway and walkway combination, the user can extrude or compress the operations to suit two adjacent walkways or two driveways. The addition of neighbouring space, even in the limited

Suburban anomalies and operations

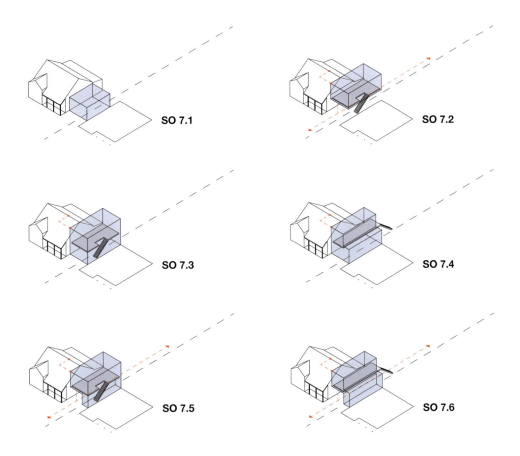

4.23
Suburban operation 7: side additions (double allotments), arranged over a combined driveway and walkway.

mode of a walkway, suggests hybrid forms where one might organise full width ground elements with partial upper-storey elements above, partial ground elements with full width upper-storey elements, or combinations of the two. Raising the additions, either in part or in full, enables access through to the rear of the allotment for pedestrians and cyclists, vehicles, or both, as indicated by the orange arrows.

SO 8. Yard arrangement

Different to SO 6 yard additions, these suggest siting strategies relative to how detached infill elements might be arrayed. Responding to street aspect, solar orientation, prevailing winds, landscape retention or creation, or programmatic requirements, these might be designed longitudinally, laterally, or as a clustered arrangement (Figure 4.24). Spread over two allotments, hybrid yard spaces might be achieved either side-by-side or back-to-back, as shown. As with the yard additions themselves, landscaped spaces might be extruded, combined, or compressed to suit local conditions and project needs.

The ambition of the suburban operations' simplified graphic mode is to speak of potential future conditions while working as a prompt for further design

Suburban anomalies and operations

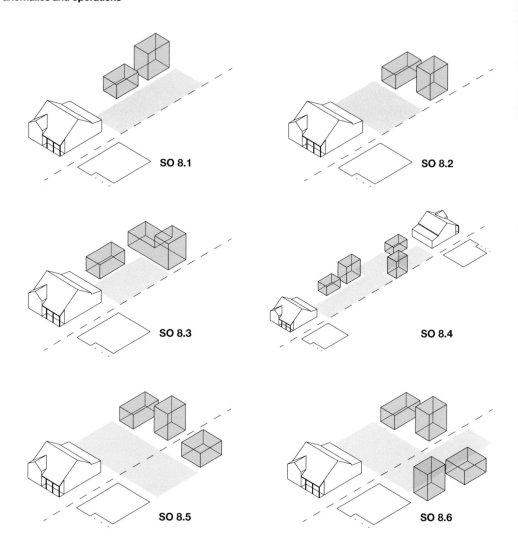

4.24
Suburban operation 8: yard arrangements (single and double allotments).

explorations, and in a manner accessible to both architects and non-architects. They work strategically across one or two lots in a deliberately smaller territorial field than the neighbourhood itself. Explaining the tactics in a single site wherever possible makes clear the individual spatial manoeuvre being discussed, as it relates to the existing house. Meanwhile the addition of one adjacent lot enables the benefits of extra space and/or another dwelling to be made evident. Once established for two sites, the moves that allow this agglomeration can be repeated in various combinations for three or more sites.

Significantly, the thinking behind the suburban operations deliberately exploits the commonly accepted anomalies found in established suburbs, reinforcing and extending them to potential alternative uses that may unlock new living patterns. As such, iteratively identifying anomalies and deploying suburban operations contributes to the evolving physical and social character of our neighbourhoods. This is explored in more detail in Part 3's design studies.

Quality-in-my-backyard

When an established suburban context is filled with quirks of physical and occupational change, what does it mean for new housing to 'fit in'?

Arguably, infill that better accommodates the complexities of contemporary household structures and offers meaningful new housing opportunities and choice where little exists, should not always have to hide behind a methodology that renders it indistinguishable from its neighbours, or be placed in a back yard as a palatable accessory. If we can understand that the character of a neighbourhood is in a constant flow that includes residential look and feel *and* shifting domestic activity as discussed in Chapter 3, perhaps we can allow our new infill housing to distinguish itself for its contribution to this mix, as necessary strategic change.

The identification of common anomalies and the deployment of suburban operations are ways of avoiding the self-limiting activity of designing a neighbourhood character 'fit' first. They are mechanisms to demonstrate in simple terms the range of possibilities older neighbourhoods already afford. It is the immediacy of their diagramming that perhaps offers their greatest value. Retaining their simplicity of analysis and, importantly, of spatial and formal expression, the most receptive audience may just be the residents of the suburbs themselves, as the anomalies and operations present both a visual demonstration of the underlying pattern found in established neighbourhoods and suggestions for how we might design strategically within this system to meet evolving needs.

The suburban operations, tailored to local conditions, help underpin the bluefield housing model described in Part 2 and form the structure of the case studies of Part 3. When coupled with an understanding of how neighbourhood housing has changed to add bathrooms for comfort, garaging for convenience, and extended space for family growth, they prompt us to question how we might add and alter for increased housing supply and choice. After all, if we already accept additions between, behind, on top of, and inside houses to make them bigger, might we accept the same amount of building mass, but configured differently to create additional and more diverse dwellings? If we already acknowledge side pods to add an extra bathroom, can we contemplate a side pod that adds a kitchen and thereby supports a second dwelling? Might we reconsider how we accommodate car parking arrangements and build a side addition that houses a second household's living room in lieu of a vehicle?

Chapter 3 discussed neighbourhood character in terms of history and activity, while this chapter has extended that conversation in relation to modes of suburban building. They have each begged the question of how we might define 'fit' or 'character' within the spectrum of neighbourhood transformation. In reassessing what has come before us in the suburbs and what is needed now, discussions around neighbourhood character can become not about preventing change completely, or halting change at the point at which we are comfortable with our surroundings, nor about pushing new development at all costs. Instead, it can be formed around an understanding that for generations we have been putting in motion the triggers for suburban housing intensification. When thought of in this way, the neighbourhood infill debate can shift from NIMBY versus YIMBY, to one of QIMBYism.

'Quality-in-my-backyard' is sometimes associated with the New Urbanist movement and its focus on the design of walkable and human-scaled communities in the tradition of past centuries.[7] It has also been used to describe a stylistic preference for new suburban housing that is aesthetically referential to traditional architectural styles. In the bluefield housing model, 'quality' and 'QIMBY' does not relate to aesthetics, but to an overall sophistication of infill strategy and execution before look and feel are considered. While understanding and responding to the continuum of neighbourhood character is a key component of bluefield housing, this does not require designing in an obsequious or reproductive manner. Rather, acknowledging suburban change and understanding how it has occurred locally at the hands of NIMBYists and YIMBYists alike, is a way to transition from discussing *if* neighbourhood change can be accepted, to determining the social and design *qualities* that our neighbourhoods need.

Notes

1 "#StopThePop Campaign," Chicago Bungalow Association, accessed 10 February 2022, www.chicagobungalow.org/additions.
2 Nishat Awan, Tatjana Schneider, and Jeremy Till, *Spatial Agency: Other Ways of Doing Architecture*. Abingdon, Oxon: Routledge, 2011, 123–125.
3 Edward Denison and Guang Yu Ren, *The Life of the British Home: An Architectural History*. Hoboken, New Jersey: Wiley, 2012.
4 Robin Boyd, *Australia's Home: Its Origins, Builders and Occupiers*. New M.U.P. ed. Carlton, Victoria: Melbourne University Press, 1987.
5 Philip Cox, Philip Graus, and Bob Meyer, *Home: Evolution of the Australian Dream*. Paddington, New South Wales: Jane Curry Publishing, 2011.
6 Anthony Di Mari and Nora Yoo, *Operative Design: A Catalogue of Spatial Verbs*. Amsterdam: BIS Publishers, 2012.
7 Accessible information on New Urbanism can be found at "Congress for the New Urbanism," Congress for the New Urbanism, accessed 30 March 2022, www.cnu.org/. and in Robert Steuteville, *25 Great Ideas of New Urbanism*. Washington, DC: Congress for the New Urbanism, 2019.

Part 2

5 From green to blue

A new definition for suburban infill

The greenfields

Private domestic yards, often decorative to the front while more operative at the rear, are defining features of suburban living. They are the spatial buffers that can cocoon a house and help establish its setting as a home within a garden. At street level, yards set thresholds that delineate the public infrastructure of roads and footpaths from the personal space of privately owned land. Behind the house, yards are the space of recreation and utility. Their offering of private amenity and neighbourly distance, as discussed in Chapter 1, helps distinguish a suburban way of life from that of urban living. So, what to do when more space is needed to extend the traditional suburban dream for an increased population? The conventional logic has been to open greenfield land for development.

The greenfields are those areas on the fringes of a city that have never been used for housing. They may be agricultural lands which are now more valuable as sites for housing than for farming. Alternatively, they could be state-owned land surplus to original requirements or strategically earmarked for future growth as a city expands. In the greenfields, new housing estates are created at the master plan level, with allotments set out based on a residential density target, maximum development yield, and market positioning. This usually results in a limited range of standardised lot sizes providing a selection of price points for the purchaser. The extent of green and recreational infrastructure across a greenfield development is planned relative to the number of allotments realised and overall scale of the new suburb, with facilities often mandated by or developed in coordination

81

DOI: 10.4324/9781003293736-8
This chapter has been made available under a CC-BY-NC-ND license.

with the local authority. Yet, expanding the city's fringes does not always result in traditional lot sizes that match the older suburbs of a city. Working within density, feasibility, and profitability targets, many new greenfield housing estates are notable for the proximity of the houses to each other and the compactness of their form. With average house sizes increasing while allotments shrink, the irony of the greenfields is that they often create a more proximate form of suburban living than the established suburbs, despite the land expanses that underpin their development. They can also offer the great contradiction of developing 'green' areas, as the push to maximise allotment numbers and dwelling footprints yields limited landscape opportunities for streets coupled with reduced private gardens. Growing out may offer suburban housing at a more affordable price point, but it does not guarantee a less compact form of living.

5.1
Fern Bay, a new greenfield suburb on the outskirts of Newcastle, north of Sydney: a compact extension of the suburban dream.
Source: Google Earth.

A common tactic to increase the number of allotments in a greenfield development and create quiet enclaves of neighbourliness is to limit the use of through-streets through culs-de-sac or dead-ends. This has the positive effect of reducing the through-traffic of cars while increasing allotment yield, as back-to-back lots fill the gaps in what would otherwise have been street intersections. When well designed, paths can link culs-de-sac, making them quiet yet connected, but when poorly designed they deny any form of through-traffic and force residents into their cars for all activities outside of the home.[1] This is exacerbated when public transport is relegated to primary roads, with little (if any) penetration into the suburb itself.

New suburbs work well when they can take advantage of existing infrastructure and services nearby, offering a manageable extension to an already well-serviced area. However, the creation of large greenfield suburbs on previously un-serviced land requires the provision of everything, from power, water, waste, and roads, to public transport, retail and recreation offerings, health and allied services, and civic functions. And the more spread out the suburbs become, the more expensive they are for a city to service. Recent research by in the US found that the most urbanised parts of a city – those with more compact urban forms –

subsidise low-rise single-family home suburbs. This is due to a simple economic fact related to distance, space, and property numbers: when compared to spread-out car-centric parts of the city, more dense areas require less infrastructure while also bringing in significantly more taxation income due to the higher number of individual properties. This results in compact downtowns returning a surplus to the city relative to the infrastructure spending incurred, while the suburbs produce a deficit. And where a city preferences car-centric single-family zoning over more compact walkable forms, it can result in most of its territory being a perpetual economic burden when it comes to infrastructure spending.[2]

Servicing the suburbs requires a multi-agency approach that mixes private and public funding and delivery. Infrastructure requirements do not come cheaply, and new satellite suburbs often present little beyond the elemental housing and requisite basic services that allow function and vehicular access. Such limitations have been brought into sharp focus with COVID-19. When Sydney went into lockdown in 2021, people were restricted to a 5 kilometres (3.1 miles) exercise radius from their homes. For one resident of Austral, a growth area southwest of the city, the shutdown demonstrated for the first time limited the facilities within the suburb:

> When you realise you couldn't get to a shop within 5 kilometres, or you couldn't get to a recreational park or anything in 5ks, you realise there really is a lack of services in the area.[3]

In some circumstances, new developments on the fringes of cities create cheaper housing options but locate residents closer to regions affected by natural disasters such as floods, fires, and weather extremes.[4] And when it comes to the design of the fringes, it is not the case that contemporary understandings of integrated design approaches are improving the outcomes of all new greenfield developments. The *Building Car Dependency* study of 20 new greenfield developments across England, from Exeter in the southwest to York in the northeast, found that all but three were places that were designed around the car, with residents forced into their cars for almost all journeys to and from their homes. Extensive internal road systems coupled with large areas of off-street parking necessary to meet zoning requirements, resulted in swathes of hard ground surfaces throughout most of the developments.[5]

With a major incentive of greenfield developments being increased affordability and entry into the housing market where it is otherwise cost prohibitive, it can be the case that the residents who can least afford the rising and fluctuating costs of running a car are those who rely on it the most. High running costs can also be incurred for household heating and cooling, exacerbated by reduced landscape amenity at the allotment scale, large expanses of hard roof and ground surfaces, and only base-level passive heating and cooling tactics incorporated within the design of many for-market volume houses themselves. It is not uncommon for those seeking affordable housing in greenfield fringes to be particularly susceptible to financial vulnerability (Figure 5.2).[6]

5.2 (overleaf)
Financial vulnerabilities in Australia's capital cities: those living on the fringes are under greater financial stress than those of inner areas, regardless of their city's size, population, or density.

Data source: The Vulnerability Analysis of Mortgage, Petroleum and Inflation Risks and Expenditure (VAMPIRE) Index, 2018.

From green to blue: a new definition for suburban infill

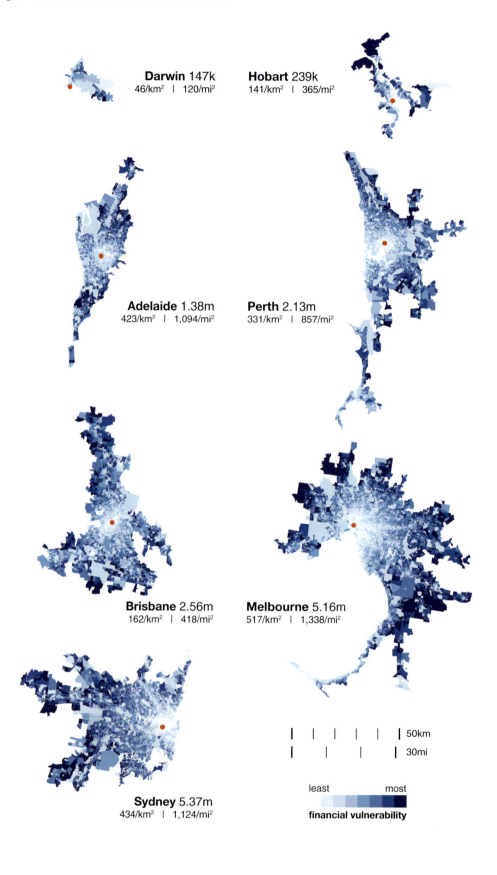

84

The brownfields

As manufacturing shifts offshore, large industrial land holdings within city boundaries can become redundant. These are the brownfields: non-residential and potentially contaminated land surrounded by or in proximity to housing, that provide the potential for residential infill opportunities as new suburbs. Because industrial sites often consist of complex and tailored designs coupled with site contamination from years of industry, retrofitting the brownfields is sometimes unfeasible, resulting in wholesale clearing of the site. The reality for some brownfields is that they are prized for their land value only, where they offer the potential for substantial new residential development within an existing suburban mix.

Due to their size, brownfield sites often require a master plan that is approved in coordination with the local planning authority or state government, the aim being to offer inward amenity for residents and the provision of broader community services and civic infrastructure that might otherwise be missing from surrounding residential areas. Often sitting adjacent homogenous single-family home suburbs, residential development in brownfield locations provide the opportunity to diversify housing offerings with a combination of multi-storey apartment buildings, townhouses, and detached housing at higher densities. When located closer to an urban centre, a brownfield development will favour larger apartment complexes.

Large brownfield developments, like their greenfield cousins, can offer a town centre with commercial, retail, hospitality, and service functions. Often, a developer's right to develop a brownfield site will be determined by government based on the residential and non-residential mix being proposed. In most contemporary brownfield developments space will be given over to shared landscape, often in the form of sporting fields, walking and cycling paths, and water

5.3
The 61ha (150 acre) Tonsley Innovation District in Adelaide: a brownfield redevelopment surrounded by low-rise residential suburbs, converting a disused car manufacturing plant into a mixed-use education, industry, civic, and residential precinct.
Source: Google Earth.

catchment areas. Landscape in the form of water reclamation and wetlands are decorative, cooling, and rehabilitative devices that often attempt to redress the balance between the brownfield site's former life as a polluter and its new existence as a model of contemporary living. This combination of remediation, landscape, commercial, civic, and residential offerings establish contemporary brownfield developments as new forms of living and working, surrounded by familiar residential territory. They are a means of generating increased housing numbers at preferred densities, whilst modelling new socially connected ways of living.

The greyfields

The greyfields can be defined both commercially and residentially. The growth of online shopping and services has seen the presence of bricks and mortar retail shrink dramatically, with swathes of vacated big box stores and their accompanying carparks forming so-called 'greyfields'. Retrofitting these 'ghostboxes', as described by Ellen Dunham-Jones and June Williamson,[7] makes environmental and social sense, particularly for civic functions that can be programmed easily into large open-plan interiors. They are well suited to 'third places': service, civic, or social environments that sit outside of where we live and work, but that we nevertheless inhabit regularly.[8] However, due to the scale of ghostboxes themselves, and of their expanses of hard-surface on-site car parking, retrofitting for residential use invariably requires a significant level of new construction and infrastructure within the site.

The greyfields have also been defined at the residential scale by Peter Newton: these are ageing suburbs with housing that is functionally, physically, and environmentally obsolescent, and subsequently under-capitalised.[9] As post-war suburbs have aged, their capital value has often been restricted to the value of the land only, with the houses themselves seen as commercially worthless. Similarly, much post-war housing has not been as socially valued as older housing stock that offers the attraction of heritage or character attributes. Offering neither the deep nostalgia of the past nor the newness value of contemporary housing, they can be demolished and replaced with new dwellings that better fit contemporary preferences and lifestyles, with little resident concern over neighbourhood character preservation.

Made up of housing that is valued neither financially nor emotionally, the greyfields are ripe for knock-down-rebuild, or 'KDR', redevelopment. This is most often seen in the form of 2- or 3-for-1 intensification on a single allotment, doubling or tripling residential densities within existing city limits; an attractive density measure for cities wishing to provide more housing in established boundaries. The model works at the scale of a single or multiple adjacent lots, and although it is a less intensive form of densification than those offered by brownfield projects it often results in sub-optimal housing outcomes. Due to the small-scale nature of greyfield development, it is generally not the domain of large developers experienced in providing a holistic mix of housing, landscape, and environmental outcomes. Instead, it is better suited to smaller home building companies that can take advantage of favourable subdivision rules to split an allotment and create free-standing homes in the absence of any overarching suburban design strategy.

Often, what yields in this form of residential intensification – even in a simple 2-for-1 duplex development – is only the size of the allotment rather than the size of the houses, with much of the new housing replicating or increasing the accommodation previously provided by the single house being replaced. This sets up two dilemmas: sites that are predominated by hard ground and roof surfaces, and a lack of housing diversity. These in turn have two negative consequences. The first is a loss of landscape amenity and an increase in urban heat island effect, as discussed in Chapter 1. The second is an affordability issue, where each new house in the land division is individually worth more than the original house it replaced, despite being on half the land.

5.4
An Australian KDR duplex in the greyfields (right) next door to the type of original home regularly being replaced (left): reduced affordability, reduced tree canopy and soft landscape surfaces, increased water run-off, and increased urban heat island effect (UHI).
Source: Google Earth.

These financial and environmental pressures have increased as greyfield KDR redevelopment activities have flourished, and they are heightened when property owners mobilise to consolidate their adjacent lots to offer a larger and thereby more valuable redevelopment site for sale. What commenced as low-intensity infill enabled by simple sub-division and unsophisticated infill techniques, now requires a more strategic and holistic approach that incorporates green urbanism principles, greater community consultation for how the greyfields turn over, and a more active and engaged presence from statutory authorities at the precinct level.[10]

The bluefields: a new definition for suburban infill

A perceived advantage of greenfield, brownfield, and greyfield residential development is that intensifying housing supply here takes the pressure off the established parts of the city having to meet increased housing targets. It is a way of attempting to meet housing targets whilst maintaining the established character of certain places. The common rhetoric, as discussed in Chapter 3, is that targeting housing increases in growth and infill zones enables large parts of a city to remain 'largely unchanged' – shielded from the challenges of intensification. However, this preservation ambition can limit the housing choice in older suburbs; locking existing residents in as their needs change, as much as it leaves potential new residents out.

Furthermore, even the most established of suburbs rarely remain 'unchanged', with incremental development happening over time. If the intention and perceived benefit of green-, brown-, and greyfield housing strategies is the avoidance of intensification challenges in character suburbs, then this leaves these older parts of the city to their business-as-usual slow burn development. But this begs the question of what this neighbourhood 'business' is, for the suburbs – regardless of their age or preservation requirements – continue to see substantial change even when they fall outside of infill policy that targets increased housing supply.

I call these established suburbs the 'bluefields'. They are neighbourhoods quarantined from strategic and formal density and diversity increases or those grappling with how to shift from single-family zoning without wholesale neighbourhood change. They are the suburbs with established character, where 'blue' represents both the perceived immutability of their traditional character, and the high financial and emotional values often in play. Blue also speaks to both the real and perceived calmness and serenity of older suburbs, qualities so often seen as being under threat by new forms of infill development.[11]

As a land definition, a bluefield area is an older neighbourhood where the retention of housing stock, streetscapes, and gardens is desirable, but where change is nonetheless observable in greyfield-like KDR minor infill. This occurs where an unprotected character house and its landscape is replaced with duplex or triplex housing. In the bluefields, change is also observable in individual alterations and additions, where houses are extended into even larger single-family homes, increasing the risk of gentrification as house values increase along with the real estate offering. As discussed in Chapter 1, in both change scenarios mature landscape is regularly the collateral damage, with many local authorities lacking the public space and operational capacity to replace tree canopy continually being lost from private land development.

Part 1 of this book touched on some intricacies and nuances of the suburbs. To be 'suburban' is to exist in a complex, politicised, and evolving housing system that guarantees only that it can never stay completely static (even if the change of pace appears glacial at times). Houses rarely remain as unchanged museum pieces, even in the most tightly regulated and protected conservation areas. People adapt their houses, moulding them to changing needs and patterns of living over time. Housing aspirations also evolve, and as the traditional suburban house in a garden setting becomes increasingly out of reach for many people

From green to blue: a new definition for suburban infill

5.5
The bluefields: older suburbs, usually quarantined from strategic and systematic change, but where change occurs nonetheless through the alterations and additions habits of private owners.

Source: GeoTIFF image courtesy of the City of Burnside.

or for others is no longer the comfortable fit that it once was, there is a growing ambition to seek new ways of living smaller and more cooperatively in an environment that is well-connected socially, civically, and commercially. Meanwhile, the leafy amenity provided by the mature landscape of suburbia continues to be beneficial and desirable but is increasingly lost to traditional forms of KDR redevelopment. Through it all, the NIMBY/YIMBY/QIMBY debates continue, led by discussions around the appropriate residential 'fit' of new housing and its new residents within an established neighbourhood.

Sociologically, the general absence of housing diversity in bluefield suburbs sees existing residents lacking downsizing options within their community, an exodus of younger residents seeking more affordable housing options as they leave home, and the locking-out of new residents seeking to enter well-serviced, high-amenity suburbs.

Beyond identifying the 'bluefields' as a fourth housing space that extends the existing green-, brown-, and greyfield land definitions, 'bluefield housing' is also offered as an accompanying infill model: an approach to systematically increasing housing numbers and introducing greater diversity of housing types into otherwise homogenous neighbourhoods. It is a way of shepherding older suburbs through change in a manner that retains their physical character while recognising their evolving social character. Leveraging the 'commonly accepted anomalies' and 'suburban operations' of Chapter 4, the bluefield housing model is strategically simple. Formed of the tropes of suburban alterations and additions that are already in play, it offers a suburban housing form that is strangely familiar, yet subtly radical.

Notes

1. Leon Van Schaik and Nigel Bertram, *Suburbia Reimagined: Ageing and Increasing Populations in the Low-Rise City*. New York: Routledge, 2019.
2. "Suburbia is Subsidized: Here's the Math," Strong Towns, last modified 8 March 2022, https://youtu.be/7Nw6qyyrTel.

3 Catherine Hanrahan, "Sydney's population is predicted to explode — this is where people will live in 20 years," *ABC News* (11 February 2022). www.abc.net.au/news/2022-02-10/populat ion-growth-outstrips-infrastructure-in-outer-sydney/100816952.

4 Jenny Schuetz, *Fixer-Upper: How to Repair America's Broken Housing Systems*. Washington, DC: Brookings Institution Press, 2022.

5 Transport for New Homes, *Building Car Dependency: The Tarmac Suburbs of the Future* (London: Transport for New Homes, 2022), www.transportfornewhomes.org.uk/the-project/ building-car-dependency/.

6 Tiebei Li, Jago Dodson, and Neil Sipe, *Vulnerability Assessment for Mortgage, Petroleum and Inflation Risk and Expenditure Index (VAMPIRE)*, 2018. RMIT University Centre for Urban Research. Accessed from AURIN on 14 January 2022, https://data.aurin.org.au/dataset/rmit-cur-vampire-2016-capital-cities-sa1-sa1-2016.

7 Ellen Dunham-Jones and June Williamson, *Retrofitting Suburbia, Updated Edition: Urban Design Solutions for Redesigning Suburbs*. Hoboken, NJ: John Wiley & Sons, 2011.

8 June Williamson and Ellen Dunham-Jones, *Case Studies in Retrofitting Suburbia: Urban Design Solutions for Urgent Challenges*. Hoboken, NJ: John Wiley & Sons, 2021.

9 Peter Newton, "Beyond Greenfield and Brownfield: The Challenge of Regenerating Australia's Greyfield Suburbs," *Built Environment* 36, no. 1 (2010): 81–104, www.jstor.org/sta ble/23289985.

10 Peter Newton, Denny Meyer, and Stephen Glackin, "Becoming Urban: Exploring the Transformative Capacity for a Suburban-to-Urban Transition in Australia's Low-Density Cities," *Sustainability* 9, no. 1718 (2017), www.mdpi.com/2071-1050/9/10/1718.

11 'Blue' has also been associated with living by water ('blue spaces') and being older ('blue rinse'). Bluefield housing relates to neither of these, as explained in the Introduction.

6 The seven principles of bluefield housing

Resilience, sustainability, and inclusivity where it is needed

Chapter 5 defined a bluefield suburb as one where broad urban infill strategies are avoided, yet where minor infill is nonetheless observable in knockdown-rebuild (KDR) development, where suburban density is increased but housing choice is not. In the bluefields, change is also observable in alterations and additions, as described in Chapter 4, where houses are extended into even larger single-family homes, further increasing the risk of gentrification. In both change scenarios mature landscape is regularly lost, with many local councils struggling to replace tree canopy lost from private land development. The general absence of housing diversity in bluefield suburbs sees existing residents lacking downsizing options within their community, an exodus of younger residents seeking more affordable housing options as they leave home, and the locking-out of new residents seeking to enter well-serviced, high-amenity suburbs.

At its heart, the bluefield housing model is about increasing housing choice while retaining and enhancing neighbourhood character: infill that is low scale, low intensity but high impact. As architect Guy Luscombe has described it,

> 'Bluefield' housing uses the existing fabric of widespread single-lot housing to create more resilient, sustainable and inclusive dwellings within our suburbs, where most people live.[1]

91

DOI: 10.4324/9781003293736-9
This chapter has been made available under a CC-BY-NC-ND license.

The seven principles of bluefield housing

Local jurisdictions face the challenges of meeting the challenges of the evolving suburban environment: how to assist their residents age-in-place, how to maintain built character and urban tree canopy, and how to increase the supply of smaller housing stock to help off-set gentrification and create avenues for new and more diverse groups of residents. The bluefield housing model has been developed as one mechanism to help address these issues and is underpinned by seven key principles.

PRINCIPLE 1   FACILITATE SHARING

The bluefield housing model is founded on a co-location strategy to leverage spatial efficiency and generate social capital. The residents of a new bluefield scheme might be a group of hitherto strangers – singles, couples, or families – who redevelop a lot together to create independent dwellings that enjoy the spatial and personal benefits that some degree of sharing can deliver. They could be a family who decide to adapt their existing home and garden to pre-emptively create the final home for the oldest members and the first independent home for the youngest. They may be any combination of unrelated individuals with similar housing ambitions to those discussed in Chapter 2. They might be a community housing provider (CHP) creating a new model of lifetime rental properties that expand their traditional portfolio.

Thought of in this way, the concept of co-located housing has a common thread: the desire for a suburban housing model that sits alongside existing single-family homes but with a downsized footprint and in a more socially connected manner. Such a model works to achieve the independence, integration, and innovation crucial to creating age-appropriate housing, while strategically avoiding any planning, aesthetic or organisational manoeuvres that can otherwise render housing as institutional, particularly for older people.[2]

The concept of sharing living arrangements with others can be challenging. Two factors are key here. The first is that the co-location strategy put forward in the bluefield housing model is for those who proactively decide to share and have control of their living choices, meaning they are predisposed to wanting to share. The second is that many people are not only happy to share, but to do so with others who are not necessarily the same as themselves. When researchers surveyed lower income older Australian residents over a decade ago when concepts of sharing were less mainstream, only 27% felt that it was important to share with those of similar religious, gender, or other characteristics.[3] In the UK, Julia Park and Jeremy Porteous link contemporary appetites for sharing with prior house-sharing experiences across the life span in both familial and friendship groups:

> Co-living arrangements seem particularly likely to gain popularity. Multigenerational living in purpose-built housing with distinct, but connected, domains would be ideal for some extended families.

The seven principles of bluefield housing

Choosing to live with friends is also beginning to feel a very natural instinct later in life – for single people and couples. Today's young people have to wait longer for a home of their own and many, perhaps even most, will have house-shared.[4]

Founded on the idea of co-locating homes on the same lot, the bluefield housing model has the capacity to modulate the degree of sharing across each development, depending on resident choices. For some, this may be a case of creating a mini cohousing scheme with a form of common house available to all. For others, it will simply be the sharing of the lot that provides the social connectedness they seek. For others still, it may be a financial incentive that draws them to the scheme, as a means of achieving suburban housing in a neighbourhood of their choice, when it may otherwise not be out of reach. What is important is that the bluefield design actively facilitates sharing, which is made possible by deploying the principles which follow.

6.1
In the bluefield housing model, something is always shared. This starts with the lot and its landscaped yard, as seen here in the Large scheme of Chapter 10, but the degrees of sharing can be increased to include common facilities.

PRINCIPLE 2 IGNORE LOT SIZE AND YIELD, AND CO-LOCATE TO AVOID LAND DIVISION

In some jurisdictions, backyard homes can be added to an existing property with no stipulation on the size of the lot required to do so, providing they fall within stated maximum footprint sizes and minimum building setbacks. This flexibility can come with other restrictions however, such as the inability to sell the backyard home independently of the main house, or the limitation of only being allowed to add one additional dwelling. The result is two dwellings that are co-dependent. By comparison, when attempting to create fully independent houses, the capacity for a neighbourhood and its individual lots to support additional infill housing is generally determined with metrics, where minimum lot sizes are determined for a policy area based on assumptions of suitable neighbourhood fit. In these circumstances, the metrics are not particularly sophisticated. If, for example, the stipulated minimum lot size for a zone is 300m^2 (3,230 sq ft), a 700m^2 (7,500 sq ft) lot could be subdivided into two new allotments providing neither fall below the minimum allowed. Assuming zoning laws are met and car and pedestrian access to each new lot can be achieved, the land division process can proceed, resulting in smaller reconfigured lots in the mould of single-family homes.

In simple terms, this traditional process of suburban land division begins with a rudimentary analysis of yield based on minimum lot size. It then proceeds through a process of site clearing in preparation for the construction of new replacement dwellings that in most cases seek to maximise the accommodation relative to zoning rules around maximum site coverage and heights, and minimum boundary setbacks. By comparison, the bluefield housing approach rethinks how allotment yield is determined. As described in the Introduction, traditional minimum lot size stipulations do not guarantee successful housing and landscape outcomes any more than interventions below these thresholds guarantee failure. Being a design-led methodology, the bluefield housing process begins with the assumptions that:

- any lot size may be considered for intensification;
- the lot is not divided;
- the number of dwellings to be achieved is not predetermined;
- dwelling numbers are decided based on a unified design approach that incorporates the other bluefield housing principles;
- at least one high amenity shared outdoor space is provided; and
- individual dwellings are co-located on the lot and are not fenced off in a way that segregates them.

BAU Battleaxe   **Bluefield**

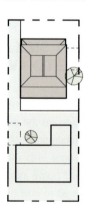 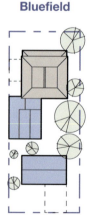

6.2
A business-as-usual (BAU) battle-axe land division (left) compared with a bluefield housing co-location development (right).

These lot-level ambitions require a bluefield development to be designed and managed such that the integrity of the co-location model is maintained over its lifetime. Given there is no mandate over minimum lot sizes for each dwelling, nor over the number of dwellings that can be created, there is a risk that the model is used as a zoning Trojan Horse to create privatised infill housing that would otherwise be disallowed. Measures to mitigate undermining of the model are discussed in Chapters 15 and 16.

PRINCIPLE 3 RETAIN AND ADAPT THE LOT'S ORIGINAL HOUSING

The business-as-usual land division approach to infill encourages KDR, resulting in poor environmental outcomes and stifled housing innovation. A common infill approach, it sits adjacent to an opposite yet common suburban act: that of adapting and extending existing homes to make them larger. These patterns of additive suburban behaviour have been discussed relative to domestic activity in Chapter 3, and in relation to physical neighbourhood change in Chapter 4. The bluefield housing model recognises this adaptive behaviour and incorporates it as a key component of its development strategy.

Whilst many houses in older neighbourhoods are precluded from demolition by precinct-wide character overlays or by individual heritage protections, there is an overriding logic to why we might keep and rework existing dwellings in the absence of such protections. As evidenced by the global suburban inclination to renovate, the retention of an existing house enables owners to tailor their homes to their personal needs and preferences, and to do so as a series of staged projects over time as their needs develop and renovation funds become available. In these circumstances, homeowners elect to retain older housing not because heritage restrictions dictate they must, but because it simply makes sense. Retaining existing housing stock makes renovations more financially feasible when the owners can remain living on site while the building work takes place. Furthermore, when the construction of older houses is robust, as is the case with many masonry homes, they resist wholesale deterioration, offering a combination of longevity and malleability.

Of course, people are often drawn to older houses for their aesthetic character traits, which extends to many neighbourhoods' garden settings and landscape amenity. The low-rise scale of older neighbourhood housing can also be attractive, and retaining and adapting original housing maintains the prevailing scale and streetscape in a way that KDR replacement dwellings cannot. Much of a neighbourhood's physical character comes from housing and landscape development that has gradually occurred over decades. While replacement dwellings may be forced to fit zoning laws that generally reinforce the prevailing neighbourhood scale, they often create a scale-creep. This occurs when a statutory authority allows a replacement dwelling to be 'slightly' over the allowed site coverage, or height, or setback because it is *generally* in accordance with the desired characteristics of the neighbourhood. Coupled with the removal of landscape, this subtle (and sometimes not-too-subtle) stretching of the rules has a cumulative effect on neighbourhood built and landscape character as the zoning breaches amplify across lots.

Retaining and adapting original housing is key to the bluefield housing model because it positions it within established modes of suburban redevelopment behaviour. Significantly, it allows streetscape character to be retained and enhanced, while using the existing housing stock as the datum by which the rhythm of the neighbourhood can be developed. Furthermore, in circumstances where a housing proponent seeks to achieve density increases that might otherwise be unachievable in a particular neighbourhood, retention and renovation of the existing house can become a bargaining chip that helps achieve a win–win outcome for the owner and the neighbourhood. Incentivising is discussed further in Chapter 14.

6.3
Many older houses accommodate physical changes that support a contemporary way of life that could not have been predicted when the houses were first built. Here, two rooms become one (left), while traditional elements are retained for their cultural memory and continuing utility (right).

PRINCIPLE 4 LEVERAGE THE PREVAILING PATTERN OF ALTERATIONS AND ADDITIONS

Underpinned by Principles 2 and 3 that retain the original street-facing house on an intact lot, the bluefield housing model functions within the existing single-family home model of suburbia. And if the adaptation of houses is a staple of older neighbourhoods, so too is the fact that the spaces around them are filled with housing additions and extras. The observations of Chapters 3 and 4 around the types of physical and behaviour changes the suburbs accommodate challenge the premise that targeting new housing in dedicated high- and medium-density zones will leave low-rise parts of the city 'largely unchanged'. The bluefield housing model leverages these behaviours. It looks to the development pattern of the local context and mimics it, not in an act of stealth, camouflage, or acquiescence, but in much simpler and more honest terms. By reconfiguring familiar single-family home site coverages to introduce additional smaller dwellings, bluefield housing challenges the notion of what it can mean to densify the suburbs. It begs the question that if additional building elements

The seven principles of bluefield housing

are acceptable for garages, bathrooms, and recreation spaces, can they not be acceptable for housing new people in the neighbourhood?

The starting point of Principle 4 is a site analysis of the existing built form of the target lot and its neighbours, and research into the prevailing zoning conditions for built-form characteristics, permitted heights, maximum site coverages, and setback requirements. This is a normative redevelopment methodology when extending a single-family home and is not innovative – but that is its point. As shown in the design studies of Part 3, building more housing on a suburban lot does not have to mean building more than what is already there. Working in this manner allows bluefield housing to achieve two key outcomes: it allows the new housing to sit comfortably within the existing neighbourhood mix, while offering the potential to be reinstated to a single dwelling that matches the scale of other extended single-family homes in the area.

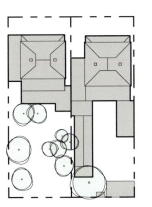
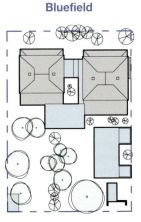

6.4
A bluefield housing development leverages the prevailing pattern of suburban alterations and additions (left) to create additional housing (right).

PRINCIPLE 5 CREATE HOUSING IN A FLAT HIERARCHY

As discussed in the Introduction, when it comes to the prevailing 'light-touch' infill responses to established neighbourhoods – ADUs, JADUs, secondary suites, 'granny flats', 'in-law suites', and the like – the defining features lie in the names. They are 'accessories' to a main dwelling, 'junior' in status, 'secondary' in performance, or prescriptive in their audience. Bluefield Principle 5 is to eschew the concept of any form of hierarchy on the lot and to instead treat all housing in the development as simply 'housing' for anyone. This may seem a semantic exercise, but its ambitions run deeper. It is a way of conceiving the housing such that none of them is a compromised dwelling. The alternative would be to define a 'main' house, relegating the new dwellings to something 'other'. This would undermine the other bluefield principles and limit the social and architectural potential for the development as a holistic entity. For the model to work as a co-location densification strategy that does not require minimum lot size thresholds, the retained street-facing house will often need to be reconfigured into a smaller dwelling, as shown in the case studies of Part 3. This adaptive reuse re-scales the single-family home into a more affordable offering while creating space for the shared landscape and/or the additional housing.

When a bluefield development is considered holistically at the scale of the entire site rather than in terms of left-over backyard space, there is no benefit to be found in treating one dwelling as more significant than any other. It is easy to assume that the retained house is the preferred choice on the lot, but in designing a flat hierarchy the potential is opened for any of the housing to be the most desirable depending on different occupant needs at different life stages. Designing this way, it is entirely possible that the new dwellings are, for example, larger than the retained house, offer better aspect, or have a higher environmental performance; qualities that may render them more attractive that the original home. Depending on the age, construction, configuration, and orientation of the retained housing stock, the designer may have to work harder to achieve amenity, performance, or aesthetic outcomes on the reworked original house than they do on the new, and the result may never match the successes of the new construction on the lot. This fact alone helps to illustrate that any concept of 'hierarchy' based on which house arrived first, or which faces the street, is irrelevant.

Strategising the housing in a flat hierarchy helps to diversify the housing stock of a neighbourhood, as it seeks to create a middle ground between the single-family home and the ADU. It also serves a social good. It declares that new small-footprint suburban housing is not something to be hidden or secreted into a back yard, and that new and innovative housing can be notable for its social and architectural contribution to the neighbourhood.

6.5
Because a bluefield housing development is designed holistically across the entire lot, it is unnecessary to differentiate between primary and secondary dwellings, even when one of those dwellings already exists on the lot.

The seven principles of bluefield housing

PRINCIPLE 6 ARRANGE HOUSING AROUND SHARED LANDSCAPE IN A UNIFIED DESIGN

The first five bluefield principles are development strategies that require a proposal to be designed holistically from boundary to boundary and with equal consideration given to each dwelling and their contribution to the whole. For many architects and planners, this is a given of residential design, particularly for any form of group dwellings. However, much production in suburban housing is design only of the house itself – its look and feel – and not of an overarching site and social strategy. This is particularly the case in pre-designed or 'standard plan' backyard homes, which are designed to fit morphologically within a broad context of suburban yards, but not always in relation to individual lot nuances. That is not to say that a system of standard plans or set designs offered by an architectural or construction company cannot be incorporated into the bluefield model, but it requires these predetermined models to work within a unified design system across the lot.

To deliver its social and neighbourhood ambitions, the bluefield approach necessitates a rethinking of private open space. It is not enough to retain an original street-facing house and its front yard landscape, and then treat the backyard as a blank slate for the creation of one or more additional houses. Principle 6 requires a deep consideration of all existing lot features, including its backyard landscape, which in many suburban settings will have taken decades to develop. A bluefield approach will look to retain as much significant backyard landscape as possible and to arrange the new housing in relation to this and to the retained home. 'Significant' landscape in this context is broad and negotiable but generally refers to woody plants such as trees and shrubs that offer amenity to the place and would require space, time, and money to replace if lost because of construction. However, retaining mature landscape does not automatically outweigh other development considerations, and a unified design approach will discover priorities here.

The bluefield starting point is to not read the lot as a blank canvas, but to instead draw the existing house and its landscape in its intact form. This project commencement approach is (or at least should be) common within architectural conceptual design. In an ideal scenario, existing ad hoc building elements that cannot be meaningfully incorporated into the scheme can be removed and given over as available territory for the new housing components. These construction zones can then be combined with the existing un-landscaped spaces on the lot to form the available territory for the building work. In many instances, this will work well for the bluefield development, as the new housing will simply occupy the footprints of the old, leaving the remnant landscape intact. Ideally, there will be an appropriate ratio of built and landscape space, with all elements working together with amenity and practicality relative to the residents' needs. This process of design will not always be possible, however, and the push to work around existing landscape may ultimately compromise the scheme to unacceptable levels. It may be, for example, that removing a particular tree allows building elements to be better positioned such that a more successful overall housing and landscape outcome is achieved. Success here may be measured by better spatial, amenity, or environmental outcomes despite the loss of existing landscape.

Where the retention of landscape is not possible, or where the backyard offers no significant landscape elements, greater freedom is afforded to the designer, but the onus to incorporate significant landscape remains the same. In all bluefield housing schemes, space for at least one deep root soil zone will be provided, around which the housing is arranged. This enables medium and large trees to be planted such that they can contribute over time to the restoration of suburban tree canopies, passive cooling of the site, and dwelling amenity. Definitions of tree sizes and further discussion around the statutory measures that can be imposed on landscape in the bluefield model is discussed in Chapter 16.

Importantly, the unified design approach must be used to resolve the bugbears of infill housing: cars, washing lines, rubbish bins, and storage. Consuming large territory on any domestic lot, car parking is obviously crucial to resolve early in the scheme to ensure sufficient space and access at the numbers determined by the relevant statutory authority. However, the successful integration of zones on site for bins, clothes drying, and overflow storage are easier to forget but must be incorporated in all bluefield housing propositions and be demonstrably resolved. A careful review of the design studies of Part 3 will show how such elements are incorporated into each scheme.

6.6
In a bluefield housing development, existing mature landscape will be integrated wherever possible. Where it is not, the housing will be arranged around deep root soil zones that can support large trees at maturity and foster social interactions in the garden.

The seven principles of bluefield housing

PRINCIPLE 7 DESIGN FOR SOCIAL, FINANCIAL, AND ENVIRONMENTAL SUSTAINABILITY

In a time of climate crisis, it should go without saying that the design and construction of new housing should be undertaken as sustainably as possible, particularly in relation to the environment. But even with climate vulnerability so widely understood, much suburban housing is offered in a notably unsustainable model. Among other factors, this is seen in suburbia's pattern of sprawled land usage, in its wastage of materials both during the construction process and through widespread demolition of existing houses, and in housing's overreliance on active heating and cooling systems for comfort due to poor design and construction. Socially, suburban housing can be isolating, while the costs of renting a home or servicing a mortgage are becoming increasingly unsustainable in many cities. The bluefield housing retrofit and co-location principles provide the opportunity to have discernibly positive environmental, social, and financial impacts in the suburbs as a sustainable form of infill development. As such, sustainability is included as a stated principle of the model, within which there are three discrete facets.

Social sustainability

Social sustainability is a founding tenet of bluefield housing. Responding to the types of desirable shared housing arrangements described in Chapter 2, the co-location model aims to facilitate more socially connected ways of living for those seeking it in a small-scale suburban setting. In designing a bluefield development, one is ultimately designing these relationships: where sharing is encouraged and facilitated, while opportunities for privacy and isolation can be accommodated. In this regard, Principle 1 is the guide.

Financial sustainability

Financial sustainability is variable, relative, and will be defined differently across locations and resident groups. The simple fact that the bluefields are most likely to be older neighbourhoods of a city and thereby of high value, bluefield housing outcomes may rarely present as 'affordable housing' by definition. Yet the ambition of bluefield housing to be a *more affordable* housing option than might otherwise be available in the same neighbourhood, should always influence project decision making and the design process. The starting point is to maximise the landscape and open space potential of Principle 6 to help resist making the housing larger than it needs to be. This can be a challenge on two fronts. First, there is an argument to be made that, wherever possible, housing should be large enough for residents to have a degree of excess space. For residents who only need one bedroom for sleeping, one can argue that the provision of a second bedroom is important to supplement what can otherwise be cramped living. The same can be said of any number of bedrooms in a dwelling; uses can usually be found for an additional unused room. Second, a bedroom is one of the cheapest parts of a house to construct. Unless it is being provided with an accompanying bathroom, an additional room costs comparatively little to construct compared with the extra space it can provide. Where space permits, it is easy to argue that a one-bedroom house can be made a two-bedroom house quite cheaply. However, the value that a second bedroom adds to a house is significantly more than the cost to create it. A fundamental step to making suburban housing more affordable – particularly in areas with high land to value (LVR) ratios – is to make it less valuable. This is anathema to broadly held views that suburban housing should offer endless financial growth, but it is a critical component of helping residents achieve financial sustainability in their housing.

Environmental sustainability

Environmental sustainability looms large over the patterns of urban growth and the construction industry, and suburban housing old and new has a role to play in how we grow our cities for climate resilience. The Sixth Assessment Report of the Intergovernmental Panel on Climate Change (IPCC) has warned that the opportunity to enable climate resilient development is rapidly diminishing, and that retrofitting our existing built environment is now more critical than ever.[5]

Environmental sustainability in the bluefield housing model begins with either the protection of existing suburban landscape and/or the design of landscape zones within the site redevelopment. It continues with the co-location of housing on an existing lot to retrofit rather than expand suburbia. Concurrently, it actively seeks to demolish only what is necessary and to rework existing housing material to make the best use of the resources already on the suburban lot. Retrofitting is not novel, but awareness of it is heightened, with the importance of the role of reworking our existing buildings in an age of climate emergency witnessed in the awarding of the 2021 Pritzker Prize to architects Anne Lacaton and Jean-Philippe Vassal, whose 30-year career is underpinned by their 'never demolish' ethos, and an impressive body of retrofitting work that achieves improved environmental, ecological, and social outcomes.[6]

The bluefield housing model aims to amplify and bring to prominence the existing modes of suburban retrofitting, with emphases across the sustainability pillars. Design tactics to help achieve this are discussed next in Chapter 8.

Notes

1 Guy Luscombe, "Where Do You Want To Live When You Grow Older?," *Architecture Australia* 110, no. 5, September/October 2021: 52–53.
2 Clare Cameron, "Housing for an Ageing Population," in *The Housing Design Handbook: A Guide to Good Practice*, ed. David Levitt and Jo McCafferty, Abingdon, Oxon: Routledge, 2019.

3   Catherine Bridge et al., *Age-specific Housing and Care for Low to Moderate Income Older People*, AHURI Final Report No. 174, Australian Housing and Urban Research Institute Limited (Melbourne, 2011), www.ahuri.edu.au/research/final-reports/174.

4   Julia Park and Jeremy Porteus, *Age-friendly Housing: Future Design for Older People*. London: RIBA Publishing, 2018, 114.

5   Hans-O Pörtner et al., eds., *Climate Change 2022: Impacts, Adaptation, and Vulnerability – Summary for Policymakers*, Working Group II Contribution to the Sixth Assessment Report of the Intergovernmental Panel on Climate Change (Cambridge: Cambridge University Press, 2022).

6   "2021 Pritzker Architecture Prize," The Hyatt Foundation, last modified 16 March 2021, www.pritzkerprize.com/laureates/anne-lacaton-and-jean-philippe-vassal.

7 Lot-level design tactics

Bugbears and joys

One rarely sees rubbish bins or washing lines in architecture images. They are temporarily moved out of frame during the photoshoot or otherwise occupy service spaces that are never photographed. Cars are sometimes observed, but usually as props, particularly when the design of the car is somehow viewed as complementing that of the house. One of the inherent difficulties in increasing densities within the reduced scale of a neighbourhood lot is factoring in the prosaics of living while designing how interactions are either actively encouraged or strategically avoided. It is a balancing act that, once achieved, establishes the groundwork for successful co-located living across a site. This chapter presents lot-level tactics that can be deployed to strategically design relationships between bluefield housing and its residents. It is not merely a case of designing-out the bugbears of infill such as car parking, rubbish bins, and washing lines, but creating amenity amongst such pragmatisms while finding opportunities to orchestrate opportunities for interaction. This will often require detailed consideration of the size and placement of garden beds, screens, and paths that can regulate how residents move throughout shared spaces, and how views are either blocked or opened to maximise amenity. This requires the designer to outsource to landscape architecture experts, or exercise their disciplinary skill to orchestrate space just enough, while creating opportunity for the residents to have agency over their homes and gardens.

DOI: 10.4324/9781003293736-10
This chapter has been made available under a CC-BY-NC-ND license.

Each of the design studies of Part 3 incorporate an overarching design strategy at the scale of the lot. They provide areas for privacy and publicity while maximising amenity in the outdoor spaces. Designed as a mini community, each case study establishes a neighbourliness within the lot boundaries whilst always maximising functionality. This chapter describes bluefield housing's lot-level design tactics.

Cars

In an ideal scenario, car parking solutions would not be an instigating design tactic, but they are ignored in design proposals at their peril. Inadequate on site and kerbside car parking provisions are low-hanging fruit for those arguing against infill housing propositions, and their under-provision can easily be weaponised in neighbourhood infill debates. Conversely, in the push to create increased housing numbers in well-serviced, walkable neighbourhoods, cars can be viewed pejoratively: our easy access to them was what enabled the suburbs to expand in the past, and our dependence on them now is one of the major restrictions to intensifying housing. The reality is, however, that in the absence of efficient, reliable, accessible, and cost-effective public transport, cars remain necessary for many suburban dwellers. Whilst we can agree that having fewer cars is a good thing for environmental and neighbourhood wellbeing, they remain fundamental to the feasibility of many suburbs. It can be the case that those arguing against the case for cars fail to appreciate that many suburbanites have no alternative means of safely and reliably accessing their work, schools, and essential services. This was a point made in the listening sessions for the LA Low-Rise Design Challenge, where academics who enjoy the benefits of living close to where they work and socialise were accused of naïvely assuming many of their fellow suburbanites can similarly get by without cars.[1]

A balance must be struck whereby onsite car parking spaces are limited or avoided where possible but provided intelligently where they cannot be. In some circumstances, local jurisdictions may determine that onsite car parking in a bluefield housing development is not required, or that additional car parking is not required above the number already stipulated for a single-family home. In others, additional parking will be required for each new dwelling created, as is often the case for backyard homes, where ADUs must sometimes be supplied with their own car parking space. As prosaic as it is, the successful incorporation of car parking is likely to be crucial for the approval of many bluefield housing proposals and in the case studies of Part 3, this is supplied at a ratio of one car space per dwelling wherever possible. This can be relatively easy to achieve in projects where two or more lots are amalgamated into the one development, as shown in Chapters 11 and 12, but can be challenging on single lot studies (see Chapter 10).

To make car parking work in a bluefield proposal, there needs to be some flexibility in how it is arranged and accessed:

Lot-level design tactics

- Car parking should be **clustered** where possible to minimise the number of cross-overs from the street, and to maximise usable space immediately adjacent to the dwellings.
- Car spaces should be **uncoupled** from specific dwellings, rather than dedicated, if this allows better use of the lot.
- Similarly, car parking should be **stacked** one behind the other if this is more spatially efficient. The costs of any inconveniences here will need to be weighed against the benefits achieved by the more spatially efficient arrangement.
- The counting of car parking should be made **relative** to the accommodation on the lot, and the lot's location within the neighbourhood. While one space per dwelling is a good benchmark, proponents may be able to successfully argue for lighter provisions based on the maximum number of residents that can be housed and their access to other forms of transit. Zero-parking allowances should be considered in neighbourhoods close to public transport and well-serviced by walkable facilities, and for developments operated by organisations that offer their own transport options.
- The design of car parking spaces should accommodate **alternative uses**, both now and into the future. The designer and residents should consider how car parking can function first as outdoor spaces if there is an over-provision of car spaces, or if the cars are temporarily moved onto the street (Figure 7.1). Consideration should also be given to how car parking spaces might be transformed into alternative uses should circumstances or legislation change in the future, and part or all of the car parking is permanently removed. The infill design work of housing researchers at Monash University is a good resource here.[2]
- **Setbacks** of dwellings located on rear laneways should be considered relative to the widths or depths required for car parking under local codes. This will allow parking to be provided when it is needed, and for gardens to establish landscaped thresholds when not (Figure 7.2).

7.1
Car parking, particularly where it impedes on otherwise useful outdoor space, should be designed for second uses.

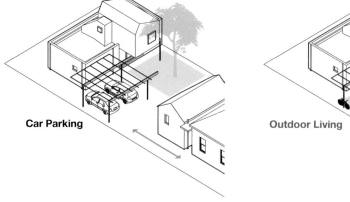
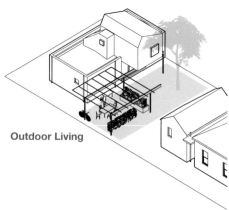

Lot-level design tactics

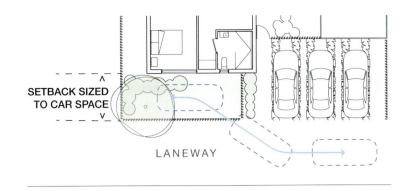

7.2
Setbacks designed relative to local car parking codes can flex between being a garden or a car park, depending on need. A car park width also serves as a workable setback from a laneway.

Ultimately, car parking arrangements will need to be considered in relation to the overall degree of sharing experienced across the development. As an example, a stacked arrangement may be impossible or at least unpalatable for residents who are looking to only share the garden, but otherwise retain maximum individuality. For others, it may be considered a minor inconvenience worth having for the sake of improving other site conditions. For others still, it will be a preferred option if they entertain a high degree of sharing, including treating cars as shared property, just as many suburban family units do.

Designing the prosaics: rubbish, laundry, and storage

One of the key factors in successfully implementing infill housing is managing the increase in utility areas necessary for each home. The consideration and organisation of rubbish bins, clothes lines, and sheds during the design process becomes increasingly important as densities on a lot increase. While it is possible (and indeed likely) that many residents will choose to locate bins, washing lines, and sheds next to their individual dwellings for both convenience and a sense of ownership, each of the design schemes of Part 3 includes deliberate strategies around either dispersing these elements across the site, consolidating them in a single location, or providing a hybrid of the two. In each case, consideration is given to screening rubbish bins and washing lines from view whilst maximising garden space, enabling ease of access, and avoiding disadvantaging one dwelling over others due to its proximity to or distance from utilities. For bluefield housing developments designed for older people, or for those with special needs, proximity of utility areas must be judiciously considered for ease and safety of use.

Including the strategic location of utility spaces in a whole-of-site design approach is crucial to the success of the overall bluefield design concept and a major factor in helping residents avoid unnecessary conflict. Rubbish bins and washing lines, for example, can create friction between residents if not designed into the scheme from the outset, and consideration must be given to factors such as the following:

- Are utility areas **unfairly located** too close to one dwelling on the site, causing that resident to be disrupted when others are not?
- Has the designer researched the **numbers, types and sizes of bins** required by the local authority and designed space for and around them?
- Have sufficiently **blank walls or fences** been provided against which utilities can be mounted?
- Is access to utilities **convenient, but sufficiently discreet**?
- Is there room for '**stuff**'? If high amenity outdoor spaces are to be maintained, is there storage for gardening equipment and the stuff of everyday life?
- For **housing built side boundary to side boundary**, what is the strategy for bins to be brought to the kerb for emptying? If not considered up front, rubbish bins need to be permanently left in the front yard, which is often an amenity compromise for residents and neighbours, and against some municipal codes (Figure 7.3).

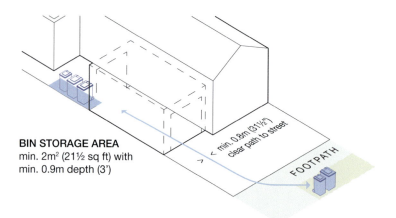

7.3
The South Australian Planning and Design Code legislates that narrow lots created through land division must accommodate storage for bins in the backyard with ease of delivery to the kerb on collection day.

The sharing of utilities and facilities can be a deal maker or deal breaker for co-located housing models depending on the design and the wishes of residents. In the Cohousing for Ageing Well project, participants in the co-design process demonstrated mixed attitudes to sharing.[3] When it came to storage, participants achieved relative consensus, with a general desire for the provision of sheds where backyard space allowed. These were seen as useful for seasonal overflow storage outside the home, helping the transition to smaller footprint living. Here, despite the spatial inefficiency, small private sheds were preferred over a single large shed which would be more efficient but messier, more difficult to access, and harder to control (Figure 7.4).

Lot-level design tactics

7.4
Where space allows, shedding should be considered for the property and for each dwelling. In this extract from the Large scheme of Chapter 10, private rubbish bins and sheds are located with a shared shed in a consolidated setting that saves space on the lot.

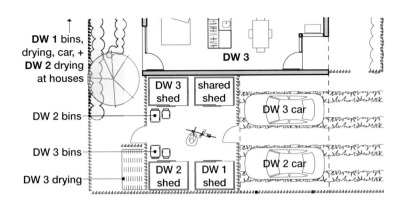

Shared washing machines and washing line were highly desirable to some participants as a means of distributing costs and reducing space, but of major concern to others, particularly in relation to who had access to whose laundry. In one instance, a participant welcomed the sharing of washing machines in a common area provided each machine was dedicated to a single dwelling. In this instance, the sharing of a washing machine was not acceptable, but the sharing of the *space* for that washing machine was. In fleshing out the issue during co-design discussions, solutions began to emerge around the use of shared washing machines for large laundry items such as bedding, but with the inclusion of smaller private washing options within each home (such as camping or portable tabletop washing machines). In all co-design processes, what becomes clear is that there will be sharing scenarios to be tested and trade-offs to be made. What is crucial in a bluefield housing proposal, is for these scenarios to be designed into the project at conception rather than applied as an overlay on completion. In all cases, there should be an overarching sharing rationale that is agreed, designed, and communicated in the design drawings. This rationale may be spatial, economical, or social, or any combination of the three. The designer should be able to articulate this, the pros and cons of the design decisions, and whether the decisions have been made from the top-down, using design expertise and experience, or bottom-up through a considered co-design with the residents. Co-design is discussed in more detail in Chapter 20.

Site separation and designed interactions

When creating a backyard home as part of a bluefield scheme, a key consideration will clearly be the separation achieved between each dwelling, particularly in relation to the size and quality of shared landscape that can be realised between the housing. And while the bluefield housing model eschews a metric approach to design, the reader may appreciate some guidance in laying out housing across a site. In the absence of any local controls that dictate minimum separation, around 8m or 26' has been determined as a sound design

Lot-level design tactics

benchmark for building separation in the single lot models presented in Part 3. From a spatial perspective, it sits within the 8 to 12m (26 to 40') dwelling separation zone found to be ideal in large formal cohousing schemes.[4] Given that bluefield housing projects are substantially smaller than the multi-allotment sites of cohousing schemes, 8m – where it can be achieved – strikes the right balance for privacy and togetherness. It also provides an appropriate deep soil zone for a mature medium or large tree of up to 12m high and with a canopy spread of 8m (40' high, with a 26' canopy). This allows for the retention of an existing mature tree or the planting of a new large tree (Figure 7.5).[5] Where space is limited, permeable paving or open decking can assist in movement around the site without compromising water levels in the soil.

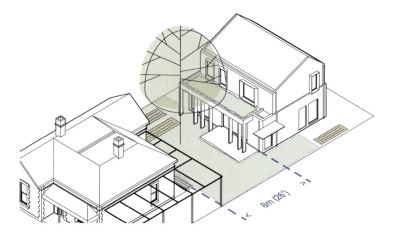

7.5
An 8m or 26' separation not only aids amenity between dwellings; it works to create deep root soil zones for medium to large trees.

Importantly, the garden spaces created by adhering to an 8m/26' rule create proportions large enough for a variety of gardens, at the residents' discretion. Activities such as mowing, planting, watering, and tending provide opportunities for individual and group activity, coupled with residual spaces for outdoor living. When looking to the variety of landscape experiences afforded by such spaces, the High Line in New York is a tangible example.[6] Here, this significant piece of public infrastructure achieves generous walkways and seating areas coupled with significant planting beds in a width of around 8m for much of its length, demonstrating how much can be provided in such a relatively small territory (Figure 7.6). It will not always be possible to achieve the 8m/26' separation benchmark in a bluefield housing project, however, this serves as a good datum from which the designer can shift relative to the idiosyncrasies of their particular project.

Lot-level design tactics

7.6
New York City's High Line by James Corner Field Operations and Diller Scofidio and Renfrow, demonstrates how much landscape program can be arranged in an 8m (26') width.

An appropriate minimum housing separation will be affected not only by the distances between front doors, but by the length or width of open space achievable in the second direction. However, in all cases a targeted strategy that designs these outdoor spaces holistically with the housing can help mitigate concerns over more dense and proximate living. In some instances, co-location experiences that were once positive, may become less desirable over time. In the example shown in Figure 7.7, a walkway has been designed directly from one dwelling, across the face of a second, and connected to a third. This forces a direct line of travel between all three dwellings, which is very good for maximum connectivity, but less so if greater privacy is required. If preferred by the residents, access can be forced through the garden and away from the housing by the simple addition of a planter box. In an ideal scenario, the designer will provide multiple means of moving people through a bluefield housing site such that positive interactions can be achieved in multiple and flexible ways.

7.7
Providing a choice of travel within a bluefield development can allow residents the flexibility of determining how their site is used.

Water-sensitive design

In dry climates, issues of water-sensitive design may be mandated in zoning principles, however, this can be limited to essentials such as minimum rainwater tank requirements. Beyond this, there are design measures that can be taken at a lot level to mitigate water loss and reduce heat loads. Excellent infill typology studies addressing improved site design in Australia include Monash's Infill Opportunities project, referenced above,[7] and Geoffrey London et al's Infill Typologies Catalogue.[8] A recent analysis found that that business-as-usual (BAU) approaches to minor residential infill increase population densities by 98% while increasing stormwater discharge to municipal systems by 44% and water imports to the lot by 85%. By comparison, selected water-sensitive architectural design responses increased population densities by 141%, while increasing stormwater discharge by only 21% and water imports by only 64%. The analysis showed that water-sensitive design strategies are also up to three times as influential in mitigating water loss and intake than technological measures.[9]

In a bluefield housing project, strategies for retaining water on site and reducing the amount potable water brought onto the lot can include the following.

- **Minimise building roofscapes** by creating smaller dwellings or arranging larger programs over two storeys.
- Minimise impervious surfaces such as concrete paths or traditional unit pavers and in lieu use **permeable paving** to return stormwater to garden beds and ground water, and to reduce the amount of runoff into the municipal stormwater system.
- Instead of paving the entirety of driveways, limit paving to **wheel tracks**, with soft ground cover in between and on each side.
- To assist car parking areas to serve double uses, create driveways and parking surfaces with **grow-through pavers** that allow soft ground cover or grass in hit-and-miss paving.
- Size **rainwater tanks**, relative to local rainfall and the catchment areas of roofs, and plumb the collected water back to the houses for use in toilets and laundries, and in kitchens where the water is potable. As with all adjunct housing elements, rainwater tanks are best thought of during the initial design phase. Tanks do not always have to be located where they can be supplied directly from overhead; they can be located away from the dwellings and fed from underground in a wet system.[10]
- With its focus on maximising shared landscape, **greywater recycling** can be considered as part of the landscape design. Kitchen, bathroom, and laundry wastewater is likely to require municipal approval and will require consideration of the types of detergents and cleaning agents used within the house, however, greywater treatment systems and onsite reed beds can be incorporated for those wishing to minimise how much waste material leaves the site.[11]

While the provision of rainwater tanks and the retention of stormwater on site will be mandated by some local authorities, the other water sensitive design strategies here are obviously an optional consideration for a bluefield housing development. They are, however, potential resources and money saving initiatives that may be desirable for residents and attractive add-ons for local decision-makers

Lot-level design tactics

looking for reasons to approve density increases without overloading municipal water and sewer systems that were designed for fewer residents.

Pets

Designing for companion animals is lot-level design strategy that responds to the understanding that pet ownership increases wellbeing, facilitates greater connectedness within a community, and increases people's engagement with nature.[12]

Beyond the amenity that generous landscape spaces can provide, a large, shared garden opens the opportunity for companion animals that may otherwise not be possible in smaller 'courtyard' gardens or in larger unit or apartment developments. With the bluefield model being a multi-unit development in a co-located suburban form, it offers the potential to house pets that require a yard. This is particularly beneficial for older residents, where pet ownership has been demonstrated as significantly positive for the health and wellbeing of people over 60. In extreme circumstances, pet ownership can reduce suicide risk, as the human-animal relationship can mitigate suicide ideation, and as pet owners worry about who will look after their animals after they have gone.[13] Meanwhile, the day-to-day ownership responsibilities of feeding, exercising, and grooming a pet contributes positively to physical and emotional wellbeing.

The provision of a consolidated large garden allows for pets that might otherwise be given up in a transition to smaller accommodation or more complex tenure arrangements. In the design studies presented in Part 3 and as shown in Figure 7.8, one can imagine an example where a dog might legally be owned

7.8
The co-location and shared garden model of bluefield housing allows for companion animals such as dogs, where residents might otherwise be unable to have them.

by the occupant(s) of one dwelling, while the companionship and responsibility benefits are shared across all residents; an arrangement well-suited to people for whom individual pet ownership might be highly desirable but impractical outside of a bluefield housing relationship.

Private and public

In more intense forms of housing where density is increased, issues of privacy and publicity are often seen in opposition: private *versus* public. In a bluefield model, as with other forms of more collaborative living, the two concepts are understood as a matched pair: private *and* public, where one relies on the other and neither is in competition. What is required, then, is a means with which to actively encourage both at the same time. Embedded in the design studies of Part 3 is an attitude towards balancing the requirements for privacy with those of engagement:

- **Positive interaction** – a staple of co-location developments and a driving reason why people choose this form of living – is achieved by creating central landscape elements that act as a fulcrum around which the housing can be sited. Living areas are strategically placed off these gardens to create strong connections between inside and out and to provide passive surveillance across the lot.
- **Decks and paved areas** are provided to encourage sitting outdoors and incidental contact between neighbours. If a resident who would normally have blinds open during the day suddenly has them shut, or they have not been seen outside for a while, a neighbour might be prompted to knock on their door to check on them.
- **Bedrooms**, however, obviously benefit from a greater level of privacy. This becomes even more important as the dwelling gets smaller. In a one-bedroom home the bedroom itself becomes an important second living space: a place to sit and read or somewhere to retreat during the day without sleeping. Replacing a larger bed with a single bed can allow for a desk or table, doubling the function of the bedroom to a study or hobby space. With this in mind, bedrooms in the case study designs are oriented away from the large common gardens where possible but given large windows (and sometimes doors) with views of and access to more private outdoor spaces (Figure 7.9).

These aspects of design for sharing and design for privacy, along with the other lot-level design tactics presented in this chapter should not be surprising nor innovative for most architects and arguably neither should they be for housing providers. However, the issues presented here can be the types of issues that get lost when an attempt is made to apply standard home designs to a non-standard siting arrangement, which is unlikely to work effectively in a co-located bluefield proposal. In the bluefields, the success of the whole will rely not only

Lot-level design tactics

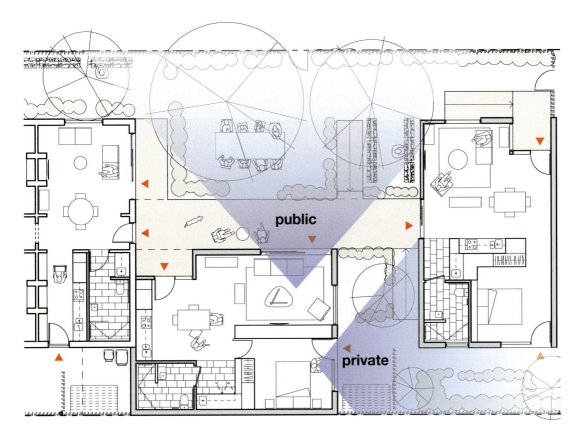

7.9
In a bluefield housing project, living areas are arranged around the shared landscape, while bedrooms are designed as private spaces that can double as secondary private spaces.

on the amenity of the housing itself, as discussed in the next chapter, but on the design of the interstitial spaces between and around them. For it is in these minor territories that the pragmatic aspects of sharing can be resolved, and the success of the scheme realised.

Notes

1   "Listening Sessions – Low Rise: Housing Ideas for Los Angeles," Los Angeles Mayor's Office, accessed 4 April 2021, https://lowrise.la/Helpful-Resources.
2   Shane Murray et al., *Infill Opportunities Design Research Report*, Department of Architecture, Monash University (Caulfield East, Victoria: Monash University, 2011), 19–21.
3   Damian Madigan, *Cohousing for Ageing Well: Design Report*, University of South Australia (Adelaide, 2020).
4   Charles Durrett, *The Senior Cohousing Handbook: A Community Approach to Independent Living*. 2nd ed. Gabriola Island, British Columbia: New Society Publishers, 2009.
5   While local municipalities may stipulate different spacings for a bluefield housing development, 8m or 26' accords with the spatial requirements for the provision of medium and large trees at maturity, as stated in the South Australian Planning and Design Code: "South Australia's Online Planning and Design Code," State Government of South Australia, accessed 9 April 2022, https://code.plan.sa.gov.au/.
6   James Corner Field Operations and Diller Scofidio and Renfro, *The High Line*. London: Phaidon Press, 2015.
7   Murray et al., *Infill Opportunities Design Research Report*.
8   Geoffrey London et al., *Infill Typologies Catalogue* (Melbourne, Victoria: Cooperative Research Centre for Water Sensitive Cities, 2020), https://watersensitivecities.org.au/content/infill-typologies-catalogue/.
9   Mojtaba Moravej et al., "What Roles do Architectural Design and On-site Water Servicing Technologies Play in the Water Performance of Residential Infill?," *Water Research* 213, 118109 (2022), https://doi.org/10.1016/j.watres.2022.118109.

Lot-level design tactics

10 Excellent water-sensitive design strategies can be found at "Water Sensitive SA," accessed 8 September 2021, www.watersensitivesa.com/.

11 Michael Mobbs, *Sustainable House*. 2nd ed. Sydney: UNSW Press, 2010.

12 Wendy Stone et al., *Housing and Housing Assistance Pathways with Companion Animals: Risks, Costs, Benefits and Opportunities*, AHURI Final Report No. 350, Australian Housing and Urban Research Institute Limited (Melbourne, 2021), www.ahuri.edu.au/research/final-reports/350.

13 Janette Young et al., "A Qualitative Analysis of Pets as Suicide Protection for Older People," *Anthrazoös* 33, no. 2 (2020): 191–205, https://doi.org/10.1080/08927936.2020.1719759.

8   Design for liveability and sustainability

A holistic approach to small suburban housing

When designing context-appropriate low-rise infill in and around existing housing, it becomes necessary to reduce the building footprints for extensions and backyard homes. Put simply, reducing the footprint of a house also helps to reduce its height, makes it easier to minimise its bulk, and retains more of the backyard for landscape. This emulates a typical suburban house with additions and garages, thereby reinforcing the prevailing neighbourhood character and the garden setting of much of suburbia.

In the design studies of Part 3, a mix of mostly one- and two-bedroom dwellings have been strategically proposed for two reasons: it allows for a doubling and tripling of existing density; and tests the amenity of small dwellings. It is easy to challenge the appropriateness and appeal of one-bedroom dwellings, and it can be argued that two bedrooms should always be provided as a minimum to provide residents with sufficient space for sundry activities and storage. However, as more and more people live alone and housing affordability moves further out of reach for many – particularly in established neighbourhoods – it is important that high quality, efficient, and adaptable one-bedroom homes be added to our suburban housing mix. As discussed in Chapter 6, while it is relatively inexpensive to add a second bedroom when building a house (due to it being an un-serviced space, unlike a bathroom), this additional accommodation not only significantly increases the building footprint over a one-bedroom offering, it increases the purchase

DOI: 10.4324/9781003293736-11

This chapter has been made available under a CC-BY-NC-ND license.

and rental prices of the property. If we are to add to our suburban housing stock at an affordable price point for both purchase and rent, it is important to provide well-designed one-bedroom dwellings. In some instances, the Part 3 design studies test how multi-bedroom dwellings can be divided into smaller one-bedroom homes and then reinstated into larger houses over time. While a mix of bedroom numbers is investigated across the studies, there is a focus in places on the provision of one-bedroom dwellings in order to achieve appropriate density increases.

In designing small, extra attention is required to maximise liveability. Whilst not a set of 'rules' by which to design increased densities on suburban lots, the design tactics presented here point to the embedded design thinking, logic, and decisions in the housing studies presented. They are the types of design and amenity considerations a proponent might put forward in a zoning application or design presentation when a bluefield housing scheme is being assessed on its merits.

Accessibility

Although not a model specifically for older people or those with special needs, bluefield housing is likely to find an audience with these cohorts, either through multigenerational living, proactive housing for a group of older friends, or as an alternative form of community or supported housing. While home modifications for elements such as grab rails and step-free doorways are often the focus of housing considerations for those with mobility issues, they are assumed as givens in the design studies of this book – constructional add-ons or design detailing that can usually be resolved with relative ease during project documentation and construction. The advantage of moving beyond such modifications towards a model that encompasses a broader housing strategy around accessibility, is that housing designed for better mobility and 'ageing well' can be considered more directly as housing for *living well*. Designing with older residents at the forefront of an imagined occupant group results in housing that can be appropriate for anyone of any age who wishes to live in a smaller suburban house but with some generosity of space. Additionally, housing that can anticipate either temporarily or permanently affected mobility can create more generous space than housing without such considerations. An example is a resident who has hip replacement or knee surgery and recuperates at home with a walker, rollator, or crutches for several weeks before transitioning to improved mobility with the reduced support of a walking stick. In such a scenario, a home designed to be fully compliant to local access and mobility codes and standards may prove temporarily useful, but a spatial over-provision in the long term.

The single lot design studies of Chapter 10 allocate such additional mobility space more prudently. Whilst not laid out to the full accessibility code, the homes

Design for liveability and sustainability

have been designed to the spatial requirements of the Livable Housing Australia (LHA) Design Guidelines, which strive to create more functional and responsive housing as occupant needs change over time.[1] LHA's liveability is measured over three spatial levels – Silver, Gold and Platinum – with the Silver level mandated as a minimum for houses, townhouses, and apartments in the 2022 update to Australia's National Construction Code. All homes in the Chapter 10 single lot design studies, including the modified existing housing, have been designed to the Gold level as a minimum. These designs see greater mobility and access than might generally be found in market housing, particularly in the case of backyard homes where space can be limited. The layouts avoid unnecessarily designing for high needs if it is not specifically required, while acknowledging that providing more generous space is prudent, given safety and movement in and around the home can become compromised as our circumstances change or as we age. Figure 8.1 demonstrates the type of space required for a fully compliant accessible bathroom under Australia's national Standard for Access and Mobility, while Figure 8.2 illustrates the reduced proportions used in the single lot design studies. No matter the age group or mobility levels designed for, the incorporation of the spatial dimensions shown here add to the amenity and usability for all, whilst helping to anticipate future needs. The case study designs also seek to demonstrate that backyard, attached, or reconfigured existing homes, while often working in tight spatial confines of the suburban lot, do not have to result in spatially mean floor plan layouts.

Externally, the single lot design studies each allow space for the creation of level walking surfaces to connect homes to the garden without the need for steps. This is achieved by creating walkways at finished floor level, connected

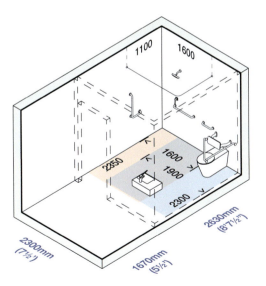

8.1
A fully accessible bathroom to Australian Standard 1428.2, showing minimum overlapping circulation zones for a shower and toilet, with overall internal dimensions and corridor space as indicated.

Fully Accessible Bathroom

Design for liveability and sustainability

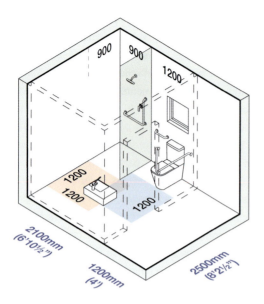

Livable Housing Australia Gold Bathroom

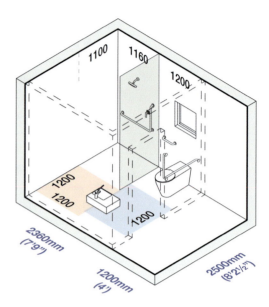

Livable Housing Australia Platinum Bathroom

down to the garden with ramps (Figure 8.3). Whilst grabrails can be provided for residents if desired, designing the ramps at a gentle pitch of 1:20 avoids the need for grabrails under Australian building codes, creating a 'light touch' approach to mobility assistance and mitigating a potentially institutionalised approach to safety. Meanwhile, creating the walkways and ramps as open

Design for liveability and sustainability

8.2
The minimum circulation zones of the single lot design studies, designed to Livable Housing Australia's Gold or Platinum standards.

8.3
The Large design study of Chapter 10. Designed in tandem with garden elements, connective timber deck walkways at finished floor level are water-sensitive design elements that provide 'light touch' mobility assistance when coupled with gentle 1:20 ramps that avoid the need for grabrails.

timber decks softens the visual impact while allowing water to reach the ground below with greater environmental benefit than would otherwise be achieved with solid paths.

Adaptability

Inasmuch as small footprint housing is a staple of the bluefield housing model, circumstances change. Houses sometimes need extending, and windows that are at least as wide and high as a door and extend down to the floor allow a simple connection to an extension by removing the glazing and frame, thereby avoiding messy reworking to the affected walls (Figure 8.4). They also maximise natural light levels and offer enhanced external views when sitting in a chair or lying on a bed. This is particularly important to increase the sense of space in a small dwelling, by extending the ground plane and views beyond the external walls of the house.

8.4
Windows that are door-sized as a minimum offer flexibility when extending, while significantly increasing amenity, particularly when a view can be extended through a garden.

Door-height windows provide flexibility

Even when homes do not require extending, their interiors need renovating or replacing over time due to domestic wear and tear or changing occupant needs. The new housing additions in each of the Part 3 design studies have been designed to adapt to future needs as easily as possible. Hard infrastructure – those components of a house that are fixed and difficult to change – is limited to bathrooms and plumbing stacks, which are organised in a group arrangement, rather than being dispersed (Figure 8.5). Timber floors on joists provide opportunities for flexible power runs within the building's floorspace and the addition or moving of floor-mounted power outlets as necessary. Flexible service runs can be accommodated in perimeter walls through battening-out wall linings from the wall structure and providing removable skirtings at the wall

Design for liveability and sustainability

bases. This can flexibly power the perimeter, allowing outlets to be moved or added over time.[2]

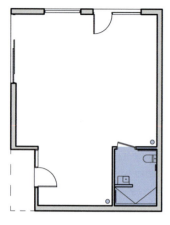
Hard Infrastructure

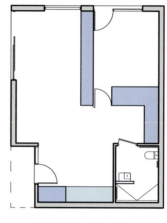
Soft Infrastructure

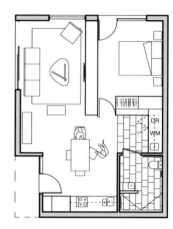
Flexible House

8.5
Hard infrastructure: plumbing and electrics. Soft infrastructure: joinery. The adaptable house, designed as an open shell for as much of the footprint as possible.

Room separation is provided not by fixed walls but by soft infrastructure; joinery which can either extend to the ceiling to maximise storage and separation or can stop short to increase light and ventilation levels while giving the increased sense of space that a continuous ceiling can provide.

Further spatial flexibility is achieved using fire-rated doors. Like adjoining rooms in a hotel, adjacent spaces in a bluefield development can utilise fire doors to either connect or separate dwellings to make them bigger or smaller (Figure 8.6). This requires the relationships between the dwellings to be designed for both independence *and* amalgamation, with the fire door simply acting as a locked or unlocked connection as needed. Further infrastructure provisions, such as the incorporation of capped plumbing in a cupboard, can anticipate the creation of an additional dwelling in the future with minimal disturbance and cost (Figure 8.7).

8.6
By designing the relationships between dwellings such that they can be larger connected spaces or smaller discrete homes, fire doors can be used to provide in-built dwelling flexibility.

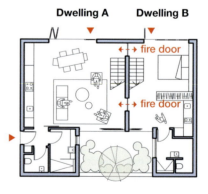

122

Design for liveability and sustainability

8.7
Servicing provisions such as capped plumbing in a cupboard can facilitate the creation of an additional dwelling with relative ease.

bedroom to living room
(removable joinery)

study and store to kitchen and laundry
(services provision in storage cupboards)

Wall space; slack space

External wall spaces, as discussed in Chapter 7, are useful for mounting washing lines or for the creation of servicing zones for bins and utilities. But they can also provide a window-free surface in one dwelling that a second dwelling can look out onto without compromising privacy, creating a backdrop for private external views. Blank walls have their advantages inside the home as well. Over time, we accumulate memories in multiple forms, such as furniture pieces, photographs, pictures, and collectibles. The housing of these memories can become difficult in small footprint living, progressively so for older residents as they accumulate more items. Participants in the Innovation in Social Housing project described that as they age and inherit items from family and friends, the storage and display of these pieces becomes increasingly important but comes with the challenge of how to adequately accommodate these additional items in a small dwelling.[3] As people get older and relocate to smaller living, they inevitably have to strike a balance between downsizing their possessions to suit living while retaining a sufficient amount of sentimental memorabilia. For some, downsizing will require disposing of more household elements than they had anticipated, including items of sentimental value.[4]

Whilst small, each new dwelling in the design studies has been designed with some form of 'slack' space, where possible – room within the dwelling that anticipates potential occupation, as described by Tatjana Schneider and Jeremy Till in *Flexible Housing*.[5] By locating windows and doors to the sides of spaces, rather than in the centre of walls, blank wall space is created for loose furniture and wall mounted items. Storage, which can take the form of cupboards or open shelves, is maximised with memory-keeping in mind. By treating the open floor plan as a series of discrete spaces with a degree of separation, loose furniture can act as a spatial divide whilst still maintaining good circulation (Figure 8.8).

Design for liveability and sustainability

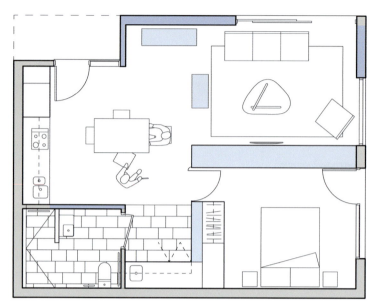

8.8
'Slack' space for memories and objects.

'Slack' space for memories

Storage

A pitched roof serves multiple purposes: it helps provide contextual fit in a neighbourhood with established older homes and, depending on the pitch, is a ready-made surface for solar panels. It also provides valuable roof-space storage. If framed traditionally, using rafters and ceiling joists in lieu of roof trusses, roof spaces can be occupied (Figure 8.9). The inclusion of a pull-down attic ladder, which can be fitted with handrails for safety and an electric motor for increased ease of use, allows for both regular and occasional use of the space. Residents with reduced mobility or concerns over safety might use the attic with the assistance of a neighbour, relative, friend, or carer who can access the space for them. In these circumstances, attic storage may not be practical for regular use, but it can be extremely useful for the rotation of seasonal storage. An example is winter or summer clothing, which can be stored in tubs in the attic when not required day-to-day in a wardrobe. Similarly, keepsakes that are important for the resident to retain but may not need to be on hand in the home can be safely stored in the attic to provide peace-of-mind that they are protected and comfort that they are nearby.

A further benefit of framing the roof conventionally is that spaces not used for attic storage can expressed to create larger internal volumes, greater light levels, and the opportunity to vent hot air during summer months. Each of the design proposals of Part 3 assumes that living spaces have high raked ceilings where possible, with seasonal attic storage provided over each bathroom and

Design for liveability and sustainability

Roof Space Storage

8.9
Conventionally framed pitched roofs, as opposed to trusses, allow for roof space to be occupied while providing more generous volumes elsewhere.

bedroom, thereby significantly increasing the liveability of these small footprint dwellings. Additionally, each shared space, such as laundries or common rooms, provides storage for all residents to use. As with all shared elements, the success of these facilities assumes a usage agreement amongst the residents to ensure equity and functionality.

Finding space in older homes

When renovating older houses, it is common to cut large openings in existing walls to extend outwards, or to combine spaces internally. Using lintels to frame the opening and support the remnant overhead building material, this can be done without affecting the ceiling lines between spaces. This also enables an opening to be filled in the future to reinstate the original rooms. Retaining the ceilings of each room and making wall openings below these allows the legibility and identity of each original room to be maintained. This opening up concept, and its capacity to significantly unlock possibilities for infill housing using existing homes, is illustrated and defined as the Porous Rooms exercise in Chapter 17.

This joining tactic can be employed successfully for hallways, which can significantly add to the usability and desegregation of spaces in an older home, where it is desired (Figure 8.10). In Australia, hallways in older houses are typically no narrower than 1.2m (4'), often 1.5m (5') wide, and sometimes as wide as 1.8m (6'). When opened to adjacent rooms they add significant space to what can otherwise be a tight floor plan, enabling improved function and easier movement. An opening in an external wall – often undertaken to add an en suite bathroom to a room being used as a bedroom – provides the opportunity to create a kitchen or new entry, unlocking the potential for a house to be divided, as discussed with Suburban Operation 2 (side pods) in Chapter 4.

Design for liveability and sustainability

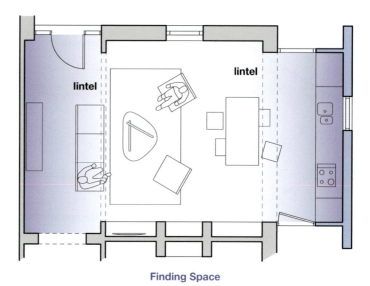

8.10
Created in internal walls, lintels allow hallways to add significant space, while opening the plan. In external walls they allow the extension of space with minimal disruption to ceiling and roof lines.

Finding Space

Environmental sustainability and climate change resilience

Principle 7 of the bluefield housing model, described in Chapter 7, is to design for sustainability, and a key component is to retrofit, rather than replace, the suburbs. However, there is an irony in retrofitting for climate resilience, as the energy and material consumption of retrofitting are themselves greenhouse gas (GHG) emitting activities. It is crucial, then, that retrofitting work reduces the amount of new construction required by reworking as much existing building stock as is feasible, and that new work is designed and constructed as sustainably as possible. This begins with passive design strategies at the scales of the lot and continues at the scale of the building, taking advantage of natural conditions where possible to reduce the reliance on artificial heating and cooling for the maximum amount of time per season. Keeping the housing small is another passive sustainability strategy, particularly when small additions can share walls with other homes on the lot, therby minimising the extent of new external walling.

Active strategies can then be deployed, specifically those aimed at eliminating the use of fossil fuels in running the housing. This is a strategy that can be argued on financial as well as environmental grounds, where the latter is at a tipping point. In launching the third report of the Intergovernmental Panel on Climate Change (IPCC),[6] United Nations Secretary-General António Guterres described investing in new fossil fuels infrastructure as 'moral and economic madness', with the countries that are increasing fossil fuel production as 'truly dangerous radicals'. There has never been a more desperate time to reduce the reliance of fossil fuels in our buildings.[7]

Sustainable design is a broad and evolutionary field, but there are some fundamental strategies that can and should be deployed in new development. The following passive and active approaches are offered here as tangible and practical steps that can be taken in any bluefield housing development. Some of them, such as photovoltaic (PV) cells and the provision of plumbed rainwater tanks, will already be mandated under some local zoning codes, thereby forcing the developer's hand. Other initiatives may be desirable but unenforcable, however, they may form part of a bargaining process with local authorities, where the sustainability offerings of a proposal help to offset other concerns over density or neighbourhood fit. This is discussed further in Chapter 14 in the context of a scorecard assessment system for zoning applications. Each bluefield case will be different, but in each the following sustainability principles – which are by no means exhaustive – can be considered for incorporation. Some are inherent to the model, as described in the preceding chapters, while others are simply common-sense good practice that should be read in conjuction with specific sustainability texts and guides.

Passive strategies

- Retain and retrofit existing housing, with as little demolition as possible.
- Retrofit insulation to the external walls, internal walls, and roofs of retained houses to improve thermal performance.
- Ensure a dispersed model across the lot to create zones for soft ground surfaces and enhanced cross ventilation.
- Design houses to be only as large as necessary.[8]
- Maximise spans and reduce structure using sustainably sourced timber, including mass timber such as cross-laminated timber (CLT) columns, beams, and panels.
- Design the depths of rooms relative to winter sun access, to allow sun penetration deep into spaces.
- Design windows that maximise daylight and reduce reliance on artificial lighting.
- Provide well-sealed double or triple glazed window units suited to local hot and cold temperature extremes.
- Design for cross ventilation to reduce reliance on air-conditioning use in warm months.
- Shade windows from undesirable sun via verandahs, sun hoods, external blinds, or screens.
- Choose materials with credentialled low- or zero-carbon production and supply qualities.
- Design using materials with embodied finishes that do not need applied finishes and paints, and that minimise or remove the need to refinish over time.
- Design using materials with high recyclability at the end of their service life.
- Design with mass insulated walls and roofs that create an efficient building envelope to maintain indoor comfort longer and reduce reliance on artificial heating and cooling.

Design for liveability and sustainability

- Design floors in sustainably sourced timber rather than concrete, using screw piles where deep foundations are required.
- Where concrete is preferred, design with it to maximise thermal mass, and use cement substitutes such as recycled fly ash or slag to reduce embedded carbon.
- Design secondary uses for onsite car spaces that may not be needed or mandated in the future.
- Design planted pergolas in lieu of hard roofed car ports.
- Design for the retention or planting of medium to large landscape that can maintain or increase urban tree canopy.
- Create deep root soil zones for the establishment and/or extension of landscape zones.
- Incorporate productive gardens in the landscape design for supplementary onsite food production, passive cooling effects, and social interaction.
- Pave hard surfaces with permeable or grow-through pavers and reduce driveway paving to wheel strips.

Active strategies

- Source green energy supply to the property from providers using renewable energy sources.[9]
- Provide solar photovoltaic (PV) arrays, fed to onsite battery storage.
- Where onsite car parking is required or mandated, provide an electric vehicle charging point.[10]
- Incorporate energy-efficient lighting and appliances.
- Substitute gas services within the house with induction cooktops for cooking, and heat pump systems for heating and cooling.
- In lieu of gas boilers for water heating, use a heat pump system or solar hot water system.
- Provide ceiling sweep fans for summer.
- Design for water vulnerability, providing rainwater tanks that are plumbed to the dwellings, as described in Chapter 7.
- Source plants indigenous to the local area that can tolerate local climates and minimise excessive watering or fertilizing.

Premised on the concept of retrofitting the suburbs, the bluefield housing model will minimise its environmental impact when its dwelling adaptation and flexibility strategies are coupled with its ecological targets of fostering suburban landsape. But in also designing-out a reliance on fossil fuels and focusing on judicious passive and active sustainable design principles, a bluefield housing proponent can further their sustainability achivements. Ultimately, a bluefield housing development should aim to pair its co-location social accomplishments with sound environmental credentials to produce a holistic response to suburban liveability and sustainability.

Design for liveability and sustainability

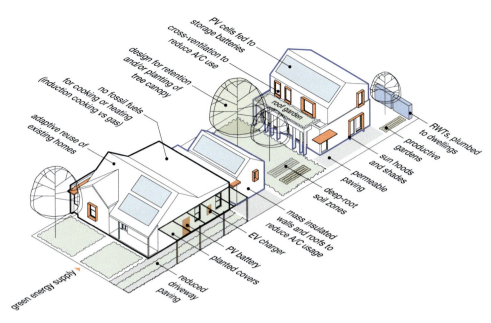

Bluefield Housing Carbon Neutral Strategy

8.11
Passive and active sustainability principles that should be considered in every bluefield housing development.

Notes

1. Livable Housing Australia, *Livable Housing Design Guidelines*. 4th ed. Forest Lodge, New South Wales: Livable Housing Australia, 2017.
2. These and other excellent flexibility tactics can be found in Tatjana Schneider and Jeremy Till, *Flexible Housing*. Oxford: Architectural Press, 2007.
3. Damian Madigan, *Innovation in Social Housing 90 Day Project: Design Principles Report*, University of South Australia (South Australia, 2017).
4. Aaron Davis et al., *Downsizing to the City: Project Report*, University of South Australia (Adelaide, 2021).
5. Schneider and Till, *Flexible Housing*.
6. Jim Skea et al., eds., *Climate Change 2022: Mitigation of Climate Change – Summary for Policymakers*, Working Group III Contribution to the Sixth Assessment Report of the Intergovernmental Panel on Climate Change (Cambridge: Cambridge University Press, 2022).
7. "Secretary-General's Video Message on the Launch of the Third IPCC Report," United Nations, last modified 4 April 2022, www.un.org/sg/en/node/262847.
8. Recent research out of the University of Toronto has demonstrated that while sustainability add-ons are good, simply building smaller houses – particularly without a basement – is the best way to reduce a dwelling's carbon footprint: Aldrick Arceo et al., "Capturing Variability in Material Intensity of Single-family Dwellings: A Case Study of Toronto, Canada," *Resources, Conservation and Recycling* 175 (2021): Article 105885, https://doi.org/https://doi.org/10.1016/j.resconrec.2021.105885.
9. In December 2021, New York City became the largest city in the US and the first cold-weather city to ban fossil fuel combustion in new buildings, focusing instead on electrification: "Mayor de Blasio Signs Landmark Bill to Ban Combustion of Fossil Fuels in New Buildings," City of New York, last modified 22 December 2021, www1.nyc.gov/office-of-the-mayor/news/852-21/mayor-de-blasio-signs-landmark-bill-ban-combustion-fossil-fuels-new-buildings.
10. There is much debate amongst urbanists around the fact that electric vehicles are still cars and do nothing to solve a city's reliance on private car use. This fact is not challenged here. However, with the bluefield housing model likely to find its audience in suburbs that still rely heavily on car usage, more sustainable forms of car use and onsite car parking will need to be incorporated in most proposals.

Part 3

9 From top-down to bottom-up

A deployable model

Top-down vs bottom-up

Bluefield housing is premised on a case study approach, a housing research strategy that often faces an unreasonable prejudice against it, specifically around a perception that such processes are too idiosyncratic to be broadly useful beyond their own study areas.[1] The alternative is to act at a city or suburb level, establishing overarching policy parameters under which individual housing outcomes can theoretically be achieved. This top-down thinking is common in housing research, particularly when policy and financial mechanisms are created as the drivers of housing supply. It is seen in data-driven research that empirically demonstrates needs and opportunities in the absence of designed housing outcomes themselves. The rationale is that robust land use, economic, and social policies, once successfully established, open housing opportunities *en masse*, without the need to interrogate the design of the housing itself: if the correct mechanisms are in place, the market will deliver fitting housing outcomes.

This is not a criticism of top-down approaches but an observation that brings into play the question of what design is, how it is understood, when it should be applied, and the roles it can play in the housing debate. It is a way of emphasising how bottom-up design approaches contribute to housing policy and strategy. Outside of design disciplines, design can be seen as an activity that occurs late in a process; an act of styling or dressing a single outcome to make it aesthetically and functionally better than it might otherwise be.

DOI: 10.4324/9781003293736-13
This chapter has been made available under a CC-BY-NC-ND license.

This is the cornerstone of zoning laws, which apply legislative metrics on the assumption they will deliver minimum acceptable housing outcomes regardless of the design of the housing itself. Lost in this assumption is a characteristic well-understood by designers: that beyond the final aesthetic and performative aspects of a finished product, design is first a process of working through a problem in a way that metrically driven approaches cannot. This is discussed relative to the concept of abstraction in Chapter 18, within the context of 'seeing the familiar with new eyes'.

Design methodology

The bluefield housing model has been borne of a case study approach, with detailed design investigations being the instrument not just of idea development, but of discovery. Rather than responding to existing zoning laws and seeking housing innovations within these parameters, a first principles approach has been taken to understand the underlying base conditions of the neighbourhood housing and lot configurations, and the types of infill housing models they might support. From this starting point, new zoning rules can then be written, as discussed in Chapter 16. This design process means stripping the lot back to its foundation conditions of original building footprint and mature landscape zones before methodically investigating infill opportunities within the established neighbourhood pattern.

Existing zoning controls such as the maximum number of dwellings, minimum building setbacks, maximum building heights and envelopes, the length of boundary wall construction, and site coverage are deliberately ignored, as they can deny new housing outcomes before they have a chance to be created for consideration. However, the architectural effects of the *spirit* of these same zoning measures inform the designs. Careful design attention is given to mass, bulk, boundary conditions, and overlooking, but this is done through architectural experience and best practice without responding to any zoning metrics. As such, whilst the case study design schemes set aside zoning policy to explore what is otherwise possible, they are designed with local amenity in mind, from both within the site and without. No limit is set on the number of additional dwellings that might be created, with the outcomes resulting from the best spatial, neighbourhood, and social fit. In breaking the rules and exploring the housing outcomes we can pose the simple question of why such housing is not currently allowed.

But this rule-breaking does not mean that the design studies are loose or lacking in realism. They are disciplined in their approach to accommodating the infill housing 'bugbears' of laundry, rubbish bins, and car parking, as discussed in Chapter 7. All car parking shown in the studies is to the Australian Standard for off-street parking,[2] but arranged and dispersed where possible to allow the space to be used for additional outdoor activity should cars be temporarily or permanently removed when desired by the residents. Following the lead of Monash University's excellent Infill Opportunities design research project, ground surfaces for car parking and driveways are conceived of as semi-permanent and permeable, allowing alternative use as outdoor space or future landscape extension if desired.[3] This ensures a balance is found between the ideal of removing on-site car parking for better amenity, and providing it where needed. Car parking provision can thereby be maximised or minimised relative to user needs, public transit availability, and local zoning requirements.

With these project parameters set, the sites of investigation are each allocated a mix of housing types, coupled with imagined occupant scenarios. Some schemes offer forms of dwelling or work-from-home flexibility via the manner of their use, or by divisibility or expandability, resulting in variable dwelling and density numbers depending on how occupants choose to utilise the spaces. Some schemes are designed to be either individual self-contained houses, larger combined single houses, or a mixed residential/commercial use, with no single form of occupation preferred over another. Some of the smaller divided dwellings have less space allocated to them for cooking, eating, and living, while the larger dwellings are provided with more generous communal areas. However, beyond making these design decisions based on spatial relationships alone, the strategy recognises that in household structures formed of familial or friendship relationships, there will be times when occupants come together and times when they do not. Providing a mix of scales allows these behaviours to occur and for formal separation of one or more entities to be achieved, if desired. The inclusion of wet areas of various scales, whilst potentially over-supplied under some occupational scenarios, not only enables additional self-contained living, but importantly unlocks the potential for parts of the schemes to be given over to small-scale commercial uses with public interfaces. While the schemes show bedrooms to test how many people can be housed, ultimately the reader can look to the floor plans and imagine alternative uses that can complement and augment the domestic settings shown.

In the design drawings, site plans describe the maximum number of bedrooms relative to the number of car spaces provided. The isometric drawings, however, refer simply to 'room': spaces that are not fixed in their programming via servicing (such as a bathroom or kitchen) or are not required to be used as access to another room. 'Room' therefore means a space that can be dedicated as a bedroom or hobby space or sitting space or workspace. A one room dwelling, for example, may function as a small one-bedroom house or as a work environment for someone who may or may not be living on the site. This opens the potential for mixed-use on a small suburban scale while still offering the ability to flex back to purely residential use. And although the buildings and landscapes are fully furnished to test usability and amenity – and are described in occupational detail relative to the uses shown – the reader can imagine alternative scenarios mapped on to the drawings. Each of the studies assumes a blurring of occupational divisions. Thought of in this manner, beds, dining tables, or sofas might be exchanged (for example) for desks, work benches, hairdressers' chairs, or even a dentist's station, triggering subtle yet meaningful occupational change. Accordingly, a living room, dining area, or bedroom might each become a waiting area, office, consulting room, or work studio.

Such reimaginings of space and use can prompt us to reconsider what is and isn't appropriate in a domestic neighbourhood setting. When we accept that a room used as a bedroom can instead serve as a home office, we also accept the fact that this home office can receive visitors for a meeting. Can we then accept that such a home office can, in fact, be a small-scale hairdresser? And if a hairdresser, then why not a dentist? And what if these workers are not the residents on the lot, but instead rent their space as a financial mechanism that helps fund the redevelopment while providing services to the local neighbourhood? These are the types of zoning discussions that can emerge when there are detailed design propositions to start the conversation.

Using real but anonymised sites, each study begins with the premise that the existing houses are Australian cottages, stripped back to their original plan form. All later additions including extensions, sheds and outbuildings are removed. As such, each of the design studies presents not as a wholesale reuse of everything on site that currently exists, but as a discussion of how the sites might have been developed differently in the first instance or how a strategic approach to redevelopment in the future might proffer alternative approaches to infill. In addition, the studies provide a prompt as to the types of new development that might be achieved, assuming the retention of only the original neighbourhood housing and the mature landscape as foundation conditions.

The result is a bottom-up approach to infill housing strategy. Because the bluefield model starts at the scale of the lot and takes a methodical approach to understanding the base housing conditions, the mature landscape, and the new additions the suburban lot can support, it is scalable. Local conditions will vary across the neighbourhoods of individual cities and across suburbanised cities themselves, but the principles of the model and its design strategy are replicable.

Design methods and data

The bluefield approach requires a nuanced reworking of the retained neighbourhood housing, and local characteristics will vary across locations and housing types. Just as the Commonly Accepted Anomalies of Chapter 4 require moulding to local adaptation typologies, so too will the lot and house typologies shown in the case studies that follow. In some instances, the studies will directly or somewhat directly translate to neighbourhoods of multiple cities, or they will at least present similarities to local conditions such that design principles are easily taken up with minor modifications. In other cities or neighbourhoods, the design methodology will require much heavier tailoring to local housing conditions. But this is where the efficacy of the model lies, as its greatest chance of acceptability rests with its capacity to reflect the prevailing neighbourhood pattern while subtly increasing its supply of smaller homes.

The case study designs respond to prevailing conditions in many Australian suburbs and will be at least somewhat familiar in other western countries. The following design methods and data have been used.

Lot sizes

For single lots, these range from 325–920m^2 (3,500–9,900 sq ft), with frontages of 11.3m–18.3m (37–60') and depths of 28.8m–50.3m (94–165'). For the two-lot studies, sites of around 650m^2 (7,000 sq ft) are amalgamated into lots of 1,300m^2 (14,000 sq ft). Some of the sizes and proportions tested in the case studies will match lots found in other cities. Where they do not, the variety of lot widths and depths tested allows the reader to adapt the examples to their local conditions.

Site area per dwelling

In a bluefield development, no subdivision occurs, and the houses are not evenly distributed across the lot. Regardless, the average site area per dwelling is provided for easy comparison with other forms of housing.

Detached house arrangements

The existing neighbourhood houses are shown as fully detached, with at least a walkway space down each side. Many aspects of the designs will therefore be directly transferrable to the detached housing arrangements common to many westernised suburbs, particularly those of North America. While there are many examples of semi-detached, row, and terrace houses in Australia, these vary in numbers by location and are vastly outweighed by detached homes. Some of the case study designs take advantage of building in (or creating access via) both a walkway and a driveway, which will not be possible in locations predominated by semi-detached homes, as is the case in many neighbourhoods in the UK, for example. In these instances, building over a single side access will need to be weighed against competing factors, such as any mandated car parking requirements behind the line of the dwelling or the ability for a backyard home to be accessed directly from the street.

Housing typology and sizes

The retained houses shown in the case studies are Victorian-era cottages c1880–1910. These share common traits of a central hallway flanked by two or three rooms on each side, and a rear lean-to that is retained in some of the studies but removed in others. This reflects the fact that some original lean-tos remain while many others have been demolished or subsumed into prior alterations. The bluefield housing model works well – or is at least clearer to illustrate as a deployable system – where the retained original housing follows a common typology and is arranged in predictable rows, as is the case with the Australian cottage. Similar examples are the Californian and Chicago bungalows, and the more varied twentieth century bungalows of the UK, Canada, and Australia. However, a common language to the foundation housing is not a pre-requisite for the bluefield model to be applied, nor is any heritage protection that mandates retention. As described by bluefield housing Principle 3 in Chapter 6, the incentive to retain and adapt existing neighbourhood housing is as much about a sustainability, construction, and staging logic as it is the retention of scale, character, and heritage. While the retained houses in the case studies share strong and identifiable traits, the model can be deployed by the reader on houses of any age or typology. Similarly, where retention of the original house is not possible, it can be replaced with a new dwelling without breaking the overall organisational and operational structure of the bluefield model, particularly where the replacement dwelling can demonstrably improve current housing provisions and performance. Inasmuch as the case studies demonstrate that density and diversity increases can be achieved within the scale and form constraints of a character neighbourhood, the bluefield approach can equally be applied to low-rise neighbourhoods in the absence of heritage or character overlays.

House sizes

The retained and reworked cottages are shown at their smallest common sizes, with rooms ranging from 3.6 x 3.8m (11'10" x 12½') up to 4.0 x 4.9m (13' x 16'). Hallways are shown as either 1.2m, 1.5m, or 1.8m wide (4', 5', or 6'). The rationale for using the smallest common size of cottage is to demonstrate utility that will only get easier to design for as the base houses become larger. When undertaking a similar process with different housing stock, the reader will need to adapt the principles accordingly. Larger houses which cater to division into multiple dwellings can also be used, providing there is sufficient space for additional dwellings and shared landscape.

Site coverage

For direct comparison, the site plans list the site coverages of the existing conditions and the bluefield design alternatives. Shown as percentages, the coverages include the ground floor footprints of the houses and garages, and exclude carports/pergolas and garden sheds.

Number of storeys

The retained houses of the case studies are all single storey, reflecting the common form of the Australian cottage. Working within these height constraints is important to demonstrate how second-storey additions and two-storey backyard homes can be accommodated within a prevailing low-rise neighbourhood scale. This is particularly important in Australia, where applications for two-storey suburban homes are often heavily scrutinised for their bulk and for their potential to overlook neighbours. For neighbourhoods where two or more storeys are common, such as those found in the UK, the US, and Canada, fitting the new housing within established heights will be easier to achieve. Houses containing basements, elevated ground levels, and second storeys or attic levels will comfortably accommodate three-storey bluefield homes within the existing neighbourhood scale.

Construction types

Contemporary Australian housing is commonly constructed in brick veneer: a 90mm (3½") deep structural timber frame with a 110mm (4¼") thick non-structural masonry exterior, separated by a 50mm (2") air gap. The older retained cottages shown in the case studies are cavity brick construction, with two leaves of structural brickwork separated by a larger air gap. Exterior walls are therefore commonly 280mm or 11" thick in total. Internal cottage walls are a single leaf of 110mm brick, while those of contemporary houses are 90mm timber studs. Whether applied to masonry construction or lightweight timber, the remodelling necessary to achieve a bluefield redevelopment are easily achieved within the existing skillset of domestic builders. Where floors in contemporary houses are commonly concrete slab on ground construction, those in the older houses of the case study designs are timber, making it easier to introduce plumbing and electrical services to previously un-serviced rooms. Contemporary roofs are formed of timber trusses, restricting their occupation as attics, but those of the retained and reworked cottages are of open conventional timber framing: rafters, beams, and ceiling joists. Where additions are made in the case studies, these keep the original cottage roof intact by the creation of linking elements that fit under the existing eaves. This serves two purposes: it limits the amount of rework to the existing roof, thereby minimising cost and the potential for leaks, while maintaining the legibility and character of the original house.

Basements

Due to Australia's temperate climate, footings do not have to be excavated below deep frost lines and are often as shallow as 600mm (2'). As a result, basements, particularly those large enough to be inhabited, are rare, and finished ground floor levels are usually set as little as 75mm (3") above the adjacent ground level. The case study designs do not therefore incorporate any basement suites as is commonly found in places such as Canada and northern parts of the US. Where a basement can be converted into a separate dwelling, particularly where it can become fully independent and not a mere 'secondary' suite, it has the potential to significantly lift the dwelling numbers of a bluefield development or otherwise allow more open space to be given over to landscape if the amount of backyard building can be reduced.

Laneways

Rear lanes are commonly found in Australian neighbourhoods that were set out prior to 1910, at which point sewer systems were established and flushing toilets were incorporated into the house. After this time, these so-called night cart lanes were no longer required to remove waste, with subsequent land releases foregoing laneways for deeper back-to-back lots. Laneway housing, although increasingly encouraged, is still relatively uncommon in Australia, with the old laneway systems often predominated by garages and shedding. For cities with extensive laneway systems and established laneway housing policy, such as Vancouver and Toronto, the bluefield housing model is likely to be much easier to incorporate into the established infill mix. In the case studies, a mix of laneway and front-loaded lots are shown to demonstrate how access can be achieved under varied conditions. Being able to make use of a rear lane significantly increases amenity and function, particularly in relation to car parking and pedestrian movement through the site, as there is less of a requirement for residents to walk from their cars directly past the windows of other homes on the lot. There is a risk with laneways, however, particularly in the case of only two dwellings, that the houses turn their backs on each other, leveraging their respective street addresses for sole access, and thereby becoming a *de facto* subdivision. This does not guarantee a bad housing outcome, but it is a potential mechanism to be exploited if the bluefield model is used to add an additional privatised dwelling where it would otherwise be precluded.

Car parking

The provisions for car parking in the designs should not be mistaken for any advocacy for a perpetuation of car dependency. Rather, on-site car parking is demonstrated to negate one of the major hurdles infill projects face when seeking neighbour buy-in and zoning approval. Importantly, car parking numbers are provided relative to the maximum number of bedrooms achieved in each development. This is important to accurately convey the car parking provisions relative to the likely number of residents. It is a particularly important argument to make in jurisdictions that mandate car parking numbers in the absence of a nuanced understanding of the number of people likely to be accommodated. For lots without a rear laneway, parking is commonly organised at the side of the house. This is different to many neighbourhoods in other countries, where parking can be found in detached garages behind the dwelling, or out in the open in front of the house. In Australia, high summer temperatures make it more amenable to park cars under cover where possible, hence cars in the designs being shaded by carports, covered pergolas, or trees. This is a deliberate strategy to demonstrate that people *and* cars can be accommodated by the model, until such point as car parking mandates can be relaxed and the space given over to other uses. Put simply, on-site car parking consumes a lot of space, particularly where cars need to turn on site to drive out while facing forward. For neighbourhoods with minimal car parking stipulations or zero-parking requirements, the bluefield model will be easier to accommodate. Any decision to forego car parking in a bluefield development should, however, be considered relative to the residents' ability to be independently mobile relative to their finances. This is discussed in Chapter 7 and is particularly pertinent to those who rely on private car use for access to work, education, and services.

Fencing

In Australia, backyard fencing is normally solid rather than transparent, with a standard height of 1.8m (6'). It is now uncommon for rear or side fencing to be low, or to be made of chain mesh or other similar open material. The case study designs therefore assume an inward-facing design that often turns its back to neighbours. In adapting the model to neighbourhoods with a greater degree of openness between lots, the reader may choose an alternative approach that leverages longer views across lots or conversely seeks additional privacy from neighbouring lots.

Overlooking

Australian zoning laws commonly contain restrictions on overlooking between neighbouring windows, and from each dwelling into the private yard spaces of its neighbours. This results in significant design restrictions for two-storey proposals, including obscured glazing and the provision of fixed privacy screens to upper-level windows and balconies. The case study designs seek to adhere to these policies relative to neighbouring lots but actively overlook the shared yard space within the development itself, to improve sociability and enable passive surveillance. This tactic is expanded in the zoning discussions of Chapter 16. For those applying the model in neighbourhoods with more relaxed overlooking requirements, the addition of two-storey elements is likely to be easier to achieve, particularly in relation to winter sun that cannot easily be gained without facing windows towards neighbouring lots.

Density calculations

Densities are described in the case studies as the number of dwellings achieved per hectare and per acre (dw/ha and dw/acre). These are all net rather than gross densities, meaning that only the area within the lot boundaries is used in the calculations, with footpaths, roads, and other public spaces excluded. In some of the studies, the dwellings are flexible, allowing connection into larger houses, or division into smaller homes. Where this occurs, multiple dwelling densities are listed. This is important to note, as it demonstrates that dwelling densities are often an abstract concept and do not take into consideration residents' patterns of use. Each of the case studies is premised on the ambition to create a medium density development of at least 34 dw/ha where possible (14 dw/acre).

Building codes

The new detached dwellings in the case studies assume design and construction compliance with local or national construction codes. The retention and adaptation of the original housing assumes that compliance with fire codes can be achieved with targeted design and construction measures. These include building up walls to the undersides of roofs with non-combustible material that creates a firebreak between newly created tenancies, and designing window and door placements that comply with local requirements for fire and acoustic separation. While the conversion of single houses into two or more independent dwellings will require approvals and potentially professional building certification advice, the requisite construction work will fall within the existing skillset of domestic builders and is not a barrier to the model.

The single lot studies

The four single lot design studies demonstrate the bluefield model across what is likely to be the most constrained neighbourhood conditions. Rather than setting a minimum lot size on which the model might operate, the work instead explores different site options that test degrees of sharing indoor and outdoor space across different sized lots. The sites are defined simply as Small, Medium, Large and Extra Large. Each case uses a real Australian lot and house, anonymised to suggest general deployability when tailored to different neighbourhoods.

The four single lots are:

- Small $325m^2$ (3,500 sq ft), two street frontages.
- Medium $530m^2$ (5,700 sq ft), one street frontage.
- Large $675m^2$ (7,265 sq ft), corner lot.
- Extra Large $920m^2$ (9,900 sq ft), one street frontage, one rear lane.

The double lot studies

The design studies for double allotments recognise three common suburban conditions that are created when consolidating two adjacent lots:

- lots joined back-to-back with two street frontages: $1,255m^2$ (13,510 sq ft);
- lots joined side-by-side with a single street access: $1,300 m^2$ (14,000 sq ft); and
- lots joined side-by-side with a front street and a rear laneway: $1,360m^2$ (14,640 sq ft).

Depending on local market conditions, the procurement of two adjacent lots can be achievable, particularly when undertaken for strategic housing gain rather than for maximum profit. In its most simple form, a property owner might purchase the house next door when it comes on the market or via private negotiation with their neighbour beforehand. This might be achieved independently, if affordable, or collaboratively with others as a form of development or investment strategy. Alternatively, two adjacent owners might joint venture and consolidate their properties without either going to market. These types of scenarios are further discussed in Chapter 13. Strategically, the amalgamation of two lots provides meaningful spatial gains over single properties. When arranged back-to-back, significant site depths between the retained housing can be achieved, providing generous territory in which to form both built and landscaped space. When two lots are arranged side-by-side, significant lateral spatial gains allow for appreciably improved site amenity over single lots.

The multiple lot study

The multiple lot study demonstrates that the bluefield strategies applied to single lots can be strategically undertaken across detached and attached lots to create a broader housing system. It explores the spatial benefits of an expanded territory and the capacity for the bluefield model to form the basis of tactical incremental development over time. The designs see new laneway housing spreading across the rear of the lots, housing additions occupying the centres, and the existing housing retained as more private housing fronting the primary street. This creates a repeatable development pattern suitable for a mix of housing types: more public and engaged at the rear and more private at the front. In total, the scheme presents:

- lots joined side-by-side with a front street and a rear laneway: 2,550m^2 (27,450 sq ft).

Imagining the residents

In developing the case studies, consideration has been given to who the imagined proponents of these housing propositions might be, without trying to limit for whom the bluefield model may be suited. In the Introduction it was disclaimed that the 'blue' in bluefield should never be considered a reference to older people, yet the model is well suited to this cohort. In many western societies, communities are ageing, with increasing numbers of older people relative to the population at large. But older residents are diverse and do not form a single homogeneous group.[4] They largely enjoy good health and make up a significant proportion of many cities' populations. In Australia, many older people are fortunate to live independently in the community, and most do so in their own home in the greater metropolitan areas of capital cities. Older people often wish to stay in their own home and within their community, however, as a city's residents age, many of them do so alone.[5]

For residents wishing to downsize to something smaller within the neighbourhood and community with which they are familiar, there can be little choice or opportunity. The same can be true for people of any age who seek to enter a suburb through the purchase or rental of a smaller and more affordable property. As discussed in Chapter 5, even as the suburbs continue to change through knock-down-rebuild urban densification, they often do so with a like-for-like replacement: a three-bedroom family home might be demolished to provide two new dwellings, but these replacement dwellings will often offer the same three-bedroom accommodation as their predecessor. The city gains the additional housing it needs to support population growth and longer life expectancies but does not gain the housing diversity required of the changing demographic.

One imagined bluefield audience, then, is residents wishing to age-in-community with family, with friends or with like-minded others. This may occur with others of the same age, or with mixed age groups. Similarly, the residents may come from one family group, from an existing friendship group, or be brought together for the first time by a housing association or similar entity. And in a post-pandemic era of increased working-from-home arrangements, some of the housing in the model may inevitably be given over to commercial use, as described above.

As such, the imagined proponents and residents of these housing propositions might be a group of hitherto strangers – singles, couples, small families, or organisations – who redevelop a property together to create independent dwellings that enjoy the spatial and personal benefits that some form of sharing can deliver. They might be a community housing provider creating a new model of lifetime rental properties that sit alongside their traditional portfolio. They could be a family who decide to adapt their existing home and garden to pre-emptively create the final home for the oldest members, a starter home for the youngest, a rental property to supplement their income, or a work-from-home arrangement that supports health and wellbeing or semi-retirement. Imagined in these ways, the concepts of co-located neighbourhood living scenarios share a common thread: the desire for a compact suburban housing model that is organised in a socially connected manner and that sits comfortably alongside existing single-family homes. Such a model works to achieve a balance between independence and integration, and between the individual and the community, while finding its place within established neighbourhood settings.

Notes

1   Jan Nijman, ed., *The Life of North Amercian Suburbs* (Toronto: University of Toronto Press, 2020), 349.
2   *AS/NZS 2890.1:2004 Parking Facilities – Part 1: Off-street car parking,* AS/NZS 2890.1:2004, (Sydney: Standards Australia / Standards New Zealand, 2004).

From top-down to bottom-up: a deployable model

3 Shane Murray et al., *Infill Opportunities Design Research Report*, Department of Architecture, Monash University (Caulfield East, Victoria: Monash University, 2011).

4 The Australian Centre for Social Innovation, *Future Directions to Support Ageing Well* (Adelaide: TACSI, 2018), 22–24.

5 The Australian Centre for Social Innovation, *Future Directions to Support Ageing Well*, 4–15.

10 Single allotments

10.1
Small: looking from the secondary street past the new Dwelling 2 and across the garden to the Dwelling 1 cottage.

Single allotments

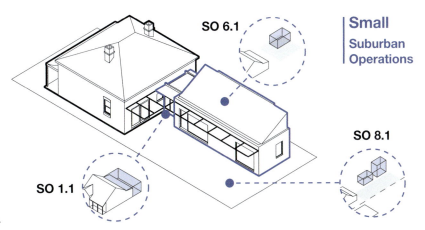

10.2
Small: Suburban Operations.

Small	325m²	3,500 sq ft	
	11.28m x 28.83m	37' x 94'7"	
Lot type	Midblock[1] with two street frontages		
Also suits	Short lots without a rear lane or second street		
	Short lots with driveway access down one side		
Existing	65% site cover, 1 dwelling		
	31 dw/ha	(325m² per dw)	
	12 dw/acre	(3,500 sq ft per dw)	
Bluefield	52% site cover, 2 dwellings		
	62 dw/ha	(163m² per dw)[2]	
	25 dw/acre	(1,750 sq ft per dw)	
Bedrooms[3]	3		
Car parking	0, with one on-street space added by removing an existing cross-over		
Sharing	Main garden, laundry, clothes drying, bin enclosure, shed		
Dwelling 1	81m² / 870 sq ft	2 rooms	renovated existing home
Dwelling 2	58m² / 625 sq ft	1 room	single-storey rear addition
Operations	SO 1.1: rear addition, single		
	SO 6.1: yard addition, single		
	SO 8.1: yard arrangement, linear		

Single allotments

Scenario

Facing the social and financial upheaval of separation from their partner, a recently single 50+ resident moves in with their 70+ parents, who own a cottage on a small lot, but with dual street access. The living arrangement is mutually beneficial: the parents receive assistance around the house from their adult child, who themself takes comfort in having secure and affordable housing. All enjoy the company that living together once more provides. Seeing the long-term benefits of the arrangement, the trio undertake a renovation together to formalise the living arrangements across two discrete dwellings.

10.3
Small: design configuration, showing two dwellings each addressing a street frontage.

A narrow footprint addition is added to the rear of the cottage to provide a one bedroom self-contained dwelling. A shared laundry links the two dwellings, freeing valuable space within the houses themselves (Figure 10.3). Determining that this could be the final housing choice for each of them, and looking to the future, each dwelling and the common laundry are designed to the Livable Housing Australia Gold standard for mobility, with space allowed for 1:20 ramps externally to create step-free movement throughout. Successfully mounting an argument that car parking is not required and that improved landscape options are preferred instead, the residents design the two dwellings such that the bedrooms are separated whilst the living rooms address the shared rear garden without looking directly into each other (Figure 10.5).

Single allotments

BAU | 325 m² | 1 dwelling | 31 dw/ha | 65% site cover
    | 3,500 sf | 1 car | 12 dw/acre |

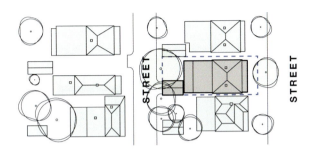

Bluefield | 325 m² | 2 dwellings | 62 dw/ha | 52% site cover
          | 3,500 sf | 0 cars for 3 BR | 25 dw/acre |

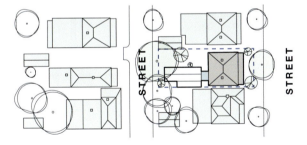

10.4
Small: site plans, showing the existing conditions (top) and the new bluefield conditions (bottom).

50m
150'

Single allotments

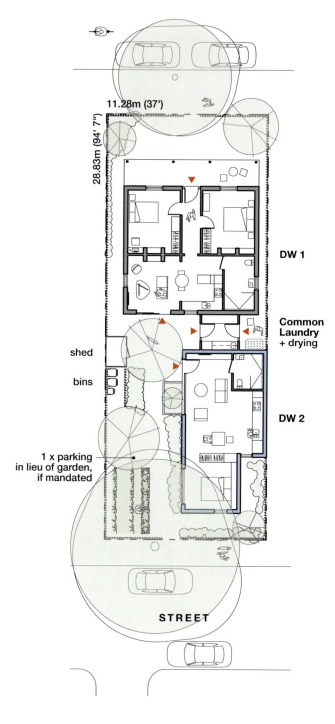

10.5
Small: floor plan.

Single allotments

10.6
Medium: an 8m (26') deep shared garden offers space for amenity, productivity, activity, and social interaction.

151

Single allotments

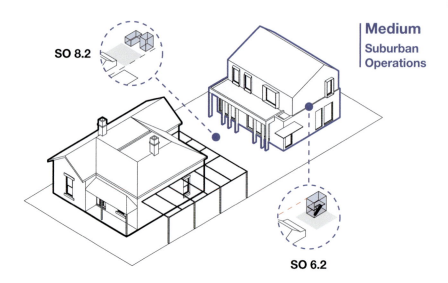

10.7
Medium: Suburban Operations.

Medium	530m²	5,700 sq ft
	15.20m x 34.89m	50' x 114½'
Lot type	Midblock with single street frontage	
Also suits	15.2m / 50' wide lots with greater depth	
Existing	48% site cover, 1 dwelling	
	19 dw/ha	(530m² per dw)
	8 dw/acre	(5,700 sq ft per dw)
Bluefield	40% site cover, 2 to 3 dwellings	
	38 to 57 dw/ha	(265 to 177m² per dw)
	15 to 23 dw/acre	(2,850 to 1,900 sq ft per dw)
Bedrooms	5	
Car parking	2	
Sharing	Main garden, parking, clothes drying, bin enclosure, shed	
Dwelling 1	112m² / 1,205 sq ft	2 rooms	renovated existing home
Option A:		
Dwelling 2	122m² / 1,315 sq ft	3 rooms	two-storey backyard home
Option B:		
Dwelling 2	64m² / 690 sq ft	1 room	ground floor of backyard home
Dwelling 3	58m² / 625 sq ft	1 room	first floor of backyard home
Operations	SO 6.2: yard addition, double	
	SO 8.2: yard arrangement, lateral	

Single allotments

Scenario

The owners of the existing home undertake a future-proofing renovation, suiting their needs now and into the foreseeable future. Targeting semi-retirement and wishing to create an independent house for their young-adult child, for whom they are carers, they undertake mobility renovations that create step-free spaces and a more open layout. The proportions of the 15.2m (50') wide lot enable them to create a backyard dwelling with 3m clearances on each side (10'). The resultant 9.2m dwelling width (30') allows for a generous one-bedroom plan suited to reduced mobility, and for a stair that provides access to an additional two bedrooms on an upper level (Figure 10.8, Figure 10.11, and Figure 10.12). Designed for flexibility, the second level is built without dividing walls and with joinery fitted with power and plumbing services. Coupled with the inclusion of two doors at the ground floor level (one external door into the stairwell and a fire-rated door between the stairwell and the ground floor) these design tactics allow for the upper floor to be fully self-contained via simple modifications (Figure 10.9). The residents thereby provide themselves dwelling flexibility into the future, and as needs change.

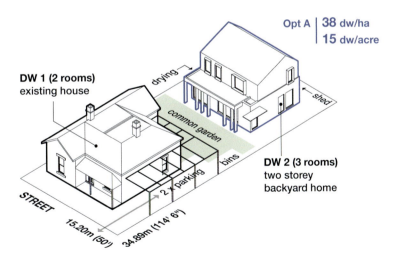

10.8
Medium: design configuration – Option A, showing two dwellings.

Single allotments

The site can be configured as one dwelling plus one work-from-home arrangement, two dwellings of two and three bedrooms respectively, three smaller dwellings, or two dwellings plus a home office. Renting parts of the accommodation is feasible, as is shifting between the accommodation. Importantly, the changes enable the owners to age-in-place with improved peace of mind for their child's independence, furthering their ability to age well. The original four-room cottage is retained and renovated into a two-bedroom dwelling, with the bedrooms and wet areas running one side of the hallway and living spaces the other. The kitchen and dining area faces the front garden, and the living space the rear garden. The scale of the backyard home complements that of the cottage and provides varied accommodation of up to three bedrooms. Each dwelling addresses a shared central garden.

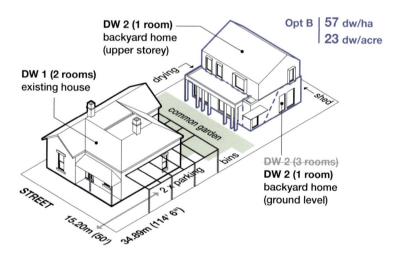

10.9
Medium: design configuration – Option B, showing three dwellings.

Single allotments

BAU	530 m² 5,700 sf	1 dwelling 2 cars	19 dw/ha 8 dw/acre	48% site cover

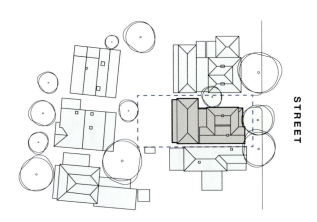

Bluefield	530 m² 5,700 sf	2-3 dwellings 2 cars for 5 BR	38-57 dw/ha 15-23 dw/acre	40% site cover

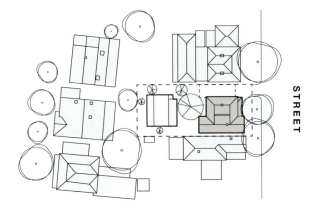

10.10
Medium: site plans, showing the existing conditions (top) and the new bluefield conditions (bottom).

50m
150'

Single allotments

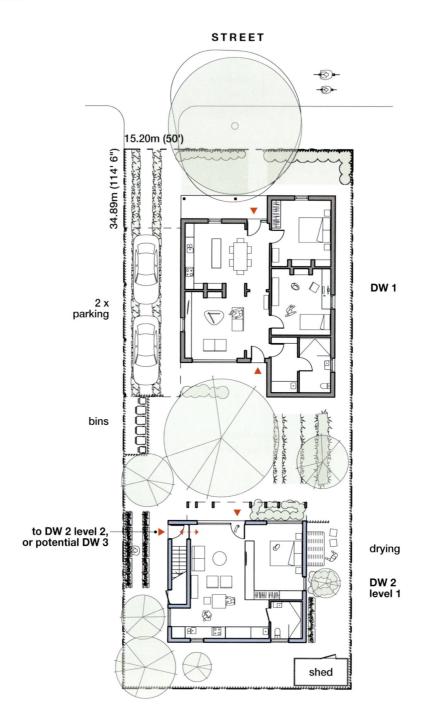

10.11
Medium: ground floor plan.

Single allotments

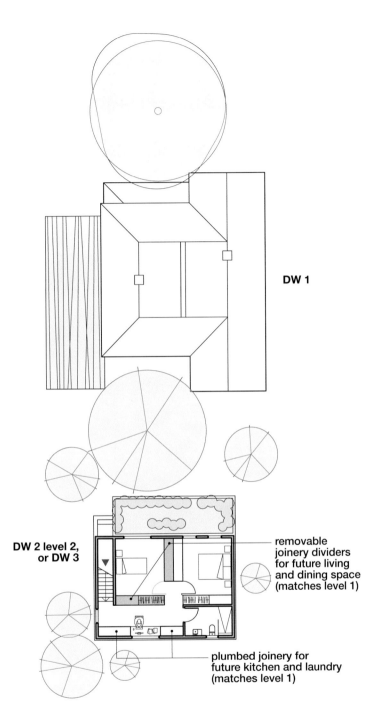

DW 1

DW 2 level 2, or DW 3

removable joinery dividers for future living and dining space (matches level 1)

plumbed joinery for future kitchen and laundry (matches level 1)

10.12
Medium: upper-level floor plan, showing the Option A configuration and the requirements to turn the upper level into the Option B third dwelling.

10m
32'

Single allotments

10.13
Large: looking from the roof of the Dwelling 3 backyard home across the garden, with Dwelling 2 sitting as an addition to the Dwelling 1 cottage.

Single allotments

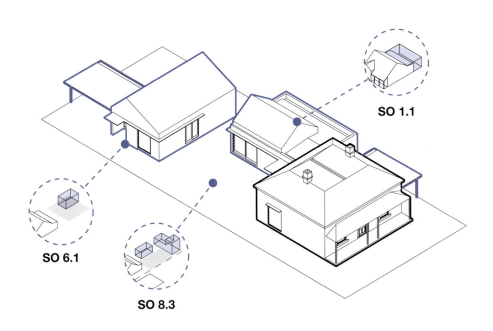

10.14 Large: Suburban Operations.	**Large**	**675m²** 16.46m x 41.00m	**7,265 sq ft** 54' x 134½'	
	Lot type	Corner lot with two street frontages		
	Also suits	Corner lots of varying sizes		
	Existing	48% site cover, 1 dwelling 15 dw/ha (675m² per dw) 6 dw/acre (7,265 sq ft per dw)		
	Bluefield	38% site cover, 3 dwellings 44 dw/ha (225m² per dw) 18 dw/acre (2,420 sq ft per dw)		
	Bedrooms	4		
	Car parking	3		
	Sharing	Main garden		
	Dwelling 1	95m² / 1,020 sq ft	2 rooms	renovated existing home
	Dwelling 2	68m² / 730 sq ft	1 room	single-storey rear addition
	Dwelling 3	67m² / 720 sq ft	1 room	single-storey backyard home
	Operations	SO 1.1: rear addition, single SO 6.1: yard addition, single SO 8.3: yard arrangement, clustered		

Single allotments

Scenario

Looking to expand its portfolio and diversify its housing mix, a Community Housing Provider (CHP) buys a home in a suburb well-serviced by public transport and close to civic, medical, service, and retail facilities. Rather than demolishing the existing house and replacing it with a unit development typical of its usual model, the CHP leverages the property's suburban characteristics to offer an alternative model for members of its client base.

The existing home is renovated to create a two-bedroom dwelling while a small footprint extension creates a second one-bedroom dwelling. Another one-bedroom dwelling is created as a backyard home that matches the size and location of garages found in the neighbourhood (Figure 10.15). Taking advantage of the lot's corner location, this backyard home addresses the side street more sympathetically than a garage would, improving the streetscape amenity in a secondary street that is otherwise dominated by garage doors, sheds, and long-sided house extensions.

The CHP sees this single allotment model as one it can replicate and disperse throughout the suburbs, and its forward-planning highlights the potential for corner sites such as this to be hubs, where one of the dwellings can be given over to a community house for residents to access for activities and mobile services.

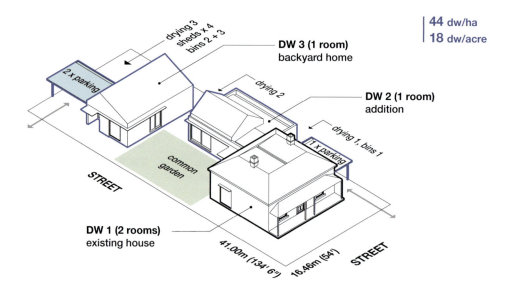

10.15
Large: design configuration, showing three dwellings that each address the two street frontages.

Each dwelling is independent, but with a shared garden and connective path or deck. The additions are arranged around a yard that strategically addresses the side street, increasing the amenity of the street itself and extending the residents' views out of their site and across the road. The bedrooms of each dwelling face away from communal areas for privacy, while the living areas deliberately address the shared garden for amenity and positive interaction (Figure 10.17).

Single allotments

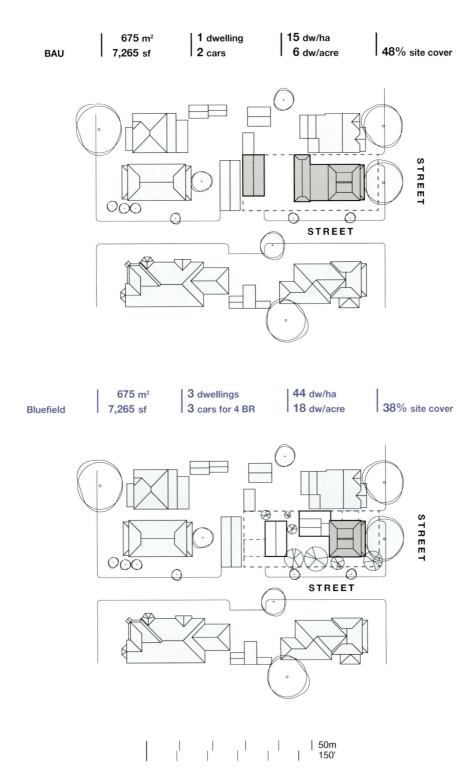

10.16
Large: site plans, showing the existing conditions (top) and the new bluefield conditions (bottom).

Single allotments

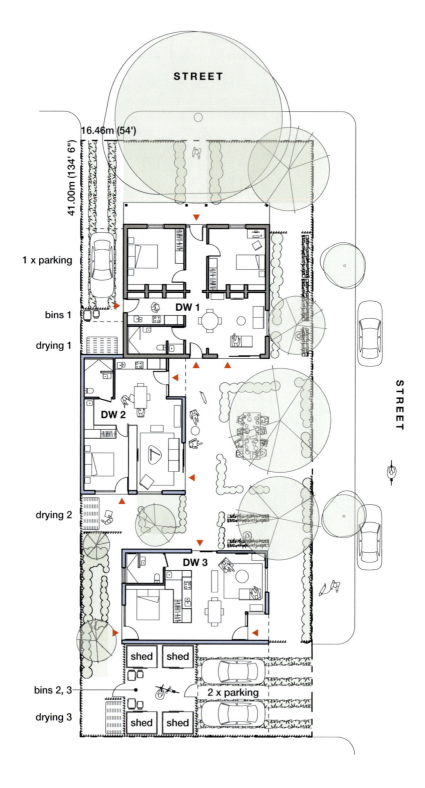

10.17
Large: floor plan.

162

10.18
Extra Large: looking past the common house across the garden to the Dwelling 3 backyard home.

Single allotments

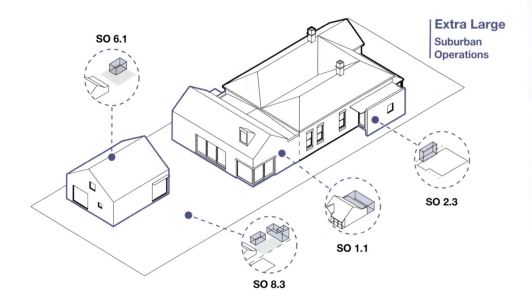

10.19
Extra Large: Suburban Operations.

Extra Large	920m²	9,900 sq ft	
	18.29m x 50.29m	60' x 165'	
Lot type	Midblock with rear lane		
Also suits	Large blocks without a rear lane		
Existing	38% site cover, 1 dwelling		
	11 dw/ha	(920m² per dw)	
	4 dw/acre	(9,900 sq ft per dw)	
Bluefield	39% site cover, 3 to 4 dwellings		
	33 to 43 dw/ha	(307 to 230m² per dw)	
	13–18 dw/acre	(3,300 to 2,475 sq ft per dw)	
Bedrooms	4		
Car parking	3–5		
Sharing	Main garden, parking, clothes drying, bin enclosure, shed		
Dwelling 1	78m² / 840 sq ft	1 room	half of renovated existing home
Dwelling 2	78m² / 840 sq ft	1 room	half of renovated existing home plus side pod
Dwelling 3	66m² / 710 sq ft	1 room	single-storey backyard home
Option A: Com. house	With shared kitchen, dining, living, laundry, bathroom, guest room		

Single allotments

Option B:
Dwelling 4   122m² / 1,315 sq ft   1 room   renovated existing home + addition

Operations   SO 1.1: rear addition, single
SO 2.3: 1.5m (5') side pod
SO 6.1: yard addition, single
SO 8.3: yard arrangement, clustered

Scenario

The owner of a large house on a traditional quarter-acre block has lived alone for three years after the loss of their spouse. They have several friends in similar circumstances, each having lived in their large family homes for many years. None of the residents wish (nor need) to give up their suburban way of life, but each would like to downsize to a house that better fits their needs now that they are older and living alone. Importantly, they would each like the company and occasional support of others, without giving up their independence. Preferring a small house over an apartment, unit or formal retirement living, the three parties come together to develop the owner's property, creating three one-bedroom dwellings and a common house (Figure 10.20).

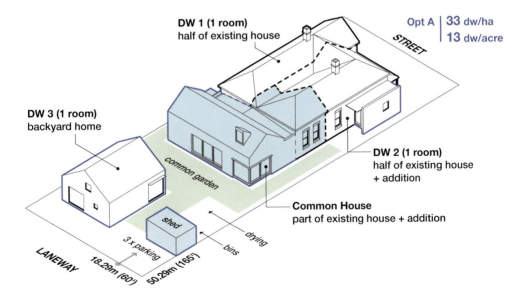

10.20
Extra Large: design configuration – Option A, showing three dwellings plus a Common House.

Together, they set the rules for their property. Each week they share a few meals and socialise in the common house. One of the residents is a keen gardener and enjoys helping the hired gardener when they visit each fortnight. For this, she pays a reduced maintenance fee, as agreed by the residents and captured in their Residents' Agreement.[4] This document also captures the agreed use of the guest bedroom in the common house, which is available should a temporary live-in carer ever be required. Ordinarily, this guest room is available for residents to use as a study or for hobbies, and on a roster basis when guests come to stay.

The original house is retained and divided into two dwellings. This is achieved by blocking the doors on one side of the central hallway and building the affected wall up to the underside of the roof for fire separation. The house receives a small kitchen addition to the side of one of the front rooms, and a rear extension similar in size and layout to those often added when homes are renovated. A small backyard home is created at the rear of the block, offset from the rear boundary to provide a garden (Figure 10.23). Although undesirable by comparison, this garden can be given over to one additional parallel car park if mandated, adding to the three spaces provided off the rear lane. A further car space is achieved in the existing front driveway.[5]

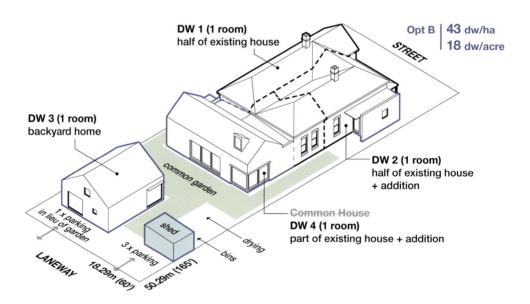

10.21
Extra Large: design configuration – Option B, showing the Common House replaced by a fourth dwelling.

Single allotments

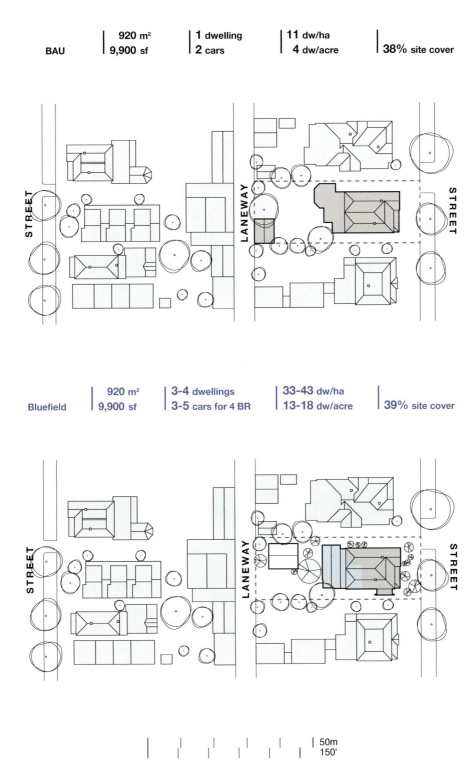

10.22
Extra Large: site plans, showing the existing conditions (top) and the new bluefield conditions (bottom).

Single allotments

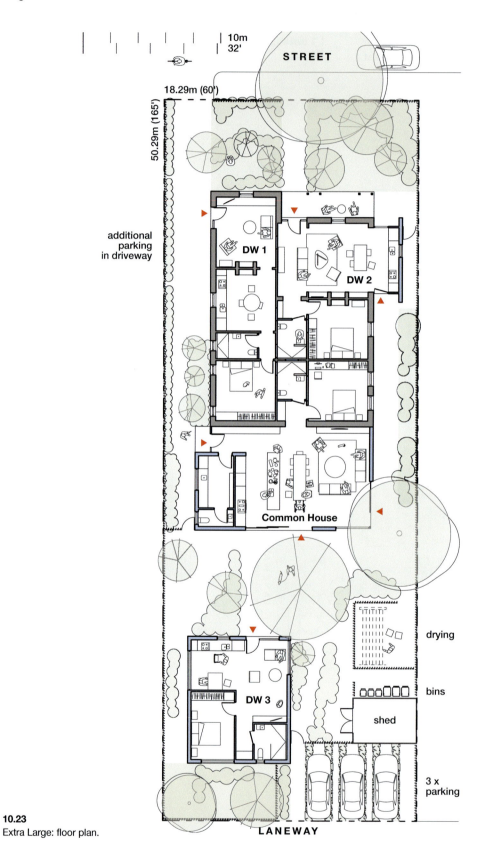

10.23
Extra Large: floor plan.

Notes

1 'Midblock' refers to a lot with neighbours on each side. Midblocks without a rear lane or second street frontage also have a neighbour to the rear.

2 Measures for site area per dwelling are clarified in Chapter 9. An equivalent average site area per dwelling figure is provided for the bluefield schemes as a comparison measure against normative minimum lot size requirements for a traditional subdivision. This allows the reader to make quantitative and qualitative comparisons of the two models relative to local zoning rules around minimum lot size.

3 'Bedrooms' are calculated as the *maximum* number of rooms that could potentially be used as bedrooms in each bluefield scheme. This assists in understanding the maximum likely occupation of a scheme, but does not guarantee that the schemes will be used at this maximum capacity. Flexibility and other potential uses are discussed in Chapter 9.

4 Residents' Agreements are discussed in Chapter 15.

5 The rationale for incorporating car parking, including as potential over-provisions, is discussed in Chapter 7. Ideally, on site car parking and car reliance can be designed out of bluefield developments, but this is contingent on local zoning rules and existing public transport infrastructure. In demonstrating how car parking can be achieved in a bluefield proposal, even at the expense of amenity and landscape, the designer reduces the risk that an absence of car parking can be weaponised against the development.

11   Double allotments

11.1
A back-to-back double lot proposal, looking down the driveway of an original home: a new connective path through the site from street to street.

Double allotments

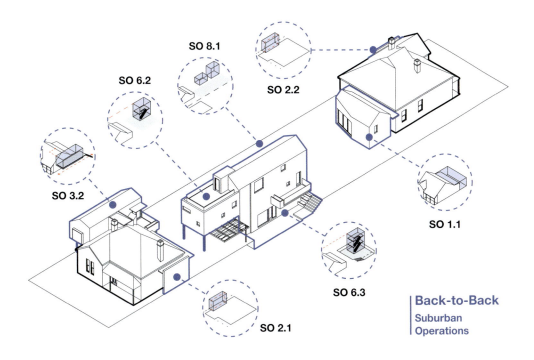

11.2
Back-to-back: Suburban Operations.

Back-to-back	1,255m2	13,510 sq ft		
	15.85m x 79.25m	52' x 260'		
Lot type	Back-to-back midblocks with two street frontages, off-set driveways			
Also suits	Back-to-back lots with in-line driveways			
Existing	39% site cover, 2 dwellings			
	16 dw/ha	(628m^2 per dw)		
	6 dw/acre	(6,755 sq ft per dw)		
Bluefield	34% site cover, 5 to 6 dwellings			
	40 to 48 dw/ha	(251 to 209m^2 per dw)		
	16 to 19 dw/acre	(2,704 to 2,253 sq ft per dw)		
Bedrooms	11			
Car parking	5, with one on-street space added by removing an existing cross-over			
Sharing	Main garden, parking, shed			
Option A Dwelling 1	144m^2 / 1,550 sq ft	3 rooms	renovated existing home plus side addition/pod	

Double allotments

Dwelling 2	75m^2 / 805 sq ft	2 rooms	attached two-storey backyard home
Dwelling 3	113m^2 / 1,215 sq ft	2 rooms	attached three-storey backyard home
Dwelling 4	70m^2 / 755 sq ft	2 rooms	single-storey rear addition
Dwelling 5	102m^2 / 1,100 sq ft	2 rooms	renovated existing home plus side pod
Option B			
Dwelling 3	64m^2 / 690 sq ft	1 room	upper floors of three-storey backyard home
Dwelling 6	49m^2 / 530 sq ft	1 room	ground floor of three-storey backyard home
Operations	SO 1.1: rear addition, single		
	SO 2.1: 0.9m (3') side pod		
	SO 2.2: 1.2m (4') side pod		
	SO 3.2: side addition, elevated		
	SO 6.2: yard addition, double		
	SO 6.3: yard addition, triple		
	SO 8.1: yard arrangement, linear		

Scenario

The back-to-back scheme is conceived of as a normative, yet more heavily intensified, additions and alterations project providing independent houses and gardens for five to six unrelated households. Where a maximum site yield of four dwellings could be achieved across the two lots under a traditional subdivision arrangement, the bluefield approach initially sees five self-contained dwellings dispersed over three buildings. Each is designed with its own outdoor space and dedicated car park, while a shared longitudinal communal garden links the three buildings and provides pedestrian access through the site from one street to another. Designed to retain the existing mature landscape, small additions to the two existing homes are coupled with a detached mini apartment building in the centre of the lot. The combined small footprints cover 5% less of the site than the existing two houses.

Double allotments

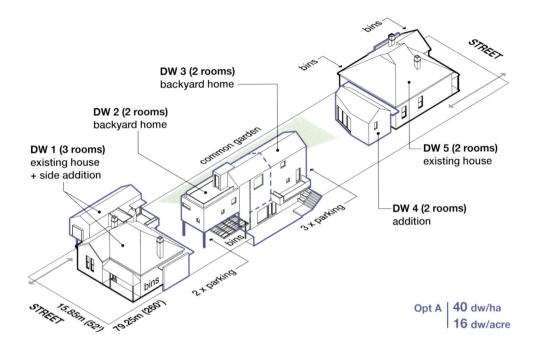

11.3
Back-to-back: design configuration – Option A, showing two retained and adapted dwellings, a third dwelling created as a small rear addition, and two more dwellings created in a central mini apartment building.

Figure 11.6 to Figure 11.9 show the housing arrangement over three levels. Dwelling 1 is conceived of as a family or share home of up to three and a half rooms. The central apartment building is arranged as two cross-over dwellings, with Dwelling 2 containing two rooms and Dwelling 3 two and a half rooms. Dwelling 3 can be split into two one-bedroom apartments. Dwelling 4 is configured as two rooms and exists as a small single-storey extension to the two and a half rooms of Dwelling 5, being the existing villa at the other end of the site.

Utilising a semi-basement for the three-storey apartment building keeps the building height to approximately 8m above ground level (26'3"), with this mass positioned toward the centre of the site and away from side boundaries. Importantly, this manoeuvre creates a high-quality sunken patio space used to access and supplement the semi-basement spaces. All existing mature trees are retained and complemented with additional plantings of varying sizes and spatial arrangements, including a 6m x 29m (20 x 95') communal productive garden running parallel with the apartment building. Additional landscape elements are provided via planter boxes to the balconies and the patio.

Double allotments

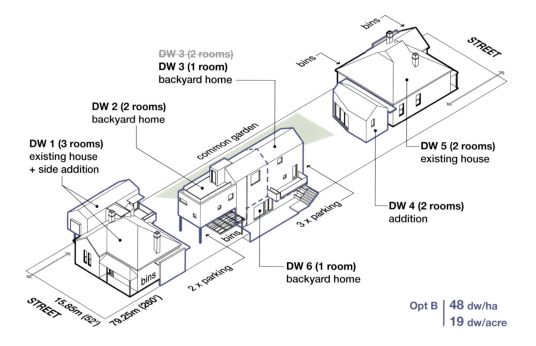

11.4
Back-to-back: design configuration – Option B, showing the central building further divided into three, creating a sixth dwelling without increasing the building footprint.

Double allotments

BAU | **1,255** m² / **13,510** sf | **2** dwellings / **4** cars | **16** dw/ha / **6** dw/acre | **39%** site cover

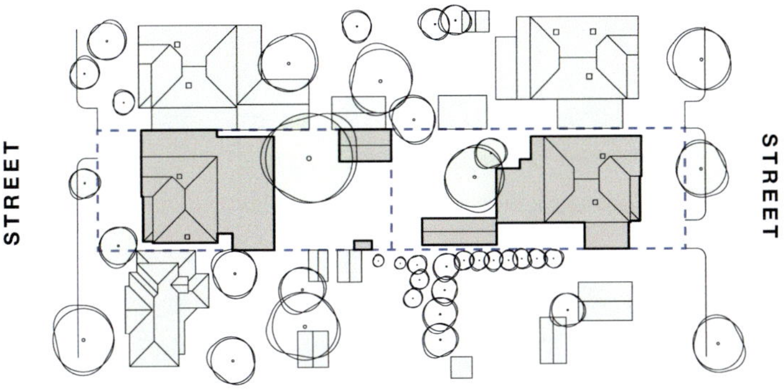

Bluefield | **1,255** m² / **13,510** sf | **5-6** dwellings / **5** cars for 11 BR | **40-48** dw/ha / **16-19** dw/acre | **34%** site cover

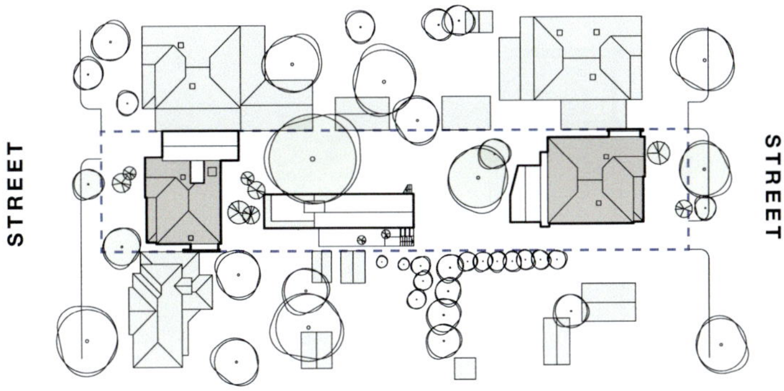

50m
150'

11.5
Back-to-back: site plans,
showing the existing conditions
(top) and the new bluefield
conditions (bottom).

Double allotments

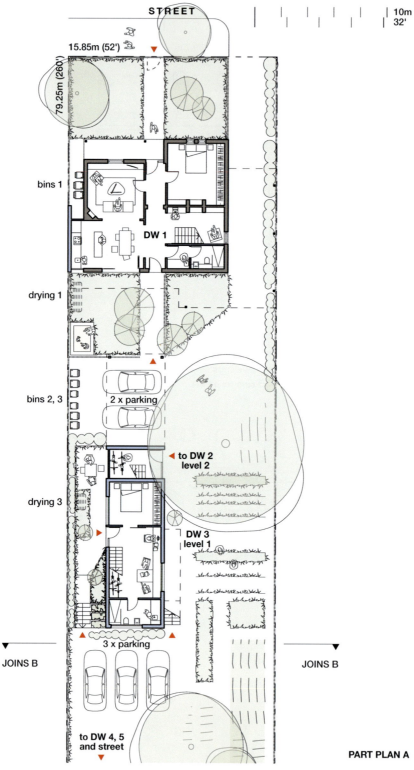

11.6
Back-to-back: ground floor plan, part A.

Double allotments

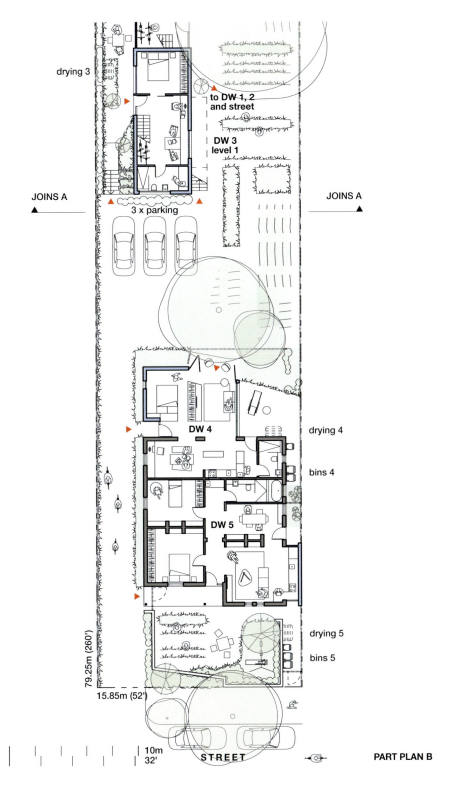

11.7
Back-to-back: ground floor plan, part B.

Double allotments

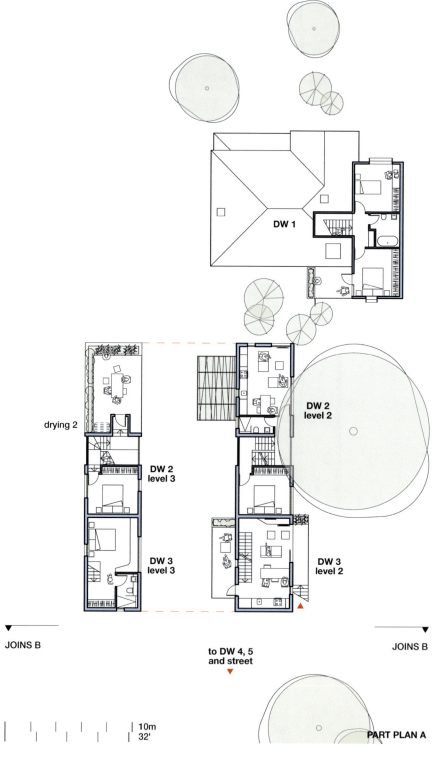

11.8
Back-to-back:
upper levels floor plan,
part A.

Double allotments

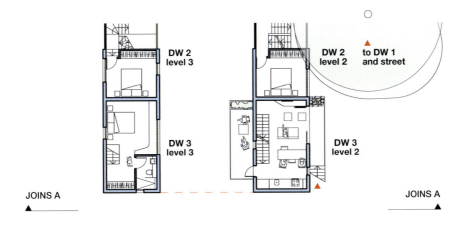

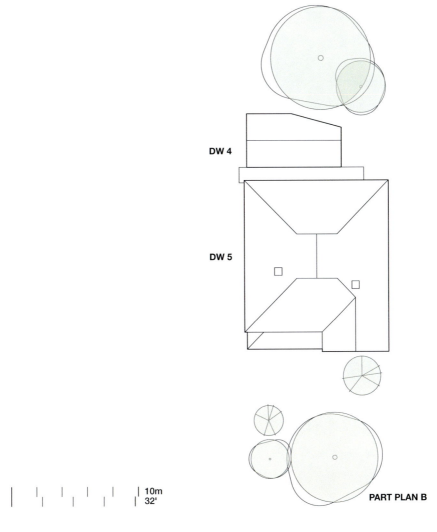

11.9
Back-to-back: ground floor plan, part B.

Double allotments

11.10
A side-by-side proposal, looking towards a new kitchen and dining infill element, where en suite bathrooms and garages commonly occupy the space between older homes.

Double allotments

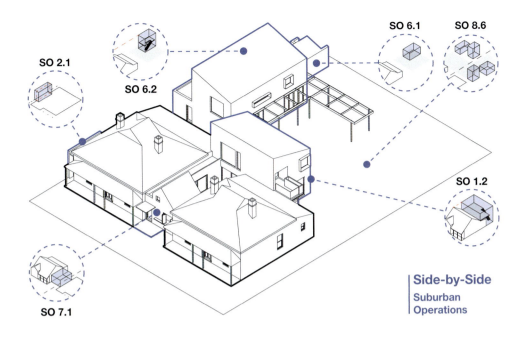

11.11
Side-by-side: Suburban Operations.

Side-by-side	1,300m2	14,000 sq ft		
	30.48m x 42.67m	100' x 140'		
Lot type	Side-by-side midblocks with single street frontage			
Also suits	Double lots with a rear lane			
Existing	42% site cover, 2 dwellings			
	15 dw/ha	(650m^2 per dw)		
	6 dw/acre	(7,000 sq ft per dw)		
Bluefield	39% site cover, 2 to 6 dwellings			
	15 to 46 dw/ha	(650 to 217m^2 per dw)		
	6 to 19 dw/acre	(7,000 to 2,335 sq ft per dw)		
Bedrooms	11			
Car parking	6			
Sharing	Main garden, parking, laundry, clothes drying, bin enclosure, shed			
Option A				
Dwelling 1	413m^2 / 4,445 sq ft	8 rooms	2 x renovated existing homes plus additions	
Dwelling 2	167m^2 / 1,800 sq ft	4 rooms	two-storey backyard home	
Option B:				
Dwelling 1	70m^2 / 755 sq ft	1 room	half of renovated existing home	

Double allotments

Dwelling 2	99m^2 / 1,065 sq ft	2 rooms	half of renovated existing home plus additions
Dwelling 3	151m^2 / 1,625 sq ft	3 rooms	half of renovated existing home plus additions
Dwelling 4	93m^2 / 1,000 sq ft	2 rooms	half of renovated existing home
Dwelling 5	100m^2 / 1,075 sq ft	2 rooms	half of two-storey backyard home
Dwelling 6	67m^2 / 720 sq ft	1 room	half of two-storey backyard home
Operations	SO 1.2: rear addition, double		
	SO 2.1: 0.9m (3') side pod		
	SO 6.1: yard addition, single		
	SO 6.2: yard addition, double		
	SO 7.1: dual lot side addition, single		
	SO 8.6: yard arrangement, clustered		

Scenario

The side-by-side scheme illustrates that density can sometimes be just a number, with flexibility-by-design allowing for anywhere from two to six dwellings without additional building. The two existing houses are reconfigured as a large, connected house of up to eight rooms over two levels. The walkway and driveway spaces between the houses are unified and infilled with a connective single-storey addition that links to a double-storey addition across the rear of the homes. A central garden is framed in the centre of these additions. The second building is a detached double-storey backyard home with single-storey elements at its boundary edge. A small boundary garden is positioned between these. At a height of approximately 7m (23'), the two-storey elements, which are both positioned towards the centre of the site, sit at a comparable height to the gabled roofs of the existing cottages in the neighbourhood. The existing mature trees are retained and supplemented with additional multi-scaled plantings in three zones. Two communal gardens and an outdoor sitting space are combined at the rear of the site, measuring 12m x 20m excluding the car parking (39' x 66'), and 21m x 20m when the car parking is amalgamated (69' x 66'). The combined front garden measures 6m x 27m including the cottage verandahs but excluding the driveway (20' x 89').

Double allotments

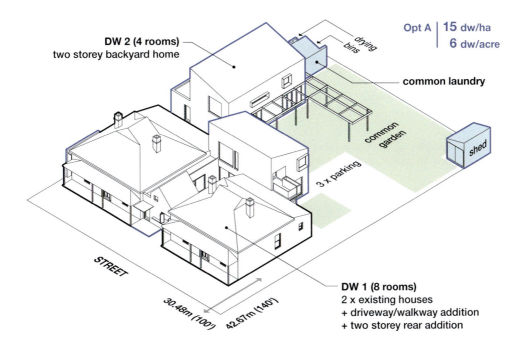

11.12
Side-by-side: design configuration – Option A, showing two dwellings.

Designed for up to four generations – a household structure that becomes increasingly likely as life expectancy increases – Dwelling 1 provides flexibility through the provision of multiple entry points and the over-provision of kitchens and bathrooms. In total it has seven entries, up to eight bedrooms, four kitchens, and five bathrooms. When conceived of as a single house as shown in Option A (Figure 11.12), it presents as a series of four living spaces connected either by hallways or landscape. Diagrammed as a simple arrangement of closed (as opposed to permanently blocked) fire doors, the large house can become as many as four smaller houses, as shown in Figure 11.15 and Figure 11.16. Similarly, the new backyard home is divisible into two by creating a fire wall over both levels, fire doors within this, multiple external entries, two bathrooms, a second kitchen (or the servicing provision for it), and a second stair, which can be constructed up-front or added at the time of division.

Double allotments

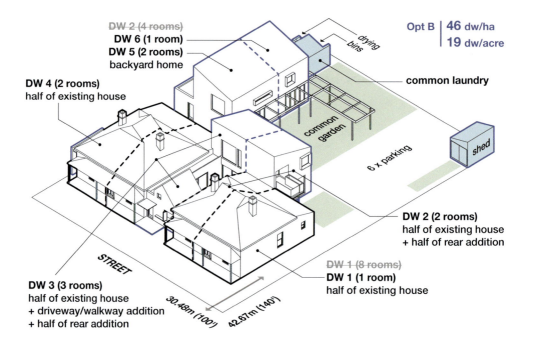

11.13
Side-by-side: design configuration – Option B, showing up to six dwellings.

184

Double allotments

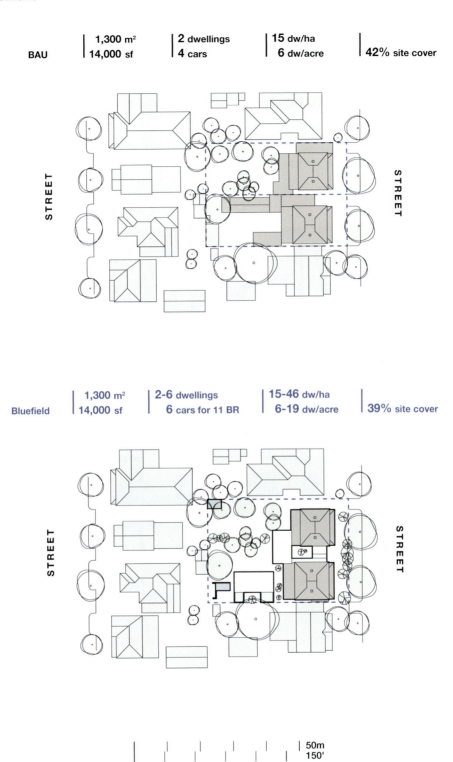

11.14
Side-by-side: site plans, showing the existing conditions (top) and the new bluefield conditions (bottom).

Double allotments

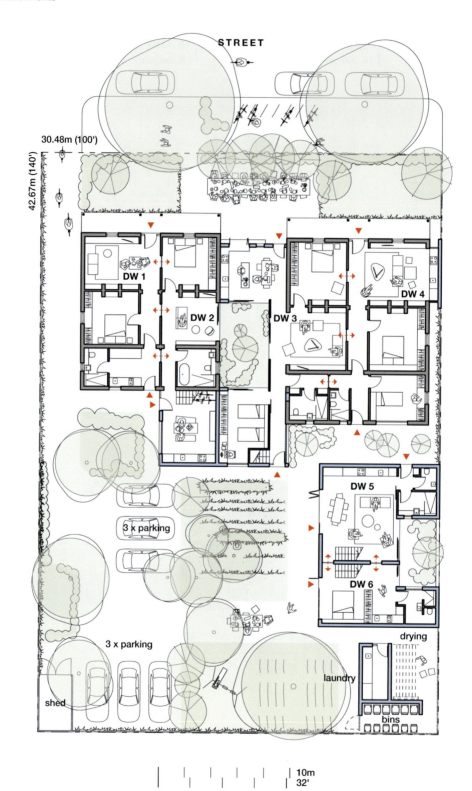

11.15
Side-by-side: ground floor plan, showing the Option B configuration of six dwellings.

Double allotments

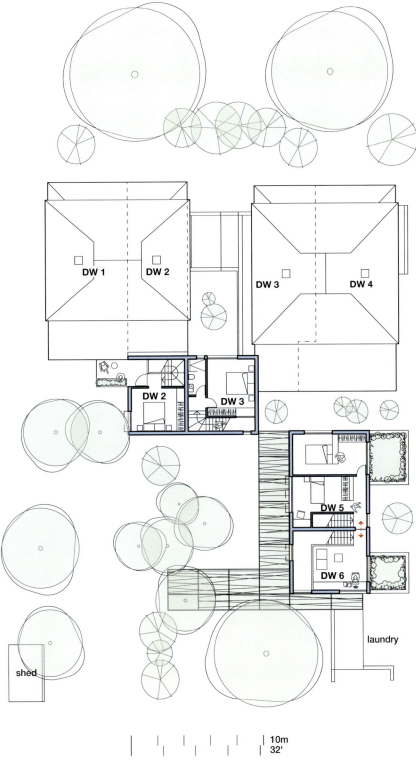

11.16
Side-by-side: upper-level floor plan, showing the Option B configuration of six dwellings.

Double allotments

11.17
A double lot laneway proposal, looking towards a two-storey addition and an adjacent common house. Operating under a cohousing model, the centre of activity is the centre of the lot. The two existing homes establish the disposition of the built elements on the site but are otherwise backgrounded in the overall design strategy of the scheme.

Double allotments

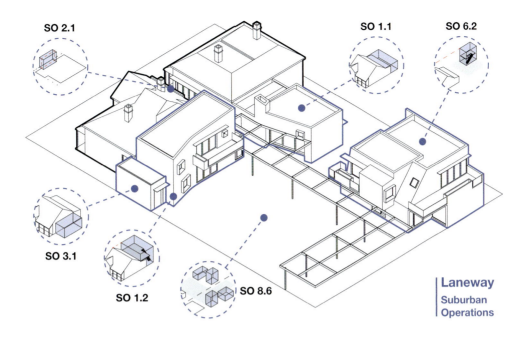

11.18
Laneway: Suburban Operations.

Laneway	1,360m²	14,640 sq ft		
	29.90m x 45.50m	98' x 149'		
Lot type	Side-by-side midblocks with a rear lane			
Also suits	Side-by-side midblocks with a single street frontage			
Existing	39% site cover, 2 dwellings			
	15 dw/ha	(680m² per dw)		
	6 dw/acre	(7,320 sq ft per dw)		
Bluefield	38% site cover, 3 to 6 dwellings			
	22 to 44 dw/ha	(453 to 227m² per dw)		
	9 to 18 dw/acre	(4,880 to 2,440 sq ft per dw)		
Bedrooms	10			
Car parking	5			
Sharing	Common house with laundry, main garden, parking, clothes drying, bin enclosure, shed			
Option A				
Com House	169m² / 1,819 sq ft	1 room	renovated existing home plus addition	
Dwelling 1	105m² / 1,130 sq ft	2 rooms	renovated existing home plus side pod	
Dwelling 2	51m² / 549 sq ft	1 room	ground floor of two-storey rear addition	

Dwelling 3	67m^2 / 721 sq ft	1 room	upper floor of two-storey rear addition
Dwelling 4	88m^2 / 947 sq ft	2 rooms	ground floor of two-storey backyard home
Dwelling 5	95m^2 / 1,023 sq ft	2 rooms	upper floor of two-storey backyard home
Option B			
Com House	169m^2 / 1,820 sq ft	1 room	renovated existing home plus addition
Dwelling 1	105m^2 / 1,130 sq ft	2 rooms	renovated existing home plus side pod
Dwelling 2	118m^2 / 1,270 sq ft	2 rooms	two-storey rear addition
Dwelling 3	183m^2 / 1,970 sq ft	4 rooms	two-storey backyard home
Option C (Option A with no Common House)			
Dwelling 6	169m^2 / 1,820 sq ft	2 rooms	renovated existing home plus addition
Operations	SO 1.1: rear addition, single		
	SO 1.2: rear addition, double		
	SO 2.1: 0.9m (3') side pod		
	SO 3.1: side addition, single		
	SO 6.2: yard addition, double		
	SO 8.6: yard arrangement, clustered		

Scenario

While retention of the prevailing streetscape pattern may be a predetermined statutory preference in older neighbourhoods, it does not need to be the starting point for a bluefield design. In this scenario, the existence of a rear lane and mature backyard landscape, coupled with the programmatic overlay of a cohousing model, has shifted the focus to the rear of the lots. The two cottages therefore become the background foundation conditions that set the pattern of development across the two amalgamated lots, whilst providing functional rooms that can be repurposed in the scheme.

The occupational overlay of cohousing, as discussed in Chapter 2, sees each of the existing houses receive rear additions. One cottage plus its new two-storey addition together operate as three small houses with a walk-through shed at the side for common use. The second cottage gets a renovation and single-storey rear addition to function as a common house with a shared kitchen, laundry, living space, and a guest bedroom. A new small two-storey backyard home at the rear of the site addresses the laneway and provides two apartments. A new pedestrian walkway separates this building from the adjacent shared car parking space, which is accessed directly off the rear lane. This is separated

Double allotments

by a small garden and fence, allowing extension of the large, shared garden if parking mandates are reduced and the residents desire it. A pergola over the car parking extends as a covered way to the common house. The new combined site coverage matches that of the existing conditions (Figure 11.19).

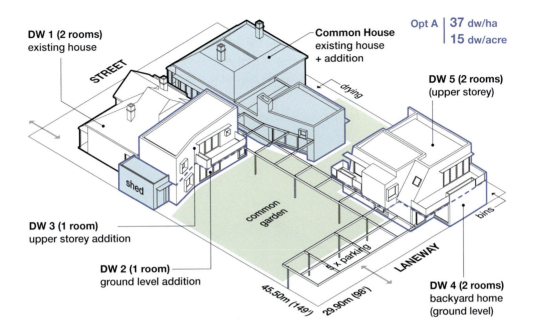

11.19
Laneway: design configuration Option A, showing five dwellings plus a common house.

Employing the same flexibility tactics seen in the Medium scheme of Chapter 10, each of the two-storey elements locate their stairs within fire-isolated walls, enabling each floor level to serve as an independent dwelling. Fire doors are provided into the stairwells from adjacent units, allowing the levels to be connected into single, larger dwellings. This allows the residents the option to configure four of the dwellings as two larger homes, without having to extend the building footprints (Figure 11.20). Further flexibility is achieved by giving over the common house to an additional two-bedroom dwelling (Figure 11.21). Together, these simple manoeuvres allow the design to be used in any combination of three to six dwellings without physical modification.

In keeping with cohousing principles, each dwelling offers either a balcony or some form of patio to connect with communal areas and to encourage incidental contact amongst residents. Communication is further enhanced by the creation of an internal pedestrian 'street' cutting through the site from the primary street to the rear lane. Another cohousing strategy, car parking is limited to the perimeter of the property to provide a pedestrian-dominated environment for the remainder of the lot. This allows space for a landscaped area of 17m wide x 18.5m long around a large existing tree (56' x 61'), extendable to a length of 24.5m (80') if the car parking space is consolidated. The productive garden and walkway adjacent this main garden and between the common dining room and

Double allotments

backyard home is 6m x 12.5m (20' x 41'), with the full width of garden across the site being 30m (98'). All existing mature trees are retained, apart from a mid-scale tree originally belonging to the cottage at the rear of the site. This is strategically removed to push the new backyard home hard up to the rear laneway, which is deemed important to give the laneway an active presence and to encourage movement through the site from front to back. Whilst a smaller, narrower apartment building could be attached to the common house, thereby retaining this tree, the overall amenity would be compromised by comparison with the scheme as designed, and a direct relationship with the laneway denied. Additional trees are planted to mitigate the loss.

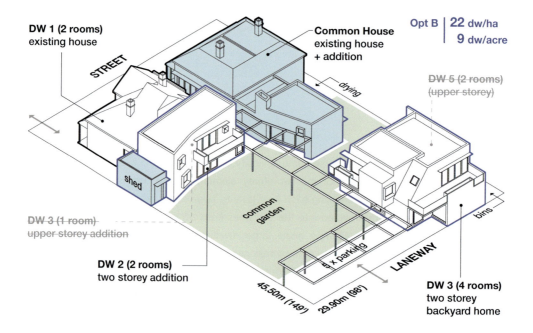

11.20
Laneway: design configuration Option B, showing three dwellings plus a common house.

Double allotments

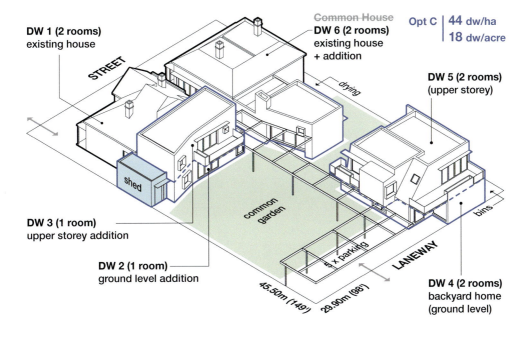

11.21
Laneway: design configuration Option C, showing the common house given over to a sixth dwelling.

Double allotments

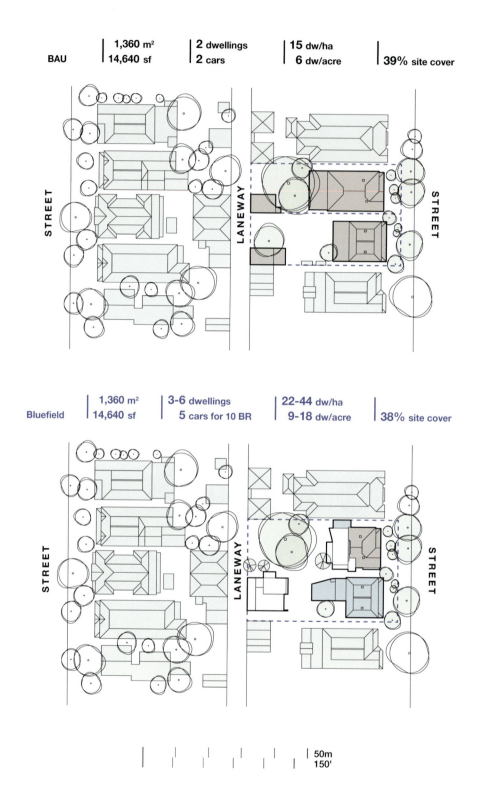

11.22
Laneway: site plans, showing the existing conditions (top) and the new bluefield conditions (bottom).

Double allotments

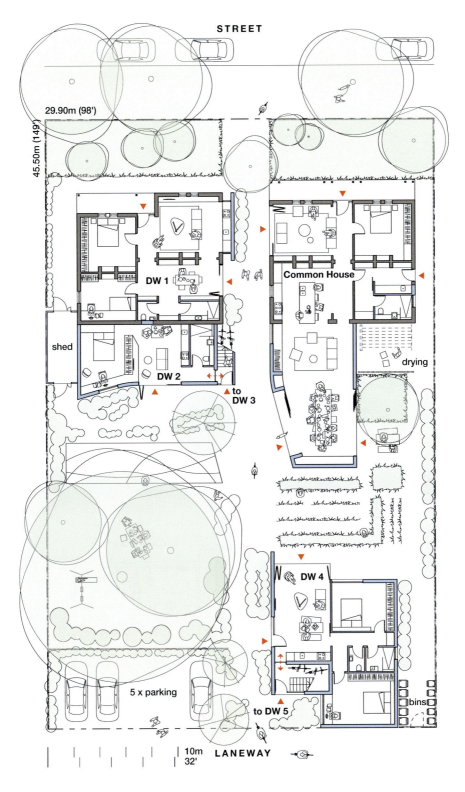

11.23
Laneway: ground floor plan.

Double allotments

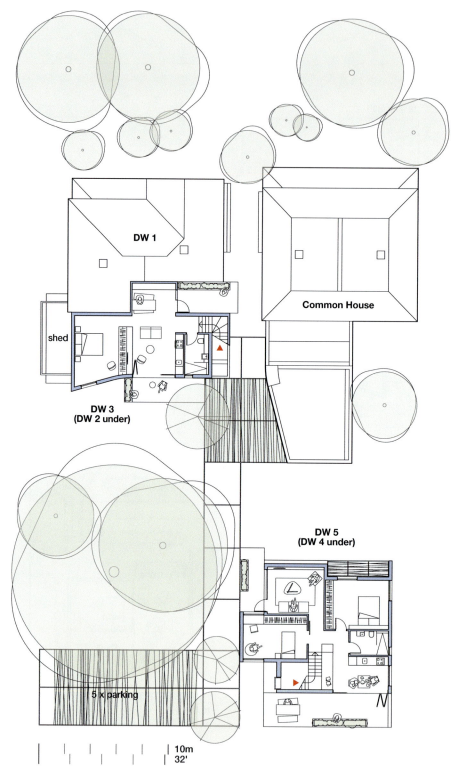

11.24
Laneway: upper level plan.

12   Multiple allotments

When viewed in the context of detached neighbourhood homes, there is a degree of normalcy in the projects presented in Chapters 10 and 11, and a sense that the design propositions could be happening now but are not. The case studies prioritise a greater diversity of household size but do not assume that infill development only ever triggers a shrinkage of housing; the inbuilt flexibility of some of the projects demonstrate that a dwelling's size can be the result of simple occupational and behavioural decisions, as opposed to strict ownership delineations. Thought of in this manner, density is merely a number and a measure which can be manipulated with relative ease. Arguably, the real challenges are found in the attitudinal approaches to use and privacy that are required with the potentially significant shifts in occupant make-up. But what of more widescale infill undertaken in the Bluefield model, where density increases are undertaken over an expanded neighbourhood field? Where there is a rationality to extending a single lot development across two adjacent sites, there is a further logic to expanding the bluefield thinking across three or more, particularly when undertaken strategically by a housing provider over time.

The following case studies demonstrate the potential outcome of starting the development process on a single lot before incorporating additional lots incrementally to increase housing outcomes, encourage community connectedness, and improve landscape conditions.

197

DOI: 10.4324/9781003293736-16
This chapter has been made available under a CC-BY-NC-ND license.

Multiple allotments

12.1
A multiple allotment proposal leveraging a common rear lane to unify four stages of development over time. The critical mass of housing enables the laneway to function as a new neighbourhood street.

Multiple allotments

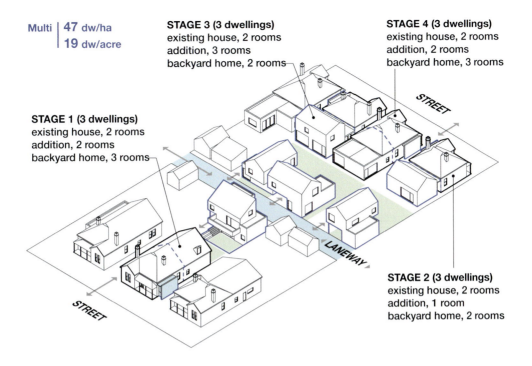

12.2
Multiple lots: a tripling of density over four stages of development.

Stage 1	700m²	7,535 sq ft	
	15.20m x 45.90m	50' x 150'7"	
Lot type	Midblock with rear lane		
Existing	39% site cover, 1 dwelling		
	14 dw/ha	(700m² per dw)	
	6 dw/acre	(7,535 sq ft per dw)	
Bluefield	34% site cover, 3 dwellings		
	43 dw/ha	(233m² per dw)	
	17 dw/acre	(2,510 sq ft per dw)	
Bedrooms	7		
Car parking	3: 2 off primary street + 1 off rear lane		
Sharing	Central garden, some parking		
Dwelling 1	92m² / 990 sq ft	2 rooms	renovated existing home plus side pod
Dwelling 2	83m² / 895 sq ft	2 rooms	renovated existing addition
Dwelling 3	139m² / 1,495 sq ft	3 rooms	three-storey backyard home
Operations	SO 2.3: 1.5m (5') side pod		
	SO 6.3: yard addition, triple		
	SO 8.2: yard arrangement, lateral		

Multiple allotments

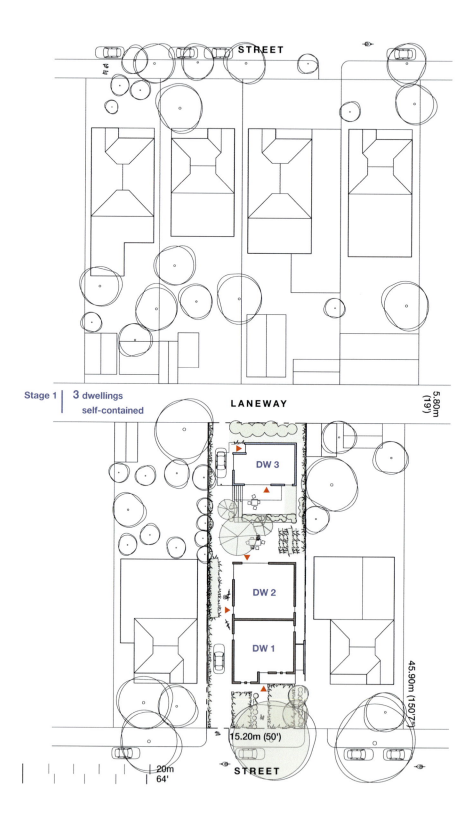

Stage 1 | 3 dwellings self-contained

Multiple allotments

Scenario

12.3
Multiple lots: Stage 1 plan, showing an existing dwelling divided into two and a third dwelling added off the laneway in the backyard.

A housing provider purchases a property with an existing rear addition. It divides this into two independent dwellings and creates a third via the addition of a three-storey backyard home, set down in a sunken courtyard to reduce bulk and designed to address the rear laneway and a central garden, which is shared. Car parking is via both street frontages but is discontinuous for safety, and to reduce hard surfaces while maximising landscape (Figure 12.3).

The development is fully self-contained but designed in anticipation of potential expansion over adjacent lots or those across the laneway. The laneway house is offset from the boundary by the width of a parking space and presents a blank wall to the laneway at ground level. This gives the dwelling a buffer from the street and the opportunity for landscape, while providing potential car parking space should it be needed to help gain zoning approval for a broader development in the future.

Stage 2	**560m^2**	**6,030 sq ft**
	12.20m x 45.90m	40' x 150'7"
Lot type	Midblock with rear lane	
Existing	50% site cover, 1 dwelling	
	18 dw/ha	(560m^2 per dw)
	7 dw/acre	(6,030 sq ft per dw)
Bluefield	39% site cover, 3 dwellings	
	54 dw/ha	(187m^2 per dw)
	22 dw/acre	(2,010 sq ft per dw)
Bedrooms	5	
Car parking	3: 1 off rear lane + 2 off rear lane of Stage 1	
Sharing	central garden, some parking	
Dwelling 4	90m^2 / 970 sq ft	2 rooms renovated existing home plus side pod
Dwelling 5	72m^2 / 775 sq ft	1 room single-storey rear addition
Dwelling 6	117m^2 / 1,260 sq ft	2 rooms two-storey backyard home
Operations	SO 1.1: rear addition, single	
	SO 2.2: 1.2m (4') side pod	
	SO 6.2: yard addition, double	
	SO 8.2: yard arrangement, lateral	

Multiple allotments

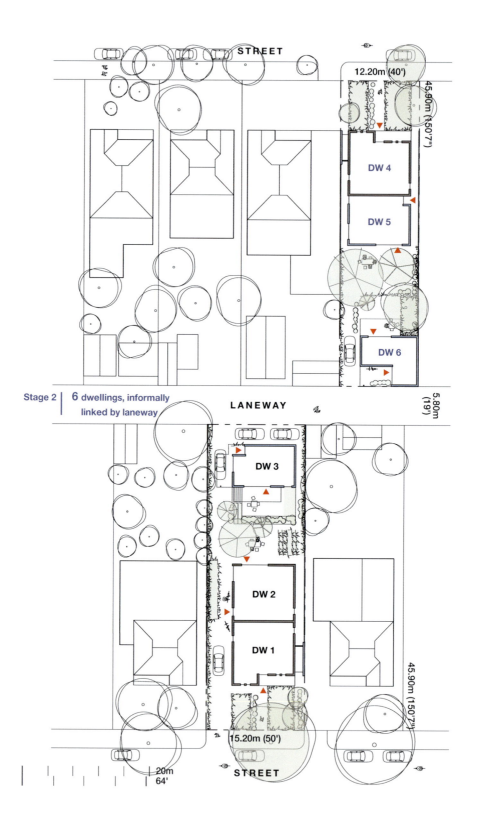

Stage 2 | 6 dwellings, informally linked by laneway

Multiple allotments

12.4
Multiple lots: Stage 2 plan, showing three additional dwellings connected to Stage 1 through shared car parking and an informal use of the laneway.

Scenario

Taking advantage of a property coming up for sale diagonally across the laneway, the housing provider purchases it with the aim of sequentially developing a dispersed field of housing across multiple lots. Deploying a similar redevelopment model to that of Stage 1, the existing house is renovated into a two-bedroom dwelling while a small footprint addition creates a second one-bedroom home. A third dwelling is created as a two-storey backyard home that addresses the rear laneway and the shared central garden. Occupying a lot that is too narrow for a front driveway, a single car park is provided off the rear lane. Leveraging the proximity and forward planning of the Stage 1 development, two additional car spaces are achieved by giving over the Stage 1 laneway garden to two parallel car parking spaces. Although not ideal from a landscape and amenity perspective, this inexpensive car parking strategy helps the housing provider achieve its development permit whilst minimising the negative impact to the Stage 1 laneway house. Additionally, the act of informally using the laneway to link the two stages begins to establish housing connections that can be amplified in potential later stages of development (Figure 12.4).

Stage 3	590m^2		6,350 sq ft
	12.80m x 45.90m		42' x 150'7"
Lot type	Midblock with rear lane		
Existing	30% site cover, 1 dwelling		
	17 dw/ha		(590m^2 per dw)
	7 dw/acre		(6,325 sq ft per dw)
Bluefield	38% site cover, 3 dwellings		
	51 dw/ha		(197m^2 per dw)
	21 dw/acre		(2,115 sq ft per dw)
Bedrooms	7		
Car parking	2: off rear lane		
Sharing	Central garden, parking		
Dwelling 7	103m^2 / 1,110 sq ft	2 rooms	renovated existing home plus side pod
Dwelling 8	121m^2 / 1,300 sq ft	3 rooms	two-storey rear addition
Dwelling 9	138m^2 / 1,485 sq ft	2 rooms	two-storey backyard home
Operations	SO 1.2: rear addition, double		
	SO 2.4: 1.8m (6') side pod		
	SO 6.2: yard addition, double		
	SO 8.2: yard arrangement, lateral		

Multiple allotments

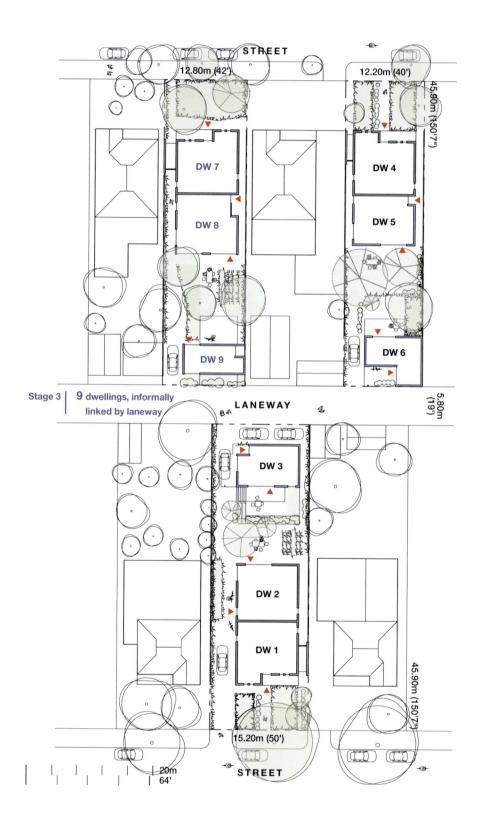

Stage 3 | 9 dwellings, informally linked by laneway

Multiple allotments

Scenario

12.5
Multiple lots: Stage 3 plan, showing three additional dwellings designed in anticipation of the middle lot being integrated in a future development.

The owners of a nearby lot, understanding the pattern of their neighbours' prior developments, approach the housing provider and negotiate a private sale. The property is two houses down from the Stage 2 lot, but more directly opposite the Stage 1 site across the lane. This new lot gets redeveloped to match the others: the existing house is remodelled, a second home is created by addition, and a new two-storey backyard home addresses the laneway. Although covering 8% more of the lot than the existing use, the adoption of the bluefield housing principles sees a 3-for-1 intensification without the loss of mature landscape (Figure 12.5).

The design is undertaken with an anticipatory design for the lot next door; it works as an independent development but can be integrated into a larger connected housing scheme should the neighbouring in-between property become available in the future. The building footprints are therefore aligned with those of Stage 2 such that landscape can eventually be made continuous between them, while the Stage 3 backyard home is built to the side boundary as one anticipatory half of a laneway duo, should the neighbouring lot be added as a fourth stage of development.

Stage 4	**700m^2**		**7,535 sq ft**	
	15.20m x 45.90m		50' x 150'7"	
Lot type	Midblock with rear lane			
Existing	53% site cover, 1 dwelling			
	14 dw/ha		(700m^2 per dw)	
	6 dw/acre		(7,535 sq ft per dw)	
Bluefield	32% site cover, 3 dwellings			
	43 dw/ha		(233m^2 per dw)	
	17 dw/acre		(2,510 sq ft per dw)	
Bedrooms	7			
Car parking	2: off rear lane			
Sharing	Central garden, parking			
Dwelling 10	89m^2 / 960 sq ft	2 rooms	renovated existing home plus side pod	
Dwelling 11	88m^2 / 950 sq ft	2 rooms	renovated existing addition	
Dwelling 12	114m^2 / 1,225 sq ft	3 rooms	two-storey backyard home	
Operations	SO 2.1: 0.9m (3') side pod			
	SO 6.2: yard addition, double			
	SO 8.2: yard arrangement, lateral			

Multiple allotments

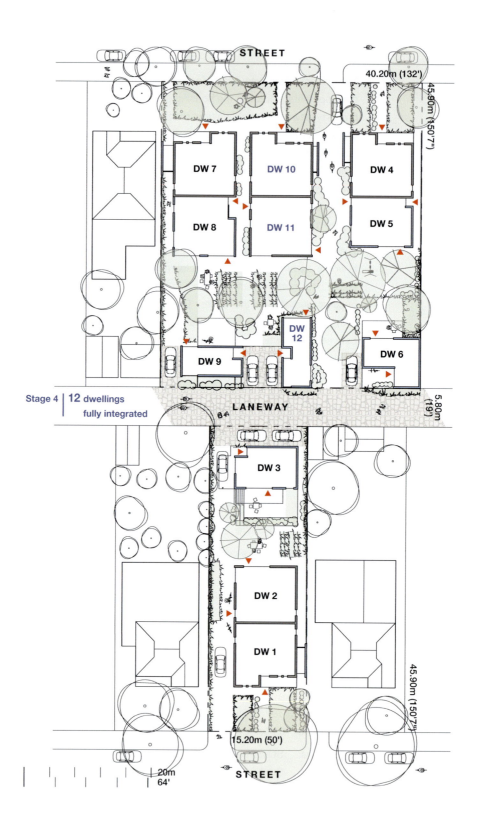

Stage 4 | 12 dwellings fully integrated

Multiple allotments

12.6
Multiple lots: Stage 4 plan, showing a fully integrated housing group of 12, with generous shared landscape and an uplifted laneway that binds the development.

Scenario

The housing provider, having established a long-term relationship with their neighbours, approaches the owner of the central lot with a proposition to integrate the property into a fully connected housing community where the owner can stay on in a newly renovated home of their choosing. They decide to move into a newly created three-bedroom laneway home, designed pre-emptively during the earlier Stage 3 redevelopment. This two-storey home completes the laneway housing, creating mews that can serve as a connective outdoor space or parking space for two cars (Figure 12.2). The existing home on the site is reconfigured to match the others: it is renovated as a two-bedroom home with a side kitchen pod, while its existing addition is reworked into another two-bedroom home. With dwellings matched in size and position, a generous shared garden of around 500m^2 (5,380 sq ft) spreads across the three lots that make up Stages 2 to 4. This provides space for additional plantings, helps to stitch together a suburban tree canopy, and brings significant amenity to the dwellings and local neighbourhood. When considered spatially, this shared landscape space is of an equivalent size to some of the lots seen in the local neighbourhood, demonstrating that the tripling of density can return landscape gains to the area (Figure 12.6).

With the four lots now addressing the laneway together, this receives an uplift of planting and resurfacing with permeable paving, while acting as a connective tissue between the previously individualised lots. This begins to shift the laneway emphasis away from simple garage access to an improved function of active street, thereby encouraging other property owners and developers to reconsider how the neighbourhood might densify in an alternative to knock-down-rebuild. However, in consolidating the lots, a degree of futureproofing is factored in, with none of the construction straddling the previous title boundaries. This allows for the dwellings to operate as a holistic development of 12 homes, but for the whole to be reinstated to any combination of the four individual lots should financial circumstances require this in the future. Where larger housing gains could be achieved by ignoring the original boundaries and creating larger mat housing footprints, designing within the original title lines offers a simple reversal that can aid in an overall development strategy. This is further discussed in the context of financing and feasibility in Chapter 15. Meanwhile, this same boundary strategy points to how multi-lot bluefield developments can incrementally increase density over time whilst continuing to contribute positively to the established pattern of the local neighbourhood (Figure 12.7).

Multiple allotments

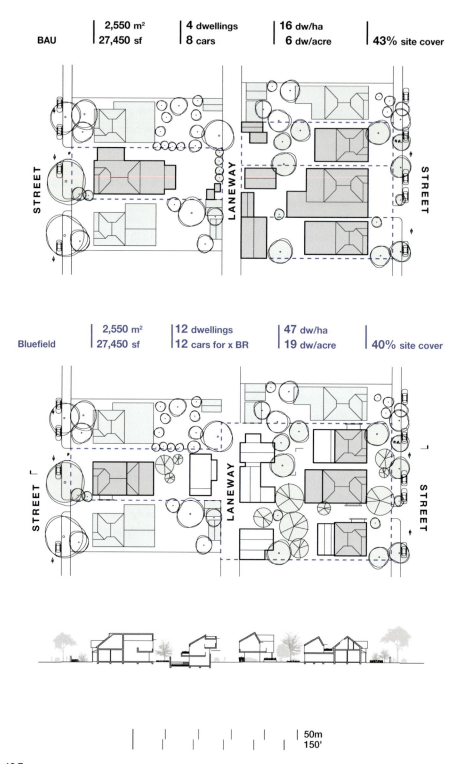

12.7
Multiple lots: Site Plan and Section, showing the retention of existing boundary lines, a tripling of density, and a compatibility of neighbourhood scale.

Part 4

13 A new normal
Leveraging established conditions

Building our way out from the inside

The strategy for addressing housing choice and affordability is complex, and an argument can be made for a three-headed approach such as that described in the California 100 report on *The Future of Housing and Community Development:*

1 the preservation of existing affordable housing for those on lower incomes;
2 increased tenant protections for better retention of and access to affordable rentals; and
3 a significant increase in housing supply.[1]

The report authors describe the tactic of supply as 'building our way out' of the housing crisis.[2] Increased supply is unlikely to ever be the only solution to relieving housing stress, but it is one critical component, and by its nature is where many NIMBY/YIMBY tensions arise. An increase in housing supply in established neighbourhoods generally raises two main concerns: how quickly multiple lots can be amalgamated and redeveloped to deliver new homes to a neighbourhood; and the resident resistance that such land assembly and housing intensification draws. As described throughout this book, the ambition of the bluefield housing co-location model is not to argue against high-density supply models any more than it is to lobby for the suburban status quo. Rather, bluefield housing is an adjunct to the supply-and-demand system of housing, particularly for older neighbourhoods that are often quarantined from densification, struggle to deliver more affordable small-footprint homes, yet nevertheless face the incremental loss of character and landscape despite NIMBY efforts to resist change.

The design studies of Part 3 demonstrate that two- and threefold suburban intensification in the bluefield mould has the potential to look very different to a suburban knock-down-rebuild model when development is driven by the incorporation of foundation housing and mature landscape. The fact that the overall site coverages in each project have principally been matched to existing conditions is an artefact of the established houses in older neighbourhoods often growing incrementally over time and thereby offering substantial terri-tory for intensification if these expanded footprints are used as the template for adding new dwellings. And whilst the designs show that density increases using the bluefield model come without significant increases in building footprint and mass and without the loss of landscape, this is not a deliberate tactic of stealth as if infill in established neighbourhoods must somehow be hidden or rendered subordinate to the prevailing streetscape pattern. Instead, it is a by-product of harnessing the additive patterns of suburban settlement.

Offered by these example projects is the possibility of large organisational change delivered via small physical change. A variety of dwelling sizes can be achieved, and in the process the reconfigured existing housing can be either foregrounded, with subtle additions behind, or backgrounded, where the existing houses establish the pattern and originating structure for the reconfigured site but are not necessarily the focus of activity. This latter condition is particularly evident in projects taking advantage of rear lanes and active central gardens. And while existing older houses can be kept for their heritage, character, and streetscape value, in the design speculations of this book their true value is found in their continued utility and demonstrated robustness for change: they are retained because it makes building and occupational sense, not because it is mandated.

Stripped of subjective analysis, the merit of retained homes is evidenced in the way they form part of an overall site and housing strategy. Similarly, whilst the new infill building elements generally sit within the volume of the existing built form, this is not a result of an obsequious or deferential architectural approach to the original housing, but rather an effect of the existing space and building mass being adequate to support the schemes' medium density targets. Similarly, the overall maintenance of existing site coverage demonstrated in each scheme is not a polemic statement, but more simply a result of preferencing the retention of mature landscape and the provision of new small footprint houses, whilst maximising dwelling separation where possible.

Demonstrating, for example, that a threefold density increase can be achieved in the absence of complicated land assemblies and without dramatically increasing building mass or reducing landscape, indicates that an uplift in neighbourhood housing supply need not be unrealistic in either an architectural or occupational sense. Challenges exist, however, in the way an alternative approach to traditional neighbourhood housing is communicated and normalised.

Similar, not different

The potential risk in describing any new housing initiative as alternative was discussed in the Introduction: where 'alternative' for a housing researcher is a positive signal of necessary change and an indicator of new housing choices, for those who are averse to change it can be off putting. Financial institutions, for example, have binding fiduciary obligations that underpin their licence to operate. They have a responsibility to the customers whose investments they protect and grow, and need returns on their investments that are risk-adjusted. Lenders therefore calculate the profits they will make on a loan taking into consideration the amount of risk to that profit that is inherent in the project. A simple way of looking at this is that lenders like certainty, and complicating the normative housing model they know and understand can introduce a level of uncertainty that must be overcome. This is discussed in more detail in Chapter 15. Similarly, statutory planners seek positive city, neighbourhood, street, and site outcomes that are as predictable as possible. In most instances, metric measures will be established on the basis that they will provide a degree of control over a built outcome, maximise its potential to impact positively on its surroundings, and minimise the negative impact to neighbours. 'Neighbours', in turn, can extend to a community of residents, property owners, and broader stakeholders who themselves can be resentful of change and be risk-averse, potentially organising themselves into a bloc to stop the approval of a development they feel is threatening to them.

Whether approaching a project from a financial, statutory, or NIMBY perspective, those responding to 'alternative' housing proposals may have experienced precedents they deem as risky and associate that risk with the proposal-at-hand. Attempting to introduce an alternative housing form to an established risk-averse system is therefore challenging, and the temptation is to discuss the proposal in ways that highlight the scheme's innovation. This is tempting when one is excited by the value of a proposition and wants others to share the same enthusiasm. But in foregrounding innovation, the proponent also highlights the project's differences and thereby its ability to introduce the perception of risk. What is required, then, is to speak of housing innovation not in terms of its differences to other housing forms, but in its similarities. This means resisting the temptation to declare how distinctive something is, to describing how much it shares with the business-as-usual approach. This may mean avoiding terms such as 'alternative' and 'innovative' altogether for the proposition to appear as normative as possible for the community, legislators, approval authorities, and lenders.

What's so new?

In some jurisdictions, the bluefield model will not be the creation of something entirely new, but an amalgam of existing neighbourhood housing practice. A common response to it is one along the lines of "this has been done for years – it's called a granny flat".[3] The instinctive answer to this statement is to highlight why it is wrong through describing the model as more than a backyard home and emphasising the differences achieved using the bluefield co-location and accommodation design tactics and principles. A more productive answer is simply "yes – it's *just* like a backyard home". Similar comparisons have been drawn between the bluefield model and established traditions of multigenerational living: "this isn't new – people in other countries have been doing this for generations". The most productive response to this is again "yes – that's right", and to extend the connection by discussing that multigenerational living has been common in cultures across the world for millennia. Similar connections can be made to the familiar, based on locations: "so what you're really talking about is a secondary suite or a junior ADU, or cohousing". The answer to all these observations is "yes", or at least "yes, *and* . . .".

In a similar way, the answer to other housing questions can be an affirmation that the bluefield approach is *not* any number of outcomes that can be negative for a neighbourhood and its residents. It is not riding the popularity wave of the transportable tiny house movement,[4] it is not exacerbating the creation of hard surfaces and urban heat island effects, it is not eroding the character of a place through complete knock-down-rebuild construction, and it is not contributing to the loss of urban tree corridors in the suburbs. Having connected and disconnected the bluefield model to established if disparate examples, the discussion is then open to why many neighbourhoods are resistant to systematising densification beyond traditional subdivision and knock-down-rebuild and why a bluefield approach should not be considered a mainstream infill alternative.

What remains is to find a way of discussing the sharing aspect of the model and to make the concept of shared housing in suburbia more normative. In presenting bluefield housing, audiences can struggle to understand what sharing in the model means. Even with disclaimers about multigenerational or cohousing being nothing new, for many a shared suburban model can be a conceptual leap. Outside of established family arrangements where sharing is more easily relatable, people may look to broader tropes of communes, boarding houses, or student share housing and attempt to reconcile these with what the bluefield model is attempting to offer on a suburban lot. Again, the most productive response is one that relates sharing to normative examples and the communicative power of scenario planning is helpful here. This is discussed in Chapter 20.

Getting to YIMBY

The act of subtly repressing a housing scheme's innovations in favour of emphasising its similarities to the norm is not to be confused with trickery. Rather, it is about framing the logic of the housing argument around existing principles to which people can relate. This is as much a benefit to the various stakeholders needing to be convinced as it is to the proponent of the model seeking a convincing argument. In drawing comparisons with BAU models, the proponent forces themselves to distil the innovations of their proposals into a set of coherent and rational principles that productively extend existing practices rather than attempt to completely reshape them. In the early stages of a project or the development of a new housing model, developing a clear narrative will require listening to what people need and not assuming you have the correct solution to their problem.

At a housing strategy level, most people involved in decision making processes have someone or some entity to whom they answer, while at the end of most decision-making processes are citizens to whom their ultimate obligations lie. As a housing advocate, it can be helpful to understand to whom or what these decision makers report. What are their KPIs? What housing and neighbourhood targets to they need to meet and report on each year? Are they ahead or behind in their targets, and importantly, how can you help these people achieve their reportable goals? How does one de-risk or at least minimise the risks being borne by decision makers and ultimately make it easy for people to say 'yes' to innovation? This can take time, and a preliminary response may not be an immediate 'yes', but a 'well . . .'. In this case, the housing proponent needs to understand 'well, what?' What are the sticking points, and what modifications are required to resolve the issues? Similarly, one of the most useful responses that can be heard from a stakeholder is 'no' or 'no, but . . .'. This gives the proponent something to which they can respond and an avenue to 'yes', should the issue be successfully resolved.

In the earliest versions of the bluefield model, before it coalesced into the principles and strategies described in this book, a sticking point was car parking, with advice from a local planning authority stating that no consideration of the model could be given if car parking was not adequately accommodated. This was despite the decision makers' personal views that car parking mandates should be relaxed, and instead related to the pain points the jurisdiction experienced with residents who are opposed to infill. This 'no' provided a way in for the model: providing multiple car parks may not be desirable from an amenity or environmental aspect, but if it could be successfully integrated it could ultimately act as a gateway for the model to be considered. It is the reason that car parking has been so heavily emphasised in this book, even as many housing experts rightfully push for zero private car parking in favour of walkable cities. Hearing 'no' to zero car parking and resolving this in the model has been essential for it to be developed with decision-makers; without it, the bluefield model will not be achievable in many jurisdictions.

In the same manner, the way the bluefield proposals are diagrammed help decision-makers say 'yes'. Seeing a suburban BAU site plan against that of a bluefield version, as diagrammed in the design studies of Part 3, helps local zoning authorities meet increased housing targets and maintain local character where it is under the threat of increased demolition. Likewise, those with responsibility for landscape infrastructure, heat mitigation, stormwater runoff control, and local planting targets can become advocates for the scheme when they can see these KPI measures met in the bluefield model.

In the bluefields, therefore, getting to the 'yes' of YIMBY is an exercise in subtlety. It means recognising and responding to the statutory and neighbourhood concerns of NIMBYism and showing that change can be minimal, but with great effect. In relating the new to the old and speaking of similarities rather than differences, we allow innovation to become apparent naturally without having to declare it loudly. And in tailoring it to local conditions, bluefield housing can become a new normal.

Notes

1 Shane Phillips et al., *The Future of Housing and Community Development: A California 100 Report on Policies and Future Scenarios*, California 100 Initiative (Los Angeles, 2022), https://california100.org/research-streams/.

2 Shane Phillips, Carolina Reid, and Dana Cuff, "A New Approach to California's Housing Politics and Policy," *The Orange County Register* (Irvine, California), 1 April 2022, www.ocregister.com/2022/04/01/a-new-approach-to-californias-housing-politics-and-policy/.

3 The term 'granny flat' is used here only for context, as it is the common term still used in Australia. The more neutral term 'backyard home' is preferred, as discussed in Chapter 2.

4 Tiny houses are those that can fit on and be transported by a trailer, and have been made popular in the media with a predominance of owners represented as younger adults looking for an affordable housing option. An alternative negative view is that tiny houses normalise the fact that housing is becoming increasingly unaffordable and that relegating people to tiny housing is acceptable.

14 Carrots and sticks
Incentivising bluefield housing

Development potential

Increasingly in Australia, houses in older neighbourhoods are advertised for sale not in terms of the what the house itself offers, but of the lot's development potential as a vacant parcel of land. Vendors and real estate agents understandably take advantage of zoning changes that have come into effect during the life of the property, resulting in the real estate offering being described only by its capacity for subdivision or ability to be replaced with a much bigger 'dream home'. In jurisdictions where demolition is allowed in the absence of a pre-approved replacement dwelling, it is common for an older house to be demolished, the land fully cleared, and the lot subdivided and offered as smaller ready-to-develop land parcels. A third method of sale sees the subdivision and redevelopment undertaken in its entirety, with the finished houses put to market as turn-key house and land packages.

To help meet the demand for housing supply, statutory authorities are increasingly moving to clearer forms of zoning metrics that give the developer some form of surety over what can be built where. This is often complemented by a fast-track approval process for projects that are deemed-to-satisfy (DTS) with the zoning requirements. The result is older housing and landscape that is easily lost and neighbourhoods that quickly transition to more dense, more built-up, and less green places than they previously were: perfectly legal, but not always desirable for local residents nor the local government responsible for managing civic and environmental priorities. The fact

DOI: 10.4324/9781003293736-19
This chapter has been made available under a CC-BY-NC-ND license.

that it is becoming increasingly easy for a property owner to redevelop in this manner begs the question of why one would choose to redevelop in another form such as bluefield housing. The answer is clear when a bluefield development is undertaken progressively by a homeowner who is seeking to remain on site but in a reconfigured form for familial, economic, or community reasons, but it is less apparent for a profit-driven developer or building company for whom knock-down-rebuild is their stock-in-trade. What is required is for the concept of 'development potential' to be reconsidered when applied to older homes and for innovative alternatives to KDR to be incentivised.

Give-and-take

Working with deemed-to-satisfy housing outcomes under carefully considered zoning metrics should theoretically deliver positive neighbourhood results. Yet suburban planning authorities working in established neighbourhoods still experience challenges of change across familiar themes:

- encouraging additional and more diverse dwellings to meet housing targets, particularly at price-points below that of single-family homes;
- limiting the erosion of character from demolition and from subsequent increases in building mass and scale;
- constraining the growth of roofscapes and hard ground surfaces, which stress existing water catchment infrastructure and disturb local microclimates;
- preserving urban tree canopies on private property for carbon storage, shade, cooling, wildlife habitat, and neighbourhood amenity;
- navigating the complexities of increased traffic flow in densified locations – particularly those that are not well serviced by public transport; and
- managing broad community expectations for what residential infill development should be and how neighbourhood transition is planned.

As discussed throughout this book, the bluefield housing model was created in response to these conditions and to specifically provide suburban infill opportunities where densification is precluded, negatively perceived, difficult to achieve, created informally, or has been realised legally but poorly. Its key points of difference are founded not in hard zoning 'rules', but in the Seven Principles of Bluefield Housing outlined in Chapter 6, underpinned by the retention of as much existing built and natural fabric as possible. It is a model that requires both a lot's developer and its approval authority to make compromises, and for the applicant to demonstrate the positive contribution the scheme will make to the local area. As such, the bluefield model contains inherent opportunities for win–win negotiations between the applicant and the approver.

Compromise around zoning principles is an integral part of the development system. Usually, these compromises are determined relative to how far removed a proposal is from the ideals of the stipulated zoning metrics. If an application's departures from the minima and maxima criteria are not too egregious, the proposal may be granted approval. However, when scaled across a neighbourhood, what might be considered 'minor' zoning indiscretions at a lot level can have lasting cumulative effects when repeated across a suburb. New and ill-considered precedents can be established, as neighbourhoods scale up at the expense of landscape and without adding housing choices to the mix. The bluefield approach seeks to redress the balance by making compromise inherent and bi-directional, bringing the give-and-take discussion forward in the application process. This collaboration commences with the statutory authority ceding on key metrics and offering density dispensations to incentivise the property owner to redevelop outside of KDR norms and in the bluefield mould:

- **housing numbers** are not capped, allowing a lot to yield more housing than it could through land division;
- **minimum lot size** is not stipulated, enabling any site to be considered for bluefield intensification;
- **car parking requirements** are not metrically derived, allowing flexibility in housing numbers.

In response, the applicant commits to delivering nuanced infill outcomes, with bargaining chips formed through a focus on adaptive reuse, landscape, housing choice, and community:

- **holistic site amenity is achieved**, demonstrated as a boundary-to-boundary design that intelligently incorporates the housing in concert with site necessities such as rubbish bins, washing lines, storage, and car parking where required, as described in the lot-level design tactics of Chapter 7;
- **existing housing is retained**, adapted, and integrated into the whole;
- **housing diversity is prioritised**, with offerings of smaller dwellings that provide more affordable housing choices to help off-set neighbourhood gentrification;
- **deep root landscape zones for medium to large trees are incorporated**, through the retention or creation of new landscape;
- **neighbourhood fit is demonstrated,** through context-specific design at the site and dwelling scales.

The aim of this relationship is simple when compared to much of the business-as-usual KDR infill: the approval authority forgoes metrics and allows more housing than would otherwise be permitted for the lot if the applicant provides better housing and landscape outcomes for the residents and for the immediate neighbourhood.

Development scorecards

Beyond these broad ambitions for positive infill outcomes, local authorities can consider a more defined set of development principles that can be established as a form of scorecard. These can be tailored to local conditions to capture nuanced neighbourhood priorities and combined with more generic goals aimed at encouraging higher level outcomes. This was the strategy employed in the 'Fourflex' entry for the LA Low Rise Design Challenge. This speculative proposal – offering a rethinking of the common LA fourplex – combined the bluefield design model with aspirational design principles developed for the Challenge by Alysia Bennett. Together, these formed a set of principles against which a zoning application could, hypothetically, be performance-assessed. In addition to two bluefield design aims of being low impact and a good neighbour, an additional eight Fourflex criteria encourage the infill proponent to provide more, where possible:

1. **Serviced**: located within *x* distance of everyday services and *x* distance of key urban centres for students and/or key workers, where 'x' is determined by local conditions.
2. **Inclusive**: individual dwellings are directly accessible from the street and/or have an outlook onto the street.
3. **Interdependent**: space on site to allow for gathering and exchange between residents separate from private spaces.
4. **Accessible**: all dwellings allow accessible occupation of toilet and living spaces for visitors and at least 50% of bedrooms.
5. **Appointed**: each dwelling includes spaces to eat, sleep, care, relax, work, study, bathe, entertain, and play independently.
6. **Safe**: each dwelling is secure and provides adequate fire separation, air conditioning, ventilation, and egress.
7. **Zero carbon**: zero-carbon building design that optimizes human health and wellbeing.
8. **Low impact** (from the bluefield model): at least 50% of existing open space within the site to be retained with minimal removal of established trees.
9. **A good neighbour** (from the bluefield model): changes to the existing fabric must be in keeping with the neighbourhood scale/character, and/or are reversible.
10. **Community design criterion**: determined in consultation with the local neighbourhood communities and the local zoning authority.[1]

Together, these ten criteria establish measurable goals across the themes of connectivity, autonomy, resilience, and equity. They are written to be pre-emptive, setting performative expectations that ask the infill applicant to demonstrate the positive outcomes of their proposal. Presented neutrally, with no single criterion outweighing the value of another, they together present a scorecard that enables an applicant to consider broad notions of social impact, environmental impact, and design excellence, and to demonstrate application, even if a criterion may not be fully met as written. An applicant could, for example, argue that they have not been able to meet the inclusivity measure as written, as not all dwellings face the street, but that the inclusivity aspirations are met by the way non-street facing dwellings address the shared spaces within the lot. Similarly, not all dwellings may achieve the stated accessibility levels, but one dwelling may achieve a higher standard in isolation. Additionally, the applicant may give over less than 50% of the site to open space but be able to demonstrate that the low impact measure is nonetheless achieved.

Importantly, the simple existence of a scorecard has the potential to act as a prompt, forcing the proponent to address opportunities of which they may otherwise be unaware or reluctant to incorporate. And by including an 'Appointed' criterion, those who may have previously sought to create informal dwellings that fail to meet legal and ethical housing standards for basic amenity and safety may be encouraged to formalise such development, encouraged by the understanding that they may create additional housing legally if the bluefield model is adopted and a range of criteria can be demonstrated.

The environmental ambitions of 'Zero Carbon' can be further extended in reference to local initiatives and opportunities already in place, whilst being supplemented by the active and passive environmental controls described in Chapter 8. Local authorities might, for example, generate a list of desirable traits for bluefield housing to assist in assessing applications and to encourage applicants to perhaps try harder than they otherwise might. This is captured in Fourflex's loosely framed yet pivotal 'Community Design Criterion', where neighbourhood communities can be brought into the zoning discussion to help define issues of local concern. This provides a wild-card measure that can prompt a more considered response to local needs. Such nuancing can be further encouraged by an application of the targets described in Part 2 of this book, with the Seven Principles of Bluefield Housing, the model's lot level design tactics, and its liveability and sustainability strategies each used as a cumulative tooklit to assess the quality of applications.

Demonstration projects, standard plans, and toolkits

Design excellence can be further promoted through the creation of demonstration projects. As the concept of bluefield developments is introduced to an area, test projects by perceived 'safe hands' are likely to be beneficial. This is particularly apt for neighbourhoods where infill is undertaken through fast-paced KDR redevelopment, but also in places where backyard homes and internal secondary suites are already allowed but are not considered as part of a holistic site redevelopment or as an organised housing intensification strategy. The 'safe hands' here may be a community housing provider or housing association with a track record of housing development and management. Alternatively, demonstration projects may be self-initiated by property owners and residents who partner with local government to test the bluefield principles, monitor post-occupancy progress, and report on outcomes for the benefit of improving the model.

Standard plan services can also play a role in incentivising the take-up of new housing models. This has been seen in the Los Angeles Department of Building and Safety (LADBS) Standard Plan Program for ADUs, where more than 50 pre-approved designs are offered for direct purchase from participating designers.[2] Presented as an online catalogue with simple descriptors of bedroom numbers, number of storeys, and overall size, the designs are pre-approved against the City's ADU zoning ordinances and require only minimal compliance checking and adjusting by LADBS relative to site-specific zoning details and footing requirements. Such a scheme could be created locally for bluefield housing for the backyard homes and potentially for the housing additions.

Similarly, design guides can help simplify potentially complex issues and help end-users navigate zoning requirements. UCLA's cityLAB has demonstrated this with its Building an ADU guidebook, which uses plain language and access-ible diagrams to describe Los Angeles' new ADU framework, clarify for the reader if they are likely to be able to add an ADU to their lot, the forms that ADU might take, and the requisite approval steps to make it happen.[3] Similar assistance can come in the form of case study descriptions, as seen in the publications of the Small Housing BC not-for-profit in Vancouver, which offers toolkits of small housing examples from across North America.[4] Taking a best-practice approach, the Chicago Bungalow Association provides a design guide for renovating and adapting multi-level bungalows in a simple 'dos-and-don'ts' arrangement,[5] while in Australia, the Design Guide for Older Women's Housing by Schored Projects and Monash University distils research into the design and construction needs for affordable housing for older women into illustrated design principles that can be read by a wide audience of practitioners and end users.[6] Together, examples such as these demonstrate the capacity for posi-tive outcomes to be fostered through examples that encourage an aspirational approach to housing supply.

Brokerages and grants

Much has been made of the negative effects of neoliberalism on housing pro-duction, with UK architect and author Paul Karakusevic highlighting the impact of government pulling away from the production of social housing:

> The general thrust of the neoliberalist argument is that if the state steps back, reducing taxes and regulation, the market will flourish and innovate. In social housing this has rarely worked, and the role of charities, the state and local municipalities has proven to be crucial in maintaining supply and standards.[7]

Given the bluefield model relies on a disaggregated approach to land supply, relying instead on increasing the capacity of individual lots to become housing intensification sites, government is unlikely to be a bluefield housing provider. The exception is if the state has a supply of properties in residential suburbs that are not substantial enough to be redeveloped as significantly higher density offerings. This is the case with low-rise state-owned duplex and triplex properties which may be of an age where they need replacing, but whose lots are neither sized nor configured in a way that enables land assembly. In this instance, the state may attempt to scale up housing production through replication of the bluefield model across its smaller sites, but in most cases, development is likely to be private.

However, this is not to say that there is no role for government in bluefield housing. The City of Los Angeles' ADU Accelerator Program is an example of how government can act as a broker between a property owner and a resident co-located on the lot. The scheme exists to match homeowners wishing to rent their ADU with older LA residents seeking a secure and affordable home.[8] This managed scheme not only orchestrates the sharing arrangement and manages the rental process, but ensures affordability for the tenant coupled with a stable rental stream for the homeowner. With rental agreements running for five years under the supervision of a dedicated case worker, tenants and homeowners can enter the sharing arrangement with the confidence that both parties are committed to a mutually-beneficial long-term housing relationship.

Further encouraging the uptake of ADU construction in the state, in 2022 the California Housing Finance Agencys (CalHFA) established its state-wide ADU Grant Program.[9] Under the scheme, property owners who wish to construct a backyard ADU, and remain in the primary dwelling as owner-occupiers rather than investors, are entitled to a grant of up to US$40,000 to cover pre-construction costs such as design work, statutory fees, permit costs, and utility connections. Applicants are means-tested but to encourage uptake income limits can be as high as US$300,000 in some counties. To qualify for the grant, an applicant must establish a loan through a lender approved by CalHFA, and have the grant monies added directly to the loan as a top-up amount that does not need to be repaid. The paperwork is managed directly between the lender and the state, isolating the grant for pre-construction work while the borrowed amount funds only the construction costs.

In Chicago, owner-occupiers of existing older homes are incentivised to uplift the energy efficiency of their homes through a partnership between the Chicago Bungalow Association and the City of Chicago.[10] Here, owners of properties that are at least 30 years old can take advantage of the Retrofit Chicago Program to have subsidised energy assessments and insulation refits undertaken on older homes to improve thermal comfort and reduce running costs. Such a scheme helps to redress the lack of insulation and associated thermal discomfort experienced in many older homes while additionally offering the property owner government-sponsored rebates on the purchase of energy efficient appliances and fittings. With its emphasis on the retrofit of existing older homes, the bluefield housing model would benefit from a targeted state-based incentive program such as this.

Tax incentives

Beyond grants, larger government-led incentives can be offered to encourage the retrofitting of existing homes. In receiving his 2022 Master of the British Empire award for services to architecture, heritage, and conservation, Edinburgh-based architect Nicholas Groves-Raines called for the removal of the UK's goods and services Value-Added Tax (VAT) from restoration and retrofit projects, mounting a sustainability argument in the process:

> Sustainability in architecture has to start with the restoration of existing buildings. Keeping what we have and reusing it is one of the best ways to save carbon. The greatest impact on this would be to remove the 20 per cent VAT rate that applies to repair on existing buildings. By removing VAT on repairs, more people would be encouraged to restore existing buildings and breathe new life into the traditional/vernacular heritage across the country.[11]

In Italy, the 'Superbonus' tax credit scheme already goes some way towards this goal. Here, homeowners are incentivised to upgrade older properties through uplifts across three core areas: insulation, heating and cooling, and structural work to reduce damage from earthquake activity. Further interventions such as the installation of solar panels and at-home charging for electric vehicles can be claimed, providing at least one of the core activities is also undertaken. The scheme operates by allowing owners to subtract the cost of upgrade works from their tax returns for five years. In the first few years of the program, up to 110% of the costs can be claimed, enabling the entire amount to be written-off plus an extra 10% to cover bank interest. The owner also has the choice to pass the credit onto the building contractor who can either sell the credit to a bank for reimbursement by the government, or alternatively claim the amount against their own taxation payments. The scheme is designed to encourage early uptake, with the credit reducing to 70% in the penultimate year, before further reducing to 65% in the final year.[12]

Other state-sponsored incentives focus on broader ambitions for building and neighbourhood revitalisation. The Illinois Property Tax Assessment Freeze, overseen by the state's Historic Preservation Division, focusses on properties with heritage status. It allows owners who undertake significant renovations to have the assessed value of the property for taxation purposes frozen for eight years, after which a four-year window is opened within which the value of the property is incrementally raised to its real value. This incentivises the owners of heritage properties to retain and rework them by offering a 12-year tax concession. To qualify, the value of the building work undertaken must exceed 25% of the original assessed property value within a two-year period, while the work must be undertaken according to ten Standards of Rehabilitation that follow standard conservation and adaptation principles.[13]

A different long-term tax strategy, aimed at encouraging multi-year investment over the quick 'flipping' of real estate assets is seen in US Opportunity Zones – identified areas that are distressed and in need of economic stimulation. In Opportunity Zones, investors can delay having capital gains calculated and applied to a redeveloped property for several years, giving them the chance to amortise their investment spending during the life of the tax exemption. To qualify, investors must spend at least 100% of the value of the property on improvements, with the value of the land excluded from the calculation. Aimed at a broad range of development opportunities across businesses and residences, Opportunity Zones can offer residential uplift incentives for investors seeking medium to long-term involvement.[14]

Large-scale tax incentives such as those described here are not necessarily directly applicable to the bluefield housing model, but they each present elements that suggest where government involvement may help to incentivise it. A simple and direct incentivising mechanism would be to extend existing real estate concessions to the bluefield model. Stamp duty, a compulsory Australian land tax paid by the purchaser of a property at the point of ownership transfer, is individually calculated at a state level. It can typically be as high as around 5% of the purchase price, adding tens of thousands of dollars to the cost which must be paid up front and cannot be added to a mortgage. Several states offer permanent or temporary stamp duty savings or removal for being a first home buyer, for buying an apartment off-the-plan, or for buying a newly constructed rather than established home. A similar concession could be applied to bluefield housing in recognition of its contribution to adding more affordable housing options to a city's mix.

Together, tax exemptions such as those described here suggest multiple ways in which the owner of a property may be encouraged to redevelop in the bluefield manner as an alternative to KDR infill, particularly when the retention and reuse of existing building and landscape fabric is rewarded in the absence of mandated preservation laws.

Short-term rentals and mixed-use

A further but potentially exploitable incentive exists in allowing the dwellings in a bluefield development to be considered for short-term rentals and mixed-use. This can be negatively perceived, with concerns raised over the ability of the bluefield model to act as a front for the creation of ongoing short stay holiday rentals or commercial tenancies. The ability for a bluefield development to be formally considered for non-residential use will ultimately have to be made at a jurisdictional level. However, such uses should not always be immediately discounted as a potential incentive to develop in the bluefield manner. In some cases, it may be of broad benefit.

Short-term rentals, whilst occupying dwellings that could otherwise serve as full-time homes, may provide necessary higher yield income to help owners pay down a mortgage, particularly in the early stages of project completion. This may be part of an owner's initial bluefield strategy, forming a temporarily higher income stream that makes the development feasible or at least more financially comfortable. Similarly, bluefield properties may be developed for small commercial operations such as consulting rooms or offices, or for expanded work-from-home scenarios that allow a resident to bring a small number of employees to the site. Such functions commonly occur within neighbourhoods, often without formal approvals or oversight,[15] and should not automatically be discounted when considering the rules and regulations for how bluefield housing might be established.

There may be a tendency to assume that all mixed-use activity in a bluefield development is bad activity, however, the introduction of minor commercial or civic functions within a residential setting may prove beneficial. A community housing provider creating a dispersed collection of bluefield housing sites may give over one potential dwelling to form a small community hub. This is described in the scenario plan of the Large corner scheme of Chapter 10, where one can imagine residents of the housing association taking advantage of either permanent or visiting services at such a hub. Similarly, a bluefield development with older residents, or in a neighbourhood with a high proportion of older residents, may benefit from having one dwelling given over to commercial use by a health professional such as a physical or mental health therapist, podiatrist, or the like. Further complementary commercial uses can be found in education, where residents may, for example, use one potential dwelling for tutoring, music, or dance lessons. Again, using a lens of housing for connectivity can be useful here, as one can imagine residents benefitting from income-producing activities that encourage interaction on the lot with a small number of weekly visitors. The successful integration of such activities will depend on where they are located on the site, how they are accessed, and whether they can take advantage of street access without visitors needing to access deep into the site if this is deemed undesirable.

As an exercise, each of the design schemes of Part 3 can be revisited to map an overlay of potential non-residential uses and to discover constraints and opportunities within the bluefield system. Acknowledging non-residential functions as realistic and viable uses for bluefield housing may be a positive reflection of the model's accommodation flexibility and a recognition that privately funded projects may benefit from supplementary income streams. For uses deemed undesirable long-term, controls can be considered around capping how long a property may be used as a short-term rental or non-residential use without applying for an extension, with consideration given to setting higher council or local government rates for these functions.

Ultimately, the carrots and sticks that both encourage and control new forms of housing will operate best when considered locally and holistically. And just as the give-and-take zoning control principles will require a nuanced approach to determine a proposal's suitability for its neighbourhood, so too will considerations of the way in which bluefield dwellings function relative to the needs of the proponents, and the effects – both negative and positive – on the broader community.

Notes

1   Damian Madigan and Alysia Bennett, *Fourflex: Redefining Family Living in the LA Care Economy, Honorable Mention, LA Low Rise – Housing Ideas for Los Angeles Design Challenge,* 2021. City of Los Angeles.
2   "ADU Standard Plan Program," Los Angeles Department of Building and Safety, accessed 10 March 2022, www.ladbs.org/adu/standard-plan-program.
3   Dana Cuff and Jane Blumenfeld, *Building an ADU – Guidebook To Accessory Dwelling Units In The City Of Los Angeles*, v1.0, (Los Angeles: cityLAB: UCLA Department of Architecture + Urban Design, 2017), https://citylab.ucla.edu/adu-guidebook.
4   Small Housing BC, accessed 21 August 2021, www.smallhousingbc.org/reports/.
5   Chicago Bungalow Association, accessed 10 February 2022, www.chicagobungalow.org/design-guidelines.
6   Sophie Dyring et al., *A Design Guide for Older Women's Housing*, Monash University (Melbourne, 2022).
7   Paul Karakusevic, "A New Era of Social Housing: Architecture as the Basis for Change," *Housing as Intervention: Architecture Towards Social Equity, Architectural Design (A.D.)* 88, no. 4 (July/August 2018): 48–55.
8   "LA ADU Accelerator Program," City of Los Angeles, accessed 30 March 2022, https://adu.lacity.org/.
9   "CalHFA ADU Grant Program," California Housing Finance Agency (CalHFA), accessed 19 October 2022, www.calhfa.ca.gov/adu.
10 "Home Energy Savings Program," Chicago Bungalow Association, accessed 10 February 2022, www.chicagobungalow.org/energy-savers.
11 "Architect awarded MBE in birthday honours urges scrapping VAT on retrofit," The Architects' Journal, last modified 6 June 2022, www.architectsjournal.co.uk/news/architect-awarded-mbe-in-birthday-honours-urges-retrofit-tax-breaks.
12 "Superbonus 110%," Italian Ministry of Economy and Finance, accessed 20 April 2022, www.governo.it/it/superbonus.
13 "Property Tax Assessment Freeze," Illinois Department of Natural Resources Historic Preservation Division, accessed 19 October 2022, www2.illinois.gov/dnrhistoric/preserve/pages/taxfreeze.aspx.
14 "Can I Buy a House in an Opportunity Zone and Call It an Investment?," Realized, last modified 5 February 2021, www.realized1031.com/blog/can-i-buy-a-house-in-an-opportunity-zone-and-call-it-an-investment.
15 Alysia Bennett, "Stealth Urbanism: The Covert Advance of Suburban Density and Diversity" (Doctor of Philosophy Monash University, 2016), https://doi.org/10.4225/03/58520f78448ea.

15 Financing, operating, and selling bluefield housing

The patrons of bluefield housing

Market-driven housing systems prefer certainty, with the real estate sector fuelled by quick and predictable sales. This is one of the reasons so much suburban housing is a variation on a theme; developers build what they know will sell, which in turn drives what the market seeks, but not necessarily what is needed to respond to evolving demographics or affordability pressures. This is not to suggest that all developers are driven solely by profit and do not seek to address housing choice, but they operate in a housing system that is driven by fast production and predictable economic outcomes. This same system also implicates many in the middle-class for whom so much private wealth and housing security is tied to real estate, including in the private rental system.[1]

In traditional knock-down-rebuild infill, the development model is discernible with a relatively high degree of financial predictability:

- The value of a target site is known due to a stated asking price, or knowable due to comparable sales in the same neighbourhood coupled with current market and economic trends. This is particularly the case for so-called 'land value' lots where the existing house has little potential for renovation and re-use.
- The maximum housing yield and the resultant sizes of the new dwellings are predictable, being determined by the zoning metrics for the address.

228

DOI: 10.4324/9781003293736-20
This chapter has been made available under a CC-BY-NC-ND license.

Financing, operating, and selling bluefield housing

- The likely construction cost and time are calculable with a strong degree of accuracy, using per square metre or foot cost rates and construction schedules drawn from the developer's established and replicable methods of design, construction, and delivery.
- The likely sale prices of the dwellings and their length of time on the market are predictable, given speculatively developed homes are designed and constructed in response to prevailing market conditions within the neighbourhood.

A speculative residential developer's likely profit can therefore be predicted quite accurately in the KDR model, as throughout the process a formula is being followed based on years of local market data, industry knowledge, and established business practice. This results in housing of known types, with a common result being the largest house possible within the permitted development envelope, and a maximising of rooms and amenities within that calculable volume.

The bluefield housing model works counter to this templated KDR model:

- As with speculative development, the value of the site is known or knowable.
- The retention of an existing house, however, disrupts cost predictability: building costs may be lower (due to building less), or higher (due to construction complications that cannot be discovered until the project commences).
- Integrating existing housing stock limits repeatable templated solutions that can maximise cost savings through economies of scale. A standard plans service for bluefield housing, as described in Chapter 14, will likely help achieve cost savings, but its effect will be limited to the backyard homes aspect and possibly some house additions. Where the existing housing stock takes a repeated and predictable form, and additions can be undertaken using common methods of integration, standard plans and details for alterations may help to reduce costs.
- The likely sale price of the bluefield housing is predictable, but most likely less predictable than a speculatively built model, particularly until such time as a critical mass of bluefield housing reaches the market. Depending on the neighbourhood, it may be introducing an uncommon form of smaller housing, the value of which may be difficult to immediately determine. Furthermore, given there will be a degree of sharing across the lot, potential purchasers may choose to pay more for a home in a bluefield development or less, depending on their personal circumstances and lifestyle preferences.

These considerations point to a degree of uncertainty around value and profit should a bluefield scheme be developed speculatively for immediate sale; a profit may be realised, but until a market is established it will not be as predictable as templated business-as-usual KDR development. Due to the idiosyncratic

229

nature of each project, bluefield housing will hold limited appeal for profit-driven speculative developers. Its patrons are therefore likely to be those who see value as a long-term proposition that includes social or familial benefits: not-for-profit community housing providers and associations, a family unit, a group of related or unrelated owner-occupiers, or one or two owner-occupiers who can subsidise the entire construction and rent out one or more of the other bluefield homes, as described in the Ecoburbia example of Chapter 2. In some instances, one of the residents may already own the target site and become a partner in the redevelopment, as described by the design scenarios of Part 3. But although the developers of bluefield housing may be deliberative and amateur rather than speculative and professional, this is not to say that they are operating in a system without precedent and resources.

An established market

Residential construction undertaken by private developers is big business, whether it be done by a residential development company, property owners working with architects and domestic builders, as owners who engage a builder to undertake all design and construction work, or as amateur owner-builders who engage individual contractors directly while assuming the role of project manager. After experiencing a two-year downturn around the COVID-19 pandemic, the annual global output of private residential construction grew by 16.8% in 2021 to US$5.3 trillion, and by 2026 this is expected to grow by a further 32.2% to US$7 trillion.[2] These figures represent the total value of materials and labour, and the associated equipment and services costs of residential construction, and a large proportion of this expenditure is spent on demolition, refurbishment, and repairs and maintenance. Worldwide, 37% of residential construction is spent on these reworking activities. In Australia, this figure is lower at 29%, but this still equated to over US$15 billion in 2021 for a population of around only 26 million people.[3] In the UK, reworking accounts for 42% of all residential

15.1
Annual residential construction spending in 2021 (represented in US$ without adjustment for inflation; currency conversions calculated using constant 2021 annual average exchange rates).

construction,[4] while in the US and Canada, the proportions rise to 46% and 48% respectively (Figure 15.1).[5,6]

These construction spending figures have been used as they employ consistent data and currency calculations that enable direct comparisons across countries. However, different sources can yield alternative expenditure amounts. The Australian Housing Industry Association, for example, uses the Australian National Accounts to advocate that the country currently spends as much as US$65 billion on residential construction each year, with around $US27 billion or 40% of this being on alterations and additions.[7] These larger figures result from capturing the construction spending that falls outside of building approvals systems and is excluded from other forms of calculation. But regardless of the calculation method, what is clear is that private spending on residential construction is big. It also comes in various forms: greenfield housing in newly created suburbs, KDR infill housing, demolitions and partial demolitions, major alterations and additions, and large and small forms of refurbishments and repairs. And in suburbanised cities, much of it occurs in ever-modifying neighbourhoods by property owners themselves, either through incremental do-it-yourself (DIY) activity over time or by direct engagement with small-scale builders who specialise in low-rise domestic construction.[8]

Because bluefield housing is a mechanism of this domestic alterations and additions market, it operates within the established economy of private residential construction. It therefore does not need to seek a new economic path to realisation. In reviewing the design studies of Part 3, the normality of the bluefield approach to design and construction becomes apparent:

- The existing house is retained, remodelled, refurbished, and repaired, mirroring the existing behaviour of suburban alterations.
- The home is extended in a similarly familiar fashion. This may come in the form of a kitchen extension that transitions a non-serviced room to serviced, replicating the commonplace exercise of adding an en suite bathroom. Additional rear additions similarly match existing construction behaviours, albeit creating an extra dwelling in the process.
- Backyard homes are created in a similar manner to detached garages or ADUs.
- Contextually designed to respond to the prevailing pattern of development in the local neighbourhood, site coverage and building mass form an equivalent amount of construction mass seen in single-family house development elsewhere.
- By extension, the consolidation of outdoor space creates landscape extents that are similar in scope to the backyard zones created in normative home renovation projects.
- In total, the scale and nature of construction operates within existing domestic construction skillsets, avoiding the need for specialist trades, equipment, or materials.

Considered in these ways, bluefield housing operates at the known level of domestic suburban construction, where the existing scale of alterations and additions is harnessed to supply additional and more diverse housing. In its simplest description, it offers stock-in-trade domestic construction coupled with considered site and building design interventions to create two or more homes out of one. From a design and construction perspective, it simply replicates the BAU enterprise of homeowners, small-scale builders, and architects. The economic complexities lie in the potential for a single development to have multiple owners and in how such a model gets funded.

Borrowing for bluefield housing

Chapter 13 highlighted that lenders will understandably seek to identify risky departures from their BAU lending practices. The bluefield model therefore begs a question of how mortgages can be secured on a development where there can be multiple owners with shared tenure over parts of the whole. Beyond the borrowing and repayment power of the proponents, which is a factor in all mortgages, much of the uncertainty over lending will come down to two things: the value of the completed individual properties relative to the development costs (otherwise known as under- or over-capitalisation), and how quickly a lender can satisfactorily liquidate an individual bluefield home on the secondary market should a borrower default on their loan.

Where an entire bluefield scheme of multiple dwellings is in single ownership, the lending relationship for purchase of the property and the subsequent construction can be simple: a single borrower takes out a loan for the entire property based on the purchase price plus the value of the building contract they have in place (including associated design and other fees). The pressure of a mortgage is lessened when the development is undertaken on the owner's existing lot, as they take out or extend a loan for the cost of the construction only, using the equity they have in the property as collateral. One of the key benefits of undertaking a bluefield redevelopment in this manner is that the cost of land is removed from the scheme, as the borrowed amount is only for construction. None of this is unique to the bluefield housing model and is standard practice for residential property owners who wish to establish or extend a mortgage for construction.

However, financing for additional homes on an existing lot can be challenging. When, in 2017, California allowed every single-family home in the state to add an ADU under California Assembly Bill 2299 – the outcome of a decade of backyard housing research by UCLA's cityLAB – it radically (and positively) shifted the definition of the single-family-home. However, in altering the understanding of property ownership, it initially affected how lenders responded to the change, as described by Dana Cuff:

> At the outset, it was noted that Backyard Homes undermined the foundational thinking of American home mortgages. This is

corroborated by lenders struggling to find ways to finance secondary rental units. This problem could have a design component, (for example, if units could be designed to be dismantled and rebuilt so that they could serve as collateral to secure a loan).[9]

On face value, the bluefield approach adds what may appear to be a layer of complexity to the addition of new homes on an existing lot, by allowing these new entities to be individually owned. But in doing so, it also allows a single owner to sell these independent dwellings while retaining their own on the same site, whether this be the original house, or one of the new backyard homes. Having the capacity to be in individual ownership, bluefield housing distributes the value of the renovated and extended single-family home across multiple dwellings, allowing the separate portions to be independently mortgaged, bought, and sold by multiple parties. And there remains, of course, the opportunity for a group of individual owners to collaboratively develop and own a bluefield site, thereby sharing the cost and the mortgage risks across smaller and more affordable housing units. What enables this flexible ownership structure is a retitling of the original single-family home lot, which in turn is borne of the sharing structure across each bluefield site.

Community land titling

A key concern in creating zoning policies for bluefield housing, which are discussed in the next chapter, is how to stop the necessary code amendments for the model forming a Trojan Horse for standard land divisions below existing acceptable lot sizes. Given the logic behind the bluefield siting method is to use co-location and lot sharing to create better neighbourhood and landscape outcomes while enabling more houses to be added to a land parcel than might otherwise be allowed, a statutory mechanism is required to prevent each bluefield home from being isolated into smaller and less amenable segregated lots within the lot. Should this occur, the potential negative consequences are an increase in hard surfaces as dwelling access becomes more convoluted, less deep root soil zones due to open space being compartmentalised with fencing, and less social connection between what will be privatised dwellings. Protecting against these concerns requires bluefield development sites to be retitled from a freehold system in a way that allows multiple ownership but restricts land division.

Strata and Community Titles, which are common in Australia for multi-unit developments, identify on the property title which parts of the lot are privately owned, and which are common to each housing unit owner. The strata title was introduced in the 1960s as a means of allowing individual ownership of apartments over multiple levels. In a strata arrangement, individual ownership is often of the space between the internal surfaces of party walls, floors, and ceilings, while construction elements such as party walls, roofs, and foundations are common property, as are shared external areas necessary to access the individual units and parking areas. A community title similarly allows a mix of private and shared ownership and is more commonly applied to larger developments. As with strata, a community title is ultimately a form of land division, as the Certificate of Title demarcates between private and common property, thereby creating opportunities for compartmentalisation of the privately-owned elements.

An alternative arrangement that allows for co-located housing while keeping the lot intact from land division is the Company Title (also known by the older Moiety Title[10]):

- residents establish a company which then owns the title over the property;
- each resident owns a share of the company;
- loans are secured over a share in the company rather than over the property itself (which may limit borrowing options);
- the shareholders are granted rights to their own private dwelling and to use of the common facilities;
- due to the company voting system, shareholders have the flexibility to make changes to how the development runs, providing flexibility over time; and
- shareholders can place restrictions on the sale or lease of dwellings, including requiring the approval of all shareholders (which may diminish the value of the property).[11]

Significantly, despite its restrictions when compared with traditional strata or community titling, a company title still enables each home to be individually bought, sold, and leased. And while the company voting system may potentially reduce property values – an obvious disincentive to those seeking a short-term return on a real estate investment – it is of benefit to bluefield housing residents seeking more affordable housing choices for established neighbourhoods. Furthermore, these same company title shareholder rights offer each bluefield community the inherent benefit of discussing and agreeing resident changeover, which is important as new residents join an established housing collaboration and begin to shape its future direction together. In essence, the shareholder process simply formalises the types of resident negotiations that will naturally have to occur in the model by default. When compared to freehold ownership, a company title may put limits on the sale and purchase of real estate, creating areas for discussion and compromise, but such effects are in-built in a collaborative housing model, and will come as little surprise to those who desire it in the bluefields.

Nevertheless, with a company title a shadow looms large over the fact that ownership and mortgaging occur on a share of a company rather than of a physical property or parcel of land; a potentially untenable proposition for owners and their lenders. For this reason, the most attractive and flexible titling arrangement for a bluefield development is likely to be a community title that is underwritten by strong and enforceable by-laws. In Australia, a community title must be accompanied by a Scheme Description once a community scheme reaches a certain size (for example six or more dwellings). In turn, by-laws apply to all scheme descriptions, tailored to the lot holders' needs. These generally relate to high-order organisational issues of the scheme, however, by-laws can be crafted to provide a finer level of detail where required. This can include pointing to a more nuanced operational document such as a bespoke Residents Agreement (described later in this chapter) or Land Management Agreement (LMA – discussed in Chapter 16). Significantly, even in the absence of a Residents Agreement, the scheme description and by-laws of a community titled development can each describe and make binding not only the obligations of the developer and the residents, but the overarching ethos and philosophies of the development. These can relate to long-term and day-to-day resident rights around general use, access to facilities, and pet ownership, and extend to ingrained principles of sustainable development and social inclusion.

What is important to note in relation to bluefield housing, then, is that mechanisms exist to bring the model under the umbrella coverage of existing community titling, which can be massaged to suit. This may necessitate minor changes to titling legislation specific to the model, including:

- the requirement for a Scheme Description for all bluefield housing projects regardless of their dwelling numbers;
- the requirement for Scheme Description by-laws that point to a tailored Residents Agreement and (where necessary) a Land Management Agreement; and
- the requirement that all these elements be created early in the bluefield creation process and be captured in the formal development approval procedure.

Once satisfactorily established, local jurisdictions can ease the process for applicants and help guide the quality of development applications by establishing model bluefield scheme descriptions, by-laws, and LMAs that template the desired spatial and operational outcomes.

Retitling in any form will, however, still carry the risk that the community title will be used as a mechanism for creating a *de facto* privatised subdivision. This may be of particular concern where all shares are held by the one person or entity. However, any premeditated use of the bluefield model for eventual subdivision would still require the proposal in the first instance to function as a truly collaborative bluefield development as desired, with all the laundry, rubbish, parking, access, open space, and housing provisions designed, approved, and then constructed in the bluefield mould. The effort this takes thereby lowers the incentive to subvert the process, as the development will have to be approved and delivered as a collaborative bluefield scheme in the first instance. And once established in this way, the requisite reverse-engineering of car parking, pedestrian access, and segregated open space aimed at privatising the scheme

Financing, operating, and selling bluefield housing

and raising the value of the properties will be difficult to achieve. In addition, in some jurisdictions the act of retitling will trigger a statutory change in land use, requiring the proponent to lodge an application to have the proposed reconfigured land parcels approved. This gives the approval authority a second look at the bluefield scheme and the opportunity to deny the retitling if it wishes.

Reversibility and strategic staging

Land titling a bluefield scheme need not be inflexible, however. While land division and housing privatisation has the possibility of subverting the ethical, operational, and suburban ambitions of bluefield housing, reinstatement of multiple bluefield homes to a single freehold property plays to the model's inherent flexibility as described in Chapter 8 and explored by the design exercises of Part 3. On social and financial grounds, the ability to return a bluefield development

15.2
Multi lot schemes developed in the bluefield manner can offer the flexibility to return to single-family homes if original lot boundaries are not constructed over.

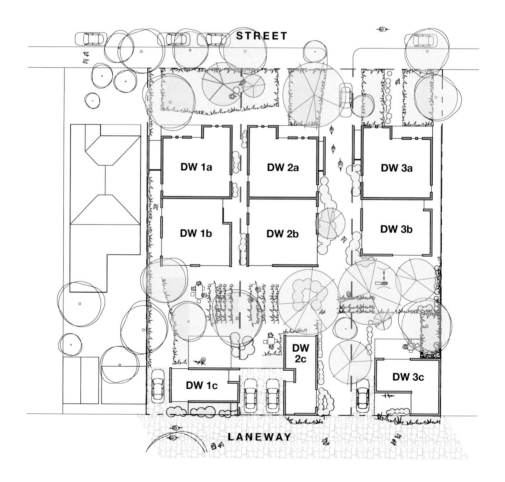

back to a single house can be of benefit to owners by providing accommodation choice that can change with needs over time.

Economically, the ability to return a bluefield housing development to a single-family home offers the chance for financiers to assess a project's lending risk differently, particularly if a single lender is financing the entire development. The fact that multiple bluefield dwellings can be reconfigured back to a single property on a single freehold title significantly reduces the risk for lenders, as the ability to liquidate the properties on the secondary market becomes much more likely. Developments undertaken over two or more lots, as shown in the dual and multi-lot schemes of Chapters 11 and 12, can offer the same reversibility if the designer can avoid construction over the dividing boundaries between the original titles (Figure 15.2). This requires the designer to consider both the extent and the construction of boundary walls to avoid encroachment and fire rating issues should the consolidated properties be returned to their original lot lines.

For bluefield schemes that connect housing across original title boundaries, such as the side-by-side scheme of Chapter 11, the ability to reinstate the lots to the two original titles may require significant reworking if construction straddles old boundaries (Figure 15.3).

15.3
The side-by-side scheme of Chapter 11 showing the original boundary line location that previously separated the original two titles. The central infill element (shown in orange) straddles the previous boundary and will require demolition if the combined property is to be reverted to two separate titles.

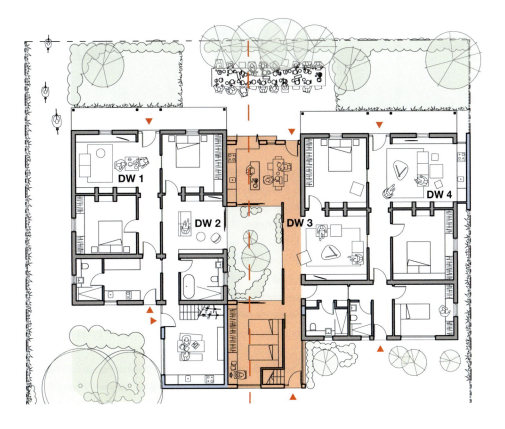

By comparison, pre-emptively designing infill elements that can predict a reinstatement of the old title boundaries, as shown in Figure 15.4, can minimise or even avoid rework, while mounting a strong argument that the full scheme is both occupationally and financially flexible.

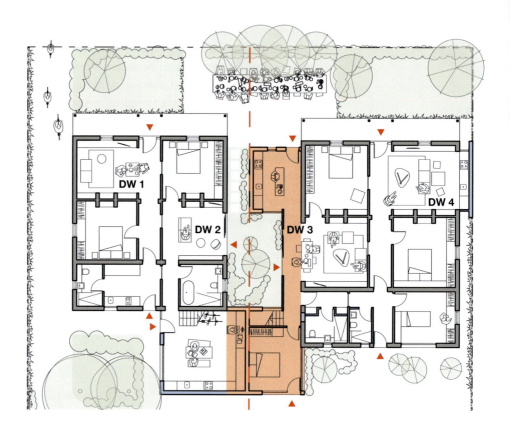

15.4
A revised version of the side-by-side scheme, with the redesigned central component pre-empting the potential reinstatement to two titles. Once reinstated, each title can accommodate two dwellings as shown. Alternatively, each pair of dwellings can be consolidated into a single-family home.

Inasmuch as a bluefield development can plan for an eventual aggregation back to a single housing form, a logical extension of this thinking is to conceive of development as a staged approach that builds up over time. The single lot studies of Chapter 10 serve as good examples here. In some instances, occupational flexibility can be inherent in the design. This is seen in the Medium proposal (Figure 15.5), where the two-storey backyard home can be configured as a three-bedroom dwelling over two levels, or two one-bedroom dwellings over one level each, or as a combination of one dwelling plus a work from home, or home business arrangement. Each mode is achievable with little to no constructional change, with the requisite building services provisions incorporated during the initial construction. This is discussed and diagrammed in more detail in Chapter 10. Similarly, works to the original house can be strategically deferred or gradually undertaken over time, particularly where development costs prohibit full completion in a single construction project. When designed for flexibility, staging of the various modes of occupation can thereby occur through patterns of use, through discrete building phases, or both. This allows the owner to intensify or reduce usage over time, while taking advantage of opportunities to monetise parts of the whole, either by renting out one or more of the components, or by taking advantage of working from home.

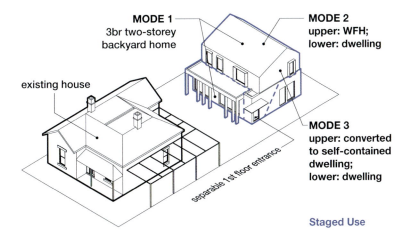

15.5
The Medium single lot scheme with three potential modes of use. Using the flexible design and construction strategies described with the case study in Chapter 10, Modes 2 and 3 are achievable as staged construction with minimal building modifications.

Flexibility by design is made simpler in detached backyard home projects such as this, as the physical separation of new and old buildings allows for obvious staging. However, flexible staging can also be realised in attached models if it is planned for, as exemplified by the Small design speculation of Chapter 10. Here, the existing cottage receives a commonplace rear extension that creates an open plan kitchen-dining-living space coupled with a study or work from home space. The cottage is thereby freed to accommodate three bedrooms and a bathroom, while an additional powder room is providing in a linking element between the old and the new (Figure 15.6). The design is undertaken in anticipation of future division into two self-contained dwellings. This is achieved through minimal construction intervention, most of which is internal. The Bedroom 3 wall is opened to the hallway and remodelled into a kitchen-dining-living space for Dwelling 1 (the cottage), with the former bedroom window widened to create a glazed entry that overlooks the garden. The linking hallway and powder room are combined to create a shared laundry, with the former powder room window replaced with a door that accesses a shared drying area. Finally, the rear addition receives two changes to become Dwelling 2: taking advantage of its proximity to the kitchen plumbing, the study is converted to a bathroom, while the living room is converted to a bedroom via the simple addition of dividing joinery. To create more generous space for the new dining and living area, the kitchen island can be removed if desired. External changes are similarly minor: a washing line is added to the side court for hidden clothes drying, while the rubbish bins are moved from behind the newly formed Dwelling 2 into the shared garden behind a screening fence.

STAGE 1 (anticipatory)
rear addition to create
3-bedroom home with study

STAGE 2 (bluefield development)
minor modifications to create
1x2br + 1x1br dwellings

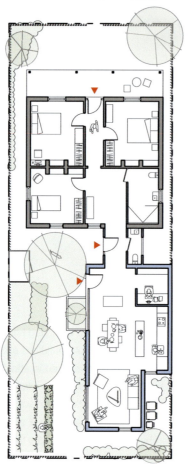
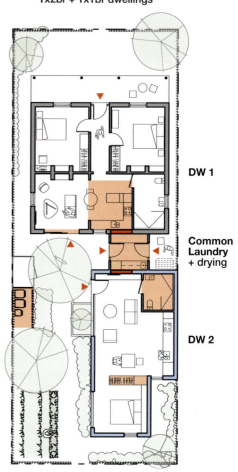

DW 1

Common Laundry + drying

DW 2

15.6
The Small single lot scheme of Chapter 10 showing a Stage 1 extension that anticipates future separation into two bluefield homes in a future Stage 2. The minor changes required to create the two dwellings are indicated in orange.

The key to minimising the amount of rework required to create the two dwellings is to forward-plan the future external doors of both dwellings, to design and construct the future party walls and their window locations for fire protection, and to arrange the footprint of the Stage 1 rear addition such that both the new and old parts of the house can address the garden. Where a common approach to creating an addition is to simply extrude the existing house with a rear extension of the same width, narrowing and elongating the addition's footprint results in the original cottage being able to address the rear of the lot instead of just the front. And of course, with the formative design and construction infrastructure being flexible, reversal back to a single-family home is possible via a simple reinstatement of the Stage 1 layout, or by other minor adjustments that allow the two dwellings to become one again.

Written family agreements and residents agreements

Like any form of multiple owner or multiple tenant housing, a bluefield housing development will require a robust agreement to be in place to protect the rights of all residents. This will be a prerequisite should the development be arranged on a new community title, as the governance structure of the community scheme will legally require it to create a scheme description with by-laws. But beyond this, written agreements over finances and function become increasingly important when individuals band together to share housing, either through moving into part of someone else's existing home, transferring one's own home to someone else whilst both parties live there, or financing construction works to someone else's home to facilitate moving in. These are common share scenarios identified by lawyer Brian Herd for families coming together to create shared housing for older parents, often under a simple oral arrangement:

> When it comes to the broader family edifice or agreements between siblings and parents, we are reluctant to reduce them to writing … many such arrangements are seeded in mutual trust but fall down on two common human frailties – memory (the 'who said what') and the vagaries of human relationships (the 'what ifs') … Lamentably, most of the arrangements within families are in the oral space or the atmosphere. As night follows day, in many cases this will lead to a disagreement about what was agreed or, at worst, total conflagration. And, need I also add, litigation … The danger is double sided. Without documentation either the parent or child may be the loser. The biggest loss, however, will be to both of them, when the lawyers are finished with them.[12]

Although 'emotionally repellent' for most people, Herd describes Written Family Agreements as essential for recording the financial obligations and expectations of parent and child while capturing the agreed relationships for everyone, including other family members not forming part of the multigenerational living arrangement itself. Furthermore, the process of establishing a written agreement will identify issues and risks that may not be considered in an informal oral arrangement. In some cases, having to agree to terms in writing can highlight the negative aspects of sharing and deter the parties from establishing an unhealthy shared housing arrangement in the first instance, before potential relationship breakdowns can occur.

Other agreements can relate to how the residents will function together within the development and with any overarching housing association, which is important not only to establish a shared understanding of what residents can and cannot do within their housing development, but to also safeguard their legal rights and obligations. In a bluefield development formal agreements will be vital, and precedents can be found in established cohousing or shared living examples. Having undertaken a series of workshops with a resident focus group, the Sharing With Friends housing association has developed a plain-English Agreement that captures residents' rights and obligations, which can serve as a template for a bluefield-style development. A not-for-profit association operating in Queensland, SwF's aim is to provide small cohousing communities of five dwellings for older women whereby residents pay a contribution to the association to secure their long-term rental and receive an exit payment on leaving. The financial, organisational, and usage arrangements are described across three key areas:

Becoming a resident

- **Residency Agreement** This is registered on the title of the land and grants a long-term exclusive rights lease to a home. It does not pertain to any of the shared spaces, but access rights to these are covered under a Community Agreement. It sets out the rights and obligations of the tenant and the Association with respect to the use and maintenance of the home. It may be surrendered by the resident at any time.
- **Community Agreement** (between the Association and the original residents) or **Residency notice** (between the Association and subsequent new residents) These describe the resident's rights and obligations, plus the right to use the shared spaces or facilities. They establish a Committee comprised by the residents and require the Committee to set budgets and agreed levies for upkeep.
- **Resident Contribution Deed** This set outs the obligation for the resident to pay for their home up front when they join the Community, and for the Association to pay an exit payment when they leave. It may include an amount for refurbishment works if joining after establishment, with works undertaken by the Association before occupation. It may obligate the Association to pay part of the resident's rent into a Sinking Fund for repairs and maintenance.
- **Introduction to residents** The Association works with the existing residents to locate and interview new residents who are eligible to join the Community.

Living in the community

- **Joint decisions by Committee** Made up of the residents and designed to give them agency over how the development operates, the Committee has a Chairperson, Treasurer, and Secretary. It sets annual budgets and contributions to Administration and Sinking Funds, and ensures maintenance is undertaken. It amends rules as necessary and makes day-to-day decisions related to running the property.

Financing, operating, and selling bluefield housing

- **Community costs and expenses** These include responsibility for the common areas, including the management of an Administration Fund for day-to-day expenses and a Sinking Fund for long-term expenses, and the establishment of an annual budget for the Community, to which residents must contribute.
- **Resident costs and expenses** These include rent on the dwelling where applicable, contributions to the Administrative Fund and the Sinking Fund, personal housing costs such as cleaning and utility bills, and home contents insurance.
- **Repairs to a residence** Responsibilities for these are outlined in the Residency Agreement. The Association may organise repairs directly or direct the Committee to organise them.
- **Noise and nuisance** These are common sense measures for the benefit of all residents: houses and common spaces are to be left clean and tidy, noise must not cause a nuisance, common areas must not be obstructed from lawful use, residents must not cause offence or embarrassment to each other, and no animals may be kept without approval.
- **The Association's rights** These relate to keeping the Association financially liquid and to identifying items requiring the Association's approval. These include approval over individual insurance policies, approval over structural works, and the Association having approval to undertake repairs and maintenance and seek reimbursement from the Administrative or Sinking Fund.

Leaving the community

- **When a resident leaves** The relates to the need to give notice when ending a Residency Agreement and outlines how the Association will agree a scope of refurbishment works with the resident. Under the agreement the Association arranges refurbishment, if necessary. It also works with the Community to find a replacement resident. This person pays a Contribution, out of which the refurbishment works are paid. The departing resident receives the balance of the Contribution less anything owed to the Association, up to the value of the contribution they initially paid when entering the development. Amounts are adjusted for CPI.
- **Winding up the Community** This outlines what happens if all residents and the Association agree to end the Community and sell the property. The Exit Payment is calculated as an equal share between residents of the sale price after deducting sale costs and the value of the unimproved land. The total is capped to the initial contribution paid by each resident, adjusted for the Consumer Price Index (CPI).

Together, these components of the Sharing With Friends Resident Agreement describe the types of written considerations necessary in a collaborative living model such as bluefield housing. These become even more important to set in place where the development is in private ownership in the absence of an attached housing association to oversee the scheme – even when the relationship between residents is familial. But this is not to say that agreements must be restrictive in the first instance or inflexible during the life of the project. With the foundations of a committee established and clear procedures and decisions communicated, each bluefield community can empower its residents to tailor their operations at commencement and amend them over time as needs change and opportunities arise.

Notes

1 Jenny Schuetz, *Fixer-Upper: How to Repair America's Broken Housing Systems*. Washington, DC: Brookings Institution Press, 2022.
2 *Marketline Industry Profile: Global Residential Construction April 2022*, Marketline (Manchester, 2022).
3 *Marketline Industry Profile: Residential Construction in Australia April 2022*, Marketline (Manchester, 2022).
4 *Marketline Industry Profile: Residential Construction in the United Kingdom April 2022*, Marketline (Manchester, 2022).
5 *Marketline Industry Profile: Residential Construction in the United States April 2022*, Marketline (Manchester, 2022).
6 *Marketline Industry Profile: Residential Construction in Canada April 2022*, Marketline (Manchester, 2022).
7 *Housing Industry Outlook, February 2022*, Housing Industry Association Limited (Canberra, 2022).
8 Leon Van Schaik and Nigel Bertram, *Suburbia Reimagined: Ageing and Increasing Populations in the Low-Rise City*. New York: Routledge, 2019, 40–41.
9 Dana Cuff, "The Architect's Lot: Backyard Homes Policy and Design," *Housing as Intervention: Architecture Towards Social Equity, Architectural Design (A.D.)* 88, no. 4 (July/August 2018): 62–69.
10 In a Moiety Title, where an individual is registered as a part-owner of the land with a right to occupy their dwelling and share the common property.
11 Chris Riedy et al., *The Collaborative Housing Guide: Legalities and Ownership Structures*, Institute for Sustainable Futures at the University of Technology Sydney (Sydney, 2019), www.collaborativehousing.org.au/larger-projects-know-the-legalities.
12 Brian Herd, *Avoiding the Ageing Parent Trap*. Newport, New South Wales: Big Sky Publishing, 2021, 134–135.

16 Zoning laws
Enabling bluefield housing

How many homes?

Established as a densification model that slots into existing single-family home neighbourhoods, bluefield housing will be subject to zoning policies at two levels: neighbourhood-level intensification measures that determine the number of dwellings permitted per lot; and building-level design metrics that will describe the permitted development envelopes for the housing based on local built patterns. For cities like Vancouver, which already allows 3-for-1 intensification via the addition of a backyard home plus a secondary suite, and 4-for-2 increases by adding secondary suites to duplexes, the density increases achieved by the bluefield model will be neither new nor challenging. However, the sizes of the new homes may be larger, and their independence increased due to their more nuanced relationships to each other and to the landscaped open space around which they are designed. The ability of the houses to flex over time – either by being divided into smaller units or combined into larger wholes – may require existing density provisions to be similarly flexible.

In low density cities, the density increases achieved in low-rise neighbourhoods will be an immediate step-change. This will require local decision makers to determine if maximum dwelling numbers per lot need to be stated or, as anticipated by Bluefield Housing Principle 2 in Chapter 6, left to the proponent to argue for based on need and demonstrated neighbourhood fit. Although the bluefield model as described in Principle 2 eschews a metrically

DOI: 10.4324/9781003293736-21

This chapter has been made available under a CC-BY-NC-ND license.

driven approach to site yield in favour of a demonstration of fit through design, the number of bluefield homes achieved on a lot may end up being capped in some jurisdictions, particularly if this is necessary for the model to be more easily adopted into the existing planning system.

What's in a name?

Terms such as 'laneway house' are what they say: a house that addresses a rear lane and by default is thereby located behind an existing home that faces a primary street. 'Secondary suite' is more elusive, not readily describing that it forms part of an existing home. The name, however, belies its hierarchy on the lot, dictating that it is subordinate to a principal home and therefore a lesser or compromised dwelling. By comparison, the houses of a bluefield develop-ment are more ambiguously definable, being a combination of original home, reconfigured home into separate dwellings under the one roof, attached homes, and backyard homes. And attempting to define each dwelling element is not a particularly fruitful exercise, as it undermines the fact that they each act together as a holistic housing proposition co-located on a lot and referred to collectively in this book as 'bluefield housing'. There is a logic to 'bluefield' extending the green-, brown-, and greyfield definitions as described in Chapter 5; it recognises that established suburbs must form part of the densification discussion while recognising ways in which they can support low-rise density in their own image. But 'bluefield housing' may be seen as too vague when used as a zoning defin-ition and 'co-located housing' may be more descriptive and deployable.

Regardless of what each jurisdiction labels the model, the simple act of establishing a new housing form will likely have corollary effects on existing forms, as in the process of creating a new housing definition we automatic-ally affect the standing definitions of all other housing forms. In other words, in defining what 'bluefield housing' is, we define what the established models are *not*. As an example, a backyard home located at the rear of a bluefield lot with a rear lane may resemble a 'laneway home' as already defined, but its relation-ship with the other dwellings on the site and the open space they share renders it somewhat different, even if the differences are subtle. In the same manner, the fact that a detached backyard home in a bluefield development behaves differently to an 'ADU' or 'laneway home' as already defined, will affect those existing definitions by default. Similarly, a dwelling created as an extension to an existing home may be constructed in the manner of a junior accessory dwelling unit (JADU), but its spatial relationships at a lot level define it as something else. Likewise, while the existing home may be reworked to achieve multiple dwellings under the one roof, such as with a secondary suite, this is unlikely to be a minor separation of one or two rooms and will be a more deliberate reworking of one house into two or more homes of similar size and function. And importantly, housing definitions will be affected by the fact that a bluefield development is a holistic reworking of the entire lot, has an overarching strategy around housing supply without hierarchy between dwellings, will offer degrees of cohousing sharing, and can be designed for individual ownership and tenure. Although a bluefield scheme may be a coalition of recognisable housing parts, each part will take on new meanings – and potentially statutory definitions – when viewed as a contributing fraction of the whole.

For these reasons, existing zoning laws that relate to established housing models may need to be tailored or rewritten specifically where bluefield housing is introduced. Depending on the existing provisions in place, some jurisdictions may find it best to first draft the policy around the model before writing its associated definition. What it will not be, however, is 'cohousing', or at least not as the cohousing model is commonly understood. 'Co-location' is a much clearer and direct way of highlighting that this model is always a shared allotment model but not always a shared facilities model, whereas 'cohousing' is usually both. In other words, the bluefield model sometimes borrows cohousing tactics to free space or create better social outcomes, but that is often where the similarities end. If some bluefield schemes utilise the co-location principles of cohousing to achieve socially connected and spatially improved outcomes, they do so as a form of cohousing 'lite', as discussed in Chapter 2 and observable in the case studies of Part 3.

Land Management Agreements

Beyond statutory definitions, one of the overarching mechanisms to protect the shared allotment ambitions of bluefield housing is to couple the zoning provisions with a Land Management Agreement (LMA) that stipulates how the lot is to be used. This is different to the day-to-day agency and autonomy provided to residents through their Committee and Resident's Agreement, as described in Chapter 15, and instead ties the developer to the agreed manner in which the lot will be developed when it is granted its initial zoning approval. An LMA can capture agreed conditions around landscape provision and preservation, and how the land may be used. Forming a binding agreement between the property owner and the relevant statutory authority (who may be the Minister for Planning, for example), an LMA gets added to the land title for the lot, thereby binding both current and future owners to the usage of the property as agreed and approved when it first transitions to a bluefield development.

When coupled with the protections of a Community Title to avoid surreptitious land division and undesirable uses, as discussed in Chapter 15, an LMA is a simple regulatory mechansim that statutory authorities can lean on as part of their zoning considerations. But as much as it can be used to tie the usage of the lot to the ambitions originally promised, an LMA can be flexible when it comes to future use, as the statutory body has the discretion to consider circumstances or needs that may have changed since the LMA was first put in place. Ultimately, however, a well-considered LMA is a management tool that can be used in concert with local zoning requirements.[1]

The zoning principles of bluefield housing

Many jurisdictions have shifted to residential zoning principles that provide clarity and surety of how lots can be developed, combined with timely approval processes that speed the redevelopment process. This streamlining relies on metric development measures that are in many instances a check-box system of deemed-to-satisfy (DTS) rules. The ability for such a fast approvals process to deliver desirable housing and neighbourhood outcomes will largely fall on the capacity of the applicant to deliver high quality outcomes within predefined zoning limits. However, a faster approvals system with clearly stated minimum requirements will go some way to limiting the worst of housing developments but it will not guarantee the quality of outcomes.

Often, zoning policies and approval decisions are based on a conditional approach; approval for new housing may be granted if certain conditions are met. Usually these are metric and relate to minimum requirements or maximum allowances for elements such as lot size, building size, site coverage, building height, number of storeys, dwelling numbers, boundary setbacks, and on-site car parking provisions. The bluefield model seeks to minimise the number of stated conditions to be met, on the basis that the prevailing neighbourhood conditions may support housing numbers beyond what metric measures might otherwise suggest. This stance is taken on the basis that quantitative stipulations are no more a guarantee of successful neighbourhood outcomes than a breaking of measurement rules are an assurance of failure.

Because the bluefield housing model is designed as a mirror of suburban houses with their varied alterations, additions, and backyard homes, many of the lot and building level zoning measures will be dictated by established local planning policies. But since the model seeks to configure housing on the lot in a way that is unlikely to have ever been intended, and to do so at densities that may be higher than its neighbours, a bluefield proposal will most likely be measured under a performance-assessed (PA) approval path. What follows is a summary of the key zoning issues considered for introduction of the bluefield housing model for the suburbs of Adelaide (where the model was developed) and where a policy response has been written to respond to these issues. Being a design-led and context responsive housing model, these policy triggers are generally performance-based relative to local conditions and can therefore be tailored in other jurisdictions. They are offered here as a roadmap to the types of zoning levers that can be used in writing bluefield housing policy.

Allotment size An allotment considered for co-location is of a suitable size for the proposed development, including for the proposed number of dwellings, any common facilities created, shared open space, and plantings.
No minimum allotment size is stipulated.

Land division The co-location of housing does not alter the prevailing pattern of allotments in the local area.

Co-location does not result in the creation of additional allotments.

Built form New co-located dwellings are located behind or within an existing dwelling in a manner which maintains the prevailing streetscape scale, pattern, and character.

New housing within the co-located development is to complement the prevailing neighbourhood character in its scale, height, design, and spacing.

Building footprints within the co-located development are designed and located to allow for communal open space and landscaping.

No maximum number of bedrooms is stipulated for co-located housing.

Building setbacks Co-located dwellings are positioned relative to each other and allotment boundaries to enable deep root soil zones for trees, reduced visual impact, and access to light and ventilation within and external to the development site.

The extent of boundary wall construction is consistent with limits already described for the Zone.

Building heights The maximum building height and rise in storeys is consistent with limits already described for the Zone.

Site coverage No maximum floor area is stipulated for co-located housing.

Total maximum site coverage is consistent with that already described for the Zone plus an additional 10%.

Open space Shared open space is provided with the development site and designed to enable social interaction.

Minimum dimensions, calculation methods, and provisions for open space are consistent with those already described for the Zone.

Privacy Appropriate overlooking within the development site is encouraged to support connections between living spaces and shared open space, social connectedness, and passive surveillance.

Bedrooms are located for privacy, with views to smaller and more private outdoor spaces.

Restrictions on overlooking into neighbouring properties are consistent with overlooking restrictions already described for the Zone.

Fencing between dwellings within the co-located development are not permitted.

Fencing between a co-located development and adjoining neighbours is consistent with fencing requirements already described in the Zone.

Car parking Zero car parking is allowed where resident needs can be demonstrated.

In all other cases, one car parking space is provided per dwelling unless a lower provision can be demonstrated.

Car parking can be consolidated or split and may be provided in an in-line formation.

Car parking is located such that it maintains the prevailing streetscape character and avoids the creation of additional driveway cross-overs.

Car parking and driveways are designed to minimise the extent of impervious hard ground surfaces.

Pedestrian access Resident access into and through the development site, and to and from car parking, is safe and minimises disruption to other residents.

Pedestrian paths are designed to minimise the extent of impervious hard ground surfaces.

Landscaping Co-located housing retains existing mature landscape, to enhance neighbourhood character and amenity, to help mitigate urban heat island effects, and to help maintain urban tree corridors.

Deep root soil zones are provided around existing mature landscape to maintain its health.

Where mature landscape cannot be retained or does not exist, deep root soil zones are provided and planted with small and/or medium and/or large trees as already described for the Zone.[2]

Landscaping incorporates water-sensitive urban design strategies and is designed to minimise hard and impermeable ground surfaces.

Design review: quality over quantity

This book has argued that the bluefield housing co-location model is first and foremost a nuanced design-led approach to suburban densification. In some cities it will be a minor variation on a housing intensification theme. In others it will directly challenge the existing pattern of single-family housing. But in all cases – due to its approach of redeveloping an entire lot rather than simply 'left over' backyard space – it will require the design proposition to be scrutinised on qualitative grounds rather than against purely quantitative zoning measures. The best mechanism for this is the system of Design Review, a formal pre-application review process that can be carried out at a state level for major projects, or at a municipal level for smaller applications such as a bluefield housing development. Consisting of independent design and planning experts, a Design Review Panel serves as an external voice that can help an applicant get the most out of their project while assisting the local authority in determining whether an application should be approved.

When discussing design, it can easily be forgotten that creating successful places, spaces, and buildings for people is difficult. If it was easy, we would have a handful of tried and tested solutions that require little oversight or debate. And while this is true of many aspects of a project, it rarely applies to the whole. There are usually competing issues which, when combined, make delivery of the built environment an extremely complex task. Design Review is, without doubt, an incredibly effective way of bringing expert opinions to a project as extra sets of eyes and ears. It allows people who have not previously been involved in the project to see things fresh and to ask important questions of a project team to determine why design decisions have been made the way they have, and which alternatives have been attempted. Set up as a collegial discussion amongst peers, Design Review allows the applicant time to come up for air, to remind themselves of the project's initial ambitions, to present their design thinking to a new audience, and to open the project to possibilities that may have been missed in the cut and thrust of getting the project to this point. This pause in proceedings for generous and intelligent discussion while change can still be affected is Design Review's strength.

Design Review can also act as a safety net. In the previous chapter it was discussed that anyone seeking to use a bluefield zoning approval to sneak in an unwanted subdivision would first have to design the scheme and have it approved as a true co-located model. This is where local Design Review can play a significant role: if a panel helps to get the scheme working well before it is approved, there will be less of an impetus to use the process as a back-door subdivision mechanism. Similarly, an applicant seeking to ultimately make the scheme function as a subdivision will have to design it to work that way before masking this intention in the application drawings and materials. To be successful, this will require the proposal to function as both a privatised *and* a co-located scheme, which should raise concerns during the Design Review process if design and operation issues are not successfully resolved. The likelihood, however, is that a rigorous review process will help deliver the intended bluefield outcomes despite the subversive ambitions of unscrupulous applicants.

Ultimately, a good design review process is generative. It sends the project team away with tangible and meaningful ways in which the proposal can be improved. It also helps establish benchmarks of excellence that can be used in subsequent panel sessions on other projects. Importantly, Design Review is undertaken by people with no vested interest in the project other than to make it the best possible outcome for its users and for the many more who will only ever experience the project externally as an addition to the evolving city or neighbourhood. And a bluefield co-location development is not too small to bother running through a Design Review process; for as our suburbs and neighbourhoods come under increasing pressure to meet the very real demands of our pressing demographic needs, having a local design review system that understands the nuances of a place is beyond timely – it is indispensable.[3]

Coda

Beyond the issues and metrics of housing need, demographic shifts, changing household structure, and current housing responses and targets, this book has been concerned with providing an alternative mechanism with which to understand infill in established suburbs, particularly those with NIMBY resistance. Its ambition has been to offer design studies of a greater variety of housing than many suburbs currently afford us, coupled with approaches to landscape that leverage off the mass and scale of vegetation that is so often at risk during redevelopment, despite the significant amenity it provides. Furthermore, this book has attempted to articulate a way of seeing and describing some of Australia's established housing using methods that the reader may deploy in neighbourhoods and cities that present with similar-enough conditions that the methods might be replicated.

The forms of infill development presented by the detailed design schemes of Part 3 sit comfortably within the broader development patterns of their suburban contexts. Together they suggest that a new form of co-located living in the established suburbs can co-exist with the predominant large single-family homes that define these neighbourhoods. And whilst a test of the realisation of such new forms of development can be found in the types of financial models required to fund them and the statutory changes necessary to permit them, perhaps a bigger and more immediate challenge lies in current preconceptions of suburban housing intensification and the ability for residents of low-density low-rise neighbourhoods to adapt to the types of behavioural concessions required of a new form of medium density suburban living.

But the built aspects of our neighbourhoods, at least, are up to the challenge and ripe for experimentation. Bluefield Housing concludes with Part 5, which offers design exercises that can help unlock our understanding of suburban housing and enable us to see how malleable our neighbourhoods can be.

Notes

1   The specifics of Land Management Agreements will vary by jurisdiction and the information provided here is correct for the South Australian context for which the bluefield model was developed. See, for example, https://plan.sa.gov.au/resources/planning/land_management_agreements, accessed 26 October 2022.
2   For Adelaide, the Urban Tree Canopy Overlay in the Planning and Design Code defines a small tree as 4m high with a 2m wide canopy and in a minimum $10m^2$ soil zone (13' x 6'5" in 108 sq ft), a medium tree as 6m x 4m in $30m^2$ (20' x 13' in 323 sq ft), and a large tree as 12m x 8m in $60m^2$ (39' x 26' in 646 sq ft): Green Adelaide, *Adelaide Garden Guide for New Homes* (Adelaide: Government of South Australia, 2022), https://plan.sa.gov.au/news/article/2022/adelaide_garden_guide.
3   For further information on the role of Design Review Panels, visit www.odasa.sa.gov.au/design-review/ or www.designcouncil.org.uk/our-work/skills-learning/resources/design-review-principles-and-practice/.

Part 5

17 The value of the diagram and studies in rooms

Communicating new dwelling forms

The challenge faced by new housing models (and indeed, by books such as this) is that the arguments for the model must often be made in the absence of having a built result to use as a tangible case study. This places enormous emphasis on the nature and quality of a proposal's visual collateral, which must convey the design thinking that underpins the work while communicating to a broad audience in different scenarios. And this material also must work against the negative preconceptions people may have over density increases and the types of environments they create.

Visual literacy is relative, as are disciplinary approaches to how drawings are created and used, and architects use drawings and diagrams for different reasons at different times. The figures in this book collectively represent the types of visual strategies used to develop and explain bluefield housing to a variety of stakeholders. In some instances, such as those presented here in Part 5, they are inward-facing design exercises that help unlock a deeper or at least different way of understanding the current conditions of a place before design solutions can be explored. These are accompanied by mapping and photographic exercises that help contextualise the housing issues before a design intervention is proposed. In later stages of project communication, the visual material becomes more recognisable as architectural drawings and designs, presented in measurable and comparable scales. Together they

DOI: 10.4324/9781003293736-23
This chapter has been made available under a CC-BY-NC-ND license.

focus attention on select issues, deploying the best representation technique for the task at hand.

Aerial photographs Aerial photographs allow a muted observation of neighbourhood conditions and can be used on face value to present a broad built context without comment. However, they also allow elements of a place to be temporarily hidden or highlighted to draw attention to key issues in a simple and powerful way, as shown in Figure 17.1.

17.1
An aerial photograph with a simple overlay that powerfully highlights the extent of change naturally occurring in a neighbourhood quarantined from strategic infill and densification.

Source: Base GeoTIFF image courtesy of the City of Burnside.

Figure and ground Figure and ground diagrams are a simple mapping of conditions that exclude detailed building or occupation information. They can be traced from aerial photographs and are particularly useful for showing the mass of elements relative to neighbours, and new conditions relative to old. They can be self-explanatory when used as a comparative tool.

Site plans Site plans convey the spatial relationships of built and landscape elements as they relate to the proportions of the lot. They can be drawn in isolation or extended to show neighbouring lots. In a bluefield housing proposal they are used comparatively to explain the existing site coverage and tree canopy conditions of the local environment and the how the bluefield intervention slots into and enhances this.

Floor plans Floor plans are an assemblage of rooms, each of which can be considered mini buildings with their own functions and requirements. Together, they form a coherent building plan that tests and demonstrates the programmatic strategy and function of the building. Furnished plans are those that present human occupation through fixed and loose furniture and by the inclusion of people. As such they can demonstrate function or dysfunction.

Landscape plans Landscape plans can be considered in the same manner as rooms, with dedicated spaces of different sizes and uses. In a bluefield proposal they are crucial for demonstrating the maintenance or enhancement of tree canopies at the neighbourhood level and local amenity at the scale of the lot. The key to incorporating rubbish bins, clothes drying, and sheds in a scheme lies in treating the landscaped site plan like a furnished room of the house: there needs to be a space for everything, and this space must be designed.

Isometrics Isometric drawings are 3D models projected at 30° angles and without any perspective. They therefore present a consistent 3D scale and allow direct comparison with other isometrics drawn at the same scale. Presenting a building's form and mass as it relates to its footprint and height, they convey just enough realism to present the overall conceptual logic and clarity of a design.

Elevations Elevations are flattened views of the sides of the building. They are useful for demonstrating its height relative to another but can offer an unrealistic representation of the constructed building, unless it can be viewed from a distance and angle that replicates the drawing. Isometrics have been used in this book to give a more accurate representation of the buildings' facades, heights, and massing.

Sections Sections similarly offer the chance to compare building heights while exploring and expressing the internal volumes of the building.

Mapping Mapping is a means of visually representing numerical data, such as the VAMPIRE scores illustrated in Figure 5.2 in Chapter 5, but maps can also be more abstract ways of drawing neighbourhood and building conditions. Examples are shown in the abstraction exercises.

Visualisations Visualisations come in various forms, but renderings that accurately describe the look and feel of a design proposal are particularly useful for communicating to a broad audience that may have difficulty interpreting other forms of representation. While aerial views can be useful and engaging, rendered perspectives taken from ground level and without distorting the field of view provide a more honest and useful representation of the proposal.

Bluefield housing design exercises

Being able to draw a home, and even having the experience of living in one, does not necessarily equip someone with the natural ability to design spaces for people. And designing spaces of dwelling can take years of experience and learning from each project along the way. This is regularly evident in architecture schools where even students in their advanced years of study can struggle to design dwellings that function as they should or provide anything more than basic accommodation. It is not uncommon to see housing designed by students (and indeed some practitioners) in the absence of their lived experience: bedrooms that house a bed and nothing more; kitchens that provide nowhere to prepare food; living spaces with a single sofa facing off against a wall at four feet; convoluted corridors that consume valuable space while performing only as corridors. When learning how to design housing in the first instance, or reflecting on our current approach to designing housing, there needs to be a way of starting or renewing the design conversation, and the following two exercises are a means of doing that. This 'back to basics' approach can be particularly useful when designing for maximum amenity within a small footprint home.

Aimed at unlocking deeper thinking around small housing, the exercises of Part 5 are not written for a particular discipline. Although some may, on face value, seem more architectural while others appear more oriented towards urban or suburban planning, they are offered as a collection of tasks that are generative of housing possibilities. Although not designed exclusively for teaching, each has been devised as a self-contained exercise that academics can set as a task or assignment as written, however, they can alternatively serve as the basis of expanded exercises. Some exercises or tasks may be set in stages (weekly, for example), and used to compile a set of iterative and cumulative design observations to be deployed. Individually and collectively, the exercises are written to help build a housing design skillset and to generate experimentation and discussion around suburban housing. And just as the exercises are not written for a particular discipline, neither are they aimed at a defined level of experience; some will present as very basic while others are more challenging. Some may at first seem *overly* simple but that is because they are written to take the designer back to first principles and to challenge their preconceptions.

Bluefield exercise 1: Stuff

Purpose of the exercise: To better understand the 'stuff' of dwelling, and its spatialisation, activity by activity, through focused studies in plan.

In *How Buildings Learn*, Stewart Brand (expanding on the work of architect Frank Duffy) described a building's six 'shearing layers': the components of a building related to permanence or impermanence, and the building's capacity for change over time: site, structure, skin, services, space plan, and stuff.[1] The most malleable of these, 'stuff', describes the loose items of everyday life which together help establish the function and utility of the space plan. These are the items necessary for living that make dwelling possible, coupled with those that make it more enjoyable.

The value of the diagram and studies in rooms

The purpose of this Stuff exercise is to marry the loose items that may occupy a room with the space required to accommodate them, their use, and the amenity they bring to the occupant. It also incorporates the fixed elements of Brand's space plan layer that give a room or zone a dedicated function. Although a simple exercise on face value, it is a structured and disciplined bottom-up way of better understanding how some aspects of spatial design are set while others are less predictable. At the end of each task, the result will be a deliberately simple rectalinear layout consisting of blocked-out zones of activity and utility, as seen by the example of Figure 17.2. In undertaking the exercise, the individual will draw upon their own experience and intelligence, observing from the world around them and from case studies that they draw on as precedents. Rather than being a completed room with walls, windows, and doors, each resulting diagram will be a strategically simplified map of scaled space that deliberately excludes views, light, or connectivity to other internal and external spaces. Together, each mapped task will present a simple catalogue of spatial allowances and relationships that together make up the primary components of a home. And being a bottom-up exercise, the individual can bring their own culture of living to the task. If undertaken in a group setting, it can be expected that the mappings will be quite varied to each other in scale, operation, and the number of imagined users.

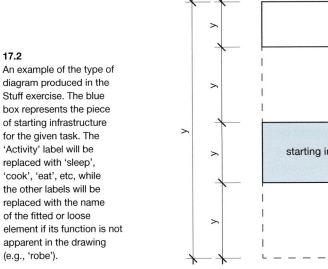

17.2
An example of the type of diagram produced in the Stuff exercise. The blue box represents the piece of starting infrastructure for the given task. The 'Activity' label will be replaced with 'sleep', 'cook', 'eat', etc, while the other labels will be replaced with the name of the fitted or loose element if its function is not apparent in the drawing (e.g., 'robe').

The value of the diagram and studies in rooms

Task 1: space maps

1. **Infrastructure**: in plan at a scale of 1:50, draw a starting piece of furniture or infrastructure as described below for each stated activity: a bed for sleeping; a stove for cooking; a table for eating. Size this starting piece by measuring existing items you know or by using manufacturers' stated dimensions. If undertaken as a student activity, typical dimensions and standards can be a facilitated in-class discussion. Activities can be mapped generically (e.g., a table for six) or specifically (e.g., a table for three generations of my extended family).

2. **Circulation**: using dashed lines, draw the associated circulation or access zones required around this starting piece. This zone(s) can be determined intuitively, by measuring an existing space with which you are familiar, in reference to a document such as the Livable Housing Australia dimensions diagrammed in Chapter 8, or in reference to precedent projects. Some elements will require access on all sides. Consider functionality and amenity: how does a bed get made? how do people sit on a sofa when watching television versus having a conversation? Note that it may be possible for these circulation zones to also be used for the additional functions/items that are to be added next.

3. **Fixtures**: draw any fixed furniture, fittings, and appliances associated with the space plan of the activity, along with any additional circulation and access zones that these may require.

4. **Loose furniture**: draw any additional loose furniture that may be associated with the activity and locate this outside the circulation zones. For examples, refer to the discussion and diagramming of slack space for memories and objects in Chapter 8.

5. **Loose items**: draw space or surfaces for any loose items often associated or at least co-located with the activity. In some instances the space for these items will double with spaces for other things. Examples include a clock, phone, charger, lamp, books, water glass, coffee cup, picture frame, medication, computer, etc. Keep in mind that we all have daily accessories around our dwellings and that these often differ from person to person. Not every loose item can be considered or known, but space for some items can and should be made.

6. **Dimensions**: once the diagram is complete, dimension the starting infrastructure element(s), the space for fixtures and loose furniture, and circulation zones. Dimension on at least two sides of the drawing such that each zone is captured, along with the overall width and length of the space (refer to the example of Figure 17.2).

7. **Label**: label the diagram with the activity (e.g.: sleep, cook, eat, etc). Each diagram should look consistent to enable easy comparison.

Activities to be mapped:

Enter: draw an entry door and the space required outside and in to accommodate movement. Consider coming or going in the rain, with another person, with a child, with a dog, with shopping, etc, and the space required to facilitate this 'stuff'.

Rise: draw a stair and the space required around it at the base, at the landing, and at the side.

Sleep: although temporary beds can be common and help make a space flexible (consider futons that roll or a Murphy bed that folds out from a wall), this exercise is about understanding a dedicated space for sleeping, so assume that the bed is the starting piece of infrastructure and is permanently set up.

Eat: draw a dining table with chairs (or a culturally appropriate alternative), the space around this, and any additional related furniture items.

Cook: begin with a single piece of kitchen infrastructure such as a sink or cooktop, and build out from this.

Live: assuming that at least two people can occupy the space without sitting next to each other, accommodate at least two pieces of furniture for sitting, such as two sofas or one sofa plus a chair. Consider that seating can also be achieved with built-in furniture.

Bathe: begin with a single piece of bathroom infrastructure such as a basin, toilet, or shower, and build out from this.

Wash: begin with a single piece of laundry infrastructure such as a sink or washing machine and build out from this; consider storage space for cleaning products, a broom, a vacuum cleaner, etc.

Do: map a second activity of your choosing. It may be for working, studying, teaching, playing, listening, hobbying, gaming, sitting, making, exercising, etc.

Task 1 extension exercise: this mapping may be undertaken a second time incorporating the local jurisdiction's mandated circulation zones for access and mobility.

Task 2: dual spaces

Incorporate the 'do' activity with one of the other spaces to create a dual function in one room: which functions naturally work well together and which require some compromise?

Task 2 extension exercise: undertake further dual mappings. Some may be obvious such as cook/eat, thereby testing spatial requirements and well-understood functionality. Others may be less normative, providing the opportunity to explore less common but potentially generative dwelling solutions.

Task 3: catalogue

Collate the 1:50 maps as a catalogue of activities. Arrange them on a single page, where room allows, equally spaced in a simple matrix. The aim is to be able to read each map individually and collectively. Together, these maps will act not as a house, but as the key components for dwelling. In some instances they may form templates exploring economic or generous spatial allowances, but they may equally be simple conversation starters for further design exploration.

'Stuff' extension task: enclosure

A fourth task is to undertake a second mapping that translates each diagrammed space to a room. For each map, add walls for enclosure and openings for access and view. Arrange these rooms into a matching matrix for direct comparison with the original maps.

Geometry extension exercise: Consider reshaping a selection of rooms to create a non-rectilinear plan form, either by skewing at least one wall or curving it. What level of geometric shifting can be undertaken without disrupting the necessary spatial allowances and programmatic function, and to what spatial or occupational benefit?

Bluefield exercise 2: Porous Rooms

Purpose of the exercise: To test the variety of uses afforded by a single room through concentrated studies, and in the temporary absence of whole-of-house programmatic complications.

Where the Stuff exercise considers the spaces of dwelling through growth – starting with a base element and building around it to determine the spatial requirements for a particular activity – Porous Rooms uses the opposite approach, taking an existing room and testing how various activities may be fitted to it. Considered another way, Stuff creates space; Porous Rooms reuses it.

Predicating the bluefield housing model on the retention and reworking of an existing neighbourhood house means that any attempt to reconfigure the design thinking around that base house risks being limited by its plan form. This is particularly the case when established neighbourhood housing consists of repeated or even similar typologies. Whether in the highly identifiable symmetrical layouts of the Australian cottages, as diagrammed in Chapter 4 and used in the Part 3 design studies, or in some other recognisable plan arrangement such as the various forms of bungalow seen in the US, Canada, and the UK, any highly identifiable assemblage of rooms about hallways resists being read as anything other than a pre-defined single entity.

However, if each part of the plan can be considered as an isolated cell and temporarily denied its relationships to other cells, rooms can be seen for their accommodative potential purely from a spatial planning perspective. In this simplified form, rooms become an abstracted sub-set of the house, liberated of the overlays of character that can inhibit investigation before it has fully begun. 'Character', then, is limited to the nuances of a room's door and window locations and any idiosyncratic elements that impact the space, such as a hearth. Character then becomes discoverable in activity rather than through architectural form or decorative appliqué. Thought of as a collection of discrete cellular rooms, the older house becomes a system formed of generative parts.

The Porous Rooms abstraction study takes this premise as its starting point and explores the types of activities one room can support, and the spatial amenity afforded each activity. In this manner, one room might be a place to live, sleep, cook, eat, bathe, work, or meet, and these activities might be studied solely in relation to their sense of fit in the room rather than to the logic of how they are arranged in the original dwelling or where they are located on a site (Figure 17.3).

Such isolation studies are not complex, but they do not have to be. Their purpose is to allow an exploration of potential usage patterns without the encumbrance of having to determine if an assemblage of the parts can constitute a coherent whole. To this end, a half-room can be tested simply for its accommodation value, divorced from any common-sense decisions of *why* such a function might be massaged into a half-space in the first instance.

The benefit of this reductive process is perhaps best be seen when a hallway is treated as a single entity. Viewed as a contained space of its own, and using a cottage as an example, it becomes clear that in a housing typology where corridors act as a spine that feeds rooms, a hallway can only be used as a connective and minor storage space to be moved through – an artefact of its narrow width coupled with multiple doors opening onto it. However, when a hallway is merged with an adjacent space, even when that space is a half-room, it has the potential to add amenity, a more generous use of space, or a more sophisticated circulation pattern.

Further agglomeration of rooms and part-rooms begins to create more identifiable small dwellings or gathering spaces. The combination of one room and two half rooms, for example, can generate a small studio apartment or a work environment, whilst the simple act of further adding a hallway to this configuration provides added amenity through improved privacy, increased space, or additional storage. Perhaps the most useful outcome of such an additive exercise is the way small spaces might be assembled to form self-contained entities with their own logic without being reliant on the building whole. This allows new or reconfigured uses to be conceived in a focussed manner from one single space up, rather than resulting from a wholesale alteration of the entire house, as per normative adaptive reuse exercises. This partial-development thinking offers the opportunity to systematically redevelop parts of the whole, potentially generating templated designs or standard plans.

The value of the diagram and studies in rooms

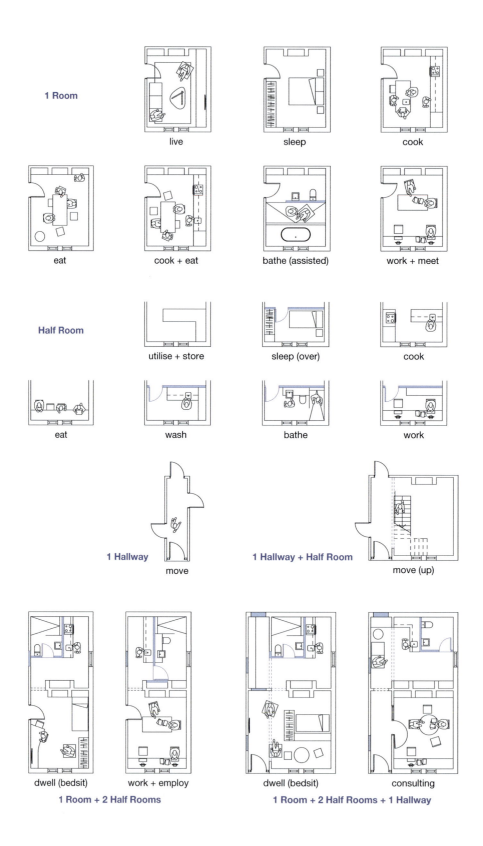

The value of the diagram and studies in rooms

17.3
Room studies: single rooms, half rooms, and hallways.

Central to the study of spatial relationships in this exercise is the ability to incorporate common building technology that is rooted in the pragmatic and evidenced in the ordinariness of building standards. Porous Rooms offers a matrix of spatial possibilities that become apparent when one room is opened to another. Such an opening-up exercise relies on portions of walls being removed to form large connective openings between rooms, with the overhead wall material supported by steel or timber lintels sized using common construction rules-of-thumb. In Australia, the technical standard for masonry design describes the widths of openings that can be efficiently formed in brick walls when using readily available proprietary steel lintels. These are the established measures builders use in routine domestic alterations without the potential time and cost impediments of designing a tailored structural solution. Whilst structural requirements vary depending on the amount of overhead building material being supported, even large openings of up to 4.2m or 13' wide can be achieved using standard lintel sizings.[2] Such larger openings take the form not of an aperture in a wall, but of almost total material removal, wherein one room is absorbed into the next. Standards for structural beams also stipulate the extent of wall or bearing material required on each side of an opening to support a lintel, typically ranging from 100–150mm (4–6"). This is simple building technology, where elements of wall must be retained to provide a seat on which to sit the lintel (Figure 17.4).

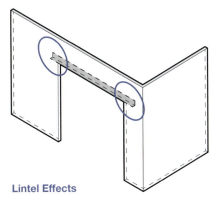

Lintel Effects

17.4
Lintel effects: the pragmatic and statutory requirement for remnant wall material to provide a bearing, as located in blue, gives rise to particular corner conditions in affected rooms.

However, these minimum bearing requirements have an unintended spatial significance, as they give rise to idiosyncratic plan forms: individual rooms with expressed corners of at least 100mm or 4" in length. And whilst it can be attractive in construction projects to deliberately work to the extents of legislation and provide the minimum statutory compliance possible to maximise space, providing supportive wall nibs greater than those stipulated by the relevant standard allows for tactical spatial manoeuvres to be made. Expressed corners of at least 600mm or 2', for example, provide niches for joinery: kitchen units, desks, wardrobes, and cupboards; elements that add convenience and utility or fix the use of a space without interfering with the spatial gains acquired by the process of opening one room to another.

A further by-product of this retained wall material is that it allows the architectural character of the original house, both physically and occupationally, to remain at least partially legible. This retention of character is perhaps most evident at ceiling level, where the introduction of a lintelled opening with remnant wall material above allows for the original ceilings to remain intact. This has clear construction cost benefits, as avoiding the need to replace the ceilings not only removes the material and labour costs associated with such work but also avoids the need to rectify ceiling height differentials which are often found from room to room in old houses. But beyond these practical construction savings measures is the less tangible benefit of retained cultural memory, witnessed in the individual's ability to read one original room as different from another, even if the current altered space blurs new uses across the two. As such, whilst new patterns of use might exist where others previously existed, it remains possible to identify elements of the original physical and human character of a place. As a result, the original character of a room plays a formative and legible role in establishing the character of the evolving new use.

Through this coupling of physical construction technology with the less tangle notions of character, Porous Rooms abstracts the house from its most intact to most degraded forms (Figure 17.5). The exercise progressively opens each room one wall at a time before combining all wall opening possibilities to reveal an almost completely porous space in plan. This creates a matrix of cells ranging from intact rooms through to semi-porous and fully porous spaces, as shown in Figure 17.6. Once established, these spaces can then be combined with the bottom-up room studies to test their ability to accommodate the utilities of storage, kitchens, bathrooms, and stairs. And whilst this exercise is useful for showing the basic fit of certain occupational elements, it is the exercise of temporarily ignoring all other building and siting context that is of most interest. Shown here as an example of the cottage form commonly found in Australian cities, the reader can apply the same strategy to other neighbourhood housing typologies. It is an exercise in careful isolation that is further tested in Chapter 18 with The Block Apartment.

17.5
An Australian cottage shown in its most intact form (left) and most degraded form after the incorporation of lintels (right).

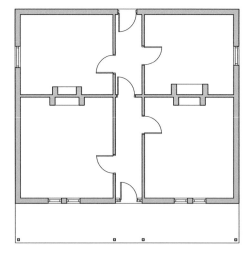
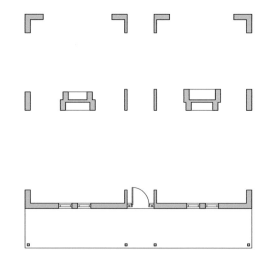

The value of the diagram and studies in rooms

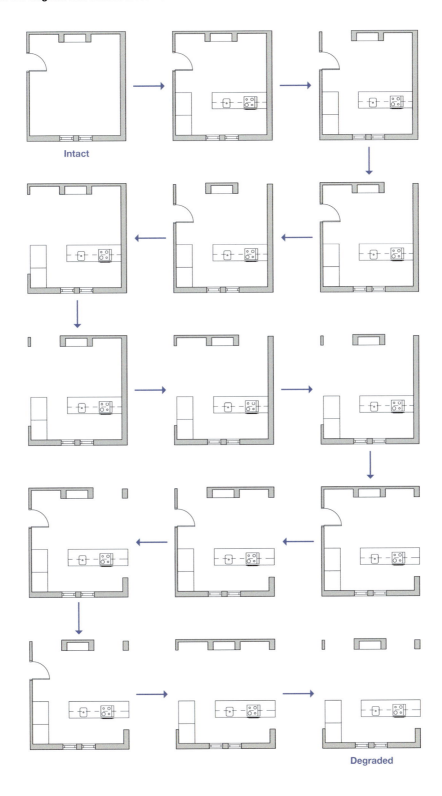

17.6
A matrix of room porosity,
demonstrated with a kitchen.

Notes

1 Stewart Brand, *How Buildings Learn: What Happens After They're Built*. New York: Penguin Books, 1995.
2 *AS 4337.1:2015 Masonry in Small Buildings – Part 1: Design,* AS 4337.1:2015, (Sydney: Standards Australia, 2015), 70.

18 Backgrounding design studies

A 'designerly' way of seeing

Seeing the familiar with new eyes

When considering how best to introduce denser forms of housing into an established neighbourhood, we can easily default to the prevailing aesthetics and housing patterns: what style are the neighbourhood houses? when were they built? how were they constructed? what are the predominant materials? and how does this new housing 'fit' with the old? These are important visual and constructional questions to engage with when considering context, but they are not the first questions that should be asked when developing new forms of infill housing that seek to spatialise the place differently. This is particularly the case if the new housing is to be considered part of a deployable system, and not merely an idiosyncratic one-off project. If zoning laws are to be written for a neighbourhood infill system such as bluefield housing, as discussed in Chapter 16, then that infill model must be demonstrably repeatable across a variety of lot scales, as demonstrated by the design studies of Part 3. This is made easier if the prevailing neighbourhood pattern can itself be understood and defined as a system. This requires temporarily switching off aesthetic conditions to better understand the suburban structure, and the ease or difficulty of this process will vary depending on how idiosyncratic or repeated the base housing is. But in all cases a systemic response requires a means of understanding the place and its housing in an identifiable base form. If the infill housing proponent is to move beyond individual bespoke

269

DOI: 10.4324/9781003293736-24
This chapter has been made available under a CC-BY-NC-ND license.

solutions and towards a scalable housing model across a neighbourhood, they must find a way to move past aesthetics to describe the generative capacity of that neighbourhood. This requires a process of abstraction and the type of design cognition that Nigel Cross has described as 'designerly' ways of knowing and thinking.[1]

In the context of bluefield housing, 'abstraction' can be defined as a design exercise that elucidates the existing context to generate new outcomes. It is a design-led activity that attempts to move beyond the idiosyncrasies of an initial study area to describe in more universal terms the underlying spatial structure at play. It is a distillation of what exists to temporarily remove the layers of fine grain and understand the foundations of a neighbourhood. The abstraction process demonstrated here takes highly specific suburban data from one neighbourhood block and distils these to a set of traits that are borne of the local area but are diagrammed to be broadly applicable elsewhere. It is not important to describe in detailed terms the actual location of the target study area (which is representative of many inner suburban neighbourhoods in Australia), nor its particular material characteristics, as its sole purpose is to provide raw physical data for analysis and dissemination. Retaining its anonymity, the character of the study area can be restricted to a discussion around abstracted and simplified spatial patterns that might support more diverse physical and social structures.

What follows are two explorations in abstraction that together – with the other five exercises – provide the freedom to reimagine suburban futures without the encumbrances that established neighbourhoods and current housing typologies present. There is an inherent risk in any attempt to make the complex simple that the desired clarified form presents as *too* naïve and therefore of little meaningful use. The potential reward, however, is that the process of distillation enables a more coherent way of seeing the familiar with new eyes. This gives rise to the question of audience and, specifically, for whom the abstraction studies of this chapter have been designed. In the first instance, the work is personal and investigative; a way to defamiliarise the well-acquainted and move beyond professional tropes that have been simultaneously established and corralled by the statutory, preservationist, constructional, financial, and programmatic requirements of suburban experience. As such, other housing practitioners may find utility in the exercises and discover clues for how they might establish a project methodology for their own design tasks at hand, whether or not those projects resemble housing studies for the established neighbourhoods of suburbanised cities. At its core, the audience for the exercises is anyone who might find it useful to reconsider the established suburbs through alternative modes of graphic, (sub)urban and architectural exploration, and might benefit from the discussions that such images invite: policy makers, urban planners, architects, students, or even building owners and occupiers.

Bluefield exercise 3: Grid Block

Purpose of the exercise: To use a method of abstraction to temporarily 'switch off' the ownership boundaries of lots and the physical nuances of houses to discover the underlying structure of a neighbourhood block.

Where the Porous Rooms exercise of Chapter 17 seeks to isolate the room from the house, Grid Block works to decouple the intricacies of individual houses from their settlement pattern across the neighbourhood block, where 'block' is a collection of single lots bounded by streets. This disassociation occurs by overlaying the nuanced suburban morphology with two-dimensional graphic explorations such as those described by Carsten Nicolai's Grid Index.[2] Nicolai's index operates as a 'visual dictionary' of the relational opportunities afforded the designer when working with multiple grids, and it serves two stated purposes. First, in identifying and overlaying contrasting grids of different sizes, Nicolai establishes graphic patterns that subdivide a surface across a range of complexity. In its simplest form, an orthogonal grid is generated by the overlay of horizontal and vertical grid lines of the same dimension (for example, 10mm) to form a uniform chequered pattern. Such a 10mm grid can then be made more complex with the overlay of an additional ½" grid to create an irregular two-dimensional field formed of the fact that one measure is not equally divisible by the other. Extended further, irregular tiling patterns arranged symmetrically might form increasingly complex patterns that grow in unexpected ways.

Beyond this patternmaking, Nicolai's second intent with *Grid Index* is to identify a graphic process of organisational arrangement that can be a useful development tool for other designers both within the discipline of graphic design and beyond. How others might use this graphic thinking is never described, and the book's utility is therefore left to the reader's interpretation. This ability to apply a two-dimensional graphic overlay of grids to an established suburban context is the starting point for the Grid Block design exercise and results in the classification of suburban block patterns that are described here as either 'known grids', 'partially known grids', and 'unknown but understandable grids'. The reader can similarly apply this grid thinking to local conditions.

The purpose of drawing an established suburban block as Nicolai might diagram an abstract graphic grid, is to defamiliarise the well-known; to find new ways of analysing and communicating its underlying structure to generate new ways of working with suburban fabric that might otherwise not be discovered. In housing terms, its ambition is to see what might be possible when traditional ownership boundaries between existing properties are denied – it is a matter of exploring through abstract analytical diagramming without a predisposed sense of what results, if any, might be found. The simple act of drawing suburban context differently to the way one ordinarily might, offers the potential to temporarily limit neighbourhood context and character to a simpler discussion of adjacencies, with all other issues of aesthetic, spatial, and occupational context removed. This is in opposition to a more normative urban diagramming process where the orders of street, footpath, allotment boundary, and building footprint are deliberately made evident and hierarchical.

As a strategy for opening thinking by overlaying one element on another, the Grid Block exercise begins by establishing the neighbourhood's known grids: streets and lanes (Figure 18.1 and Figure 18.2). Drawing all roadways neutrally, that is, with the same pen weight and with the same unbroken line type, denies the hierarchy normally observed when differentiating roads, streets, and lanes from each other based on their individual widths, capacities to carry traffic, and their abilities to create separation between lots. Creating a deliberate absence of footpaths, kerbs, or other street data aids this neutralising effect.

18.1
Known grid: streets.

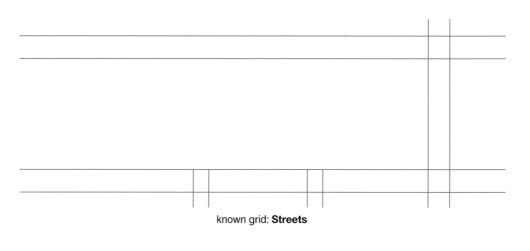

18.2
Known grid: lanes.

The individual properties within this street grid offer the final known grid system, being the setbacks of the existing houses from the street, and the houses' depths (Figure 18.3). This assumes a neighbourhood uniformity of both the setbacks and the house sizes. Where this is the case, as often occurs in older housing

18.3
Known grid: house setbacks and depths.

of repeated styles, one can establish an accurate grid system representing the alignment of the front and rear walls of the original houses, confident that this measure will represent a datum within an acceptable design tolerance of around ±1m or 3'3". Whilst such assumptions may be a limiting factor for detailed design exercises for an individual house on a single allotment, they provide a medium-scale datum that is consistent-*enough* for the sake of design experimentation across a broader territorial field. Once determined, this tertiary grid system, overlaid on that of the streets and lanes, represents the critical mass of housing across the neighbourhood block while working to substantially blur the traditional ownership boundaries of individual allotments. Furthering this abstraction is the deliberate avoidance of a grid system for lot lines between properties. Doing so would be counter-intuitive to the intentions of the exercise, in that it would undermine the goal of reading the block as a potentially continuous rather than contiguous ground plane that can be studied as a single system comprised of individual housing parts.

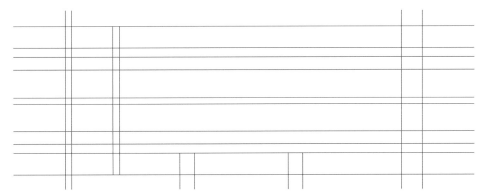

known grid: **House Setbacks and Depths**

Having established the most quantifiable grid systems of the neighbourhood block, the widths of the houses can be drawn (Figure 18.4). These are defined and represented by simply drawing the locations of the outer side walls, which can be measured using geomatic data drawn from applications such as Google Earth. Once established, these external side walls of individual houses are overlaid as dashed lines to represent their 'partially known' grid status, described as such since they can be quantified accurately but often differ from lot to lot. They operate as a grid system that is definable across the overall block but is not necessarily a constant. Significantly, when drawn in this manner, the overlay of house widths represents the spaces between the houses as equally as it does the houses themselves, while ignoring boundary lines denies them their usual hierarchical status. This deliberate subjugation of ownership divisions enables an alternative reading of the physical base conditions and is an important tactic for the types of multi-lot design studies detailed in Chapters 11 and 12. Indeed, the three two-lot studies were undertaken having first used the Grid Block exercise to reveal the infill opportunities between houses.

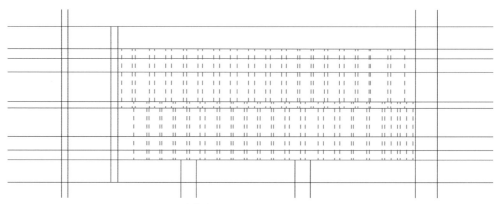

partially known grid: **House Widths**

18.4
Partially known grid: house widths.

Such abstract patterning provides the ability to see walls not as delineators of the individual territories they currently represent, but as elements that belong to a much larger field spreading across neighbouring lots to form a suburban block. Read together as a kit of parts, one might turn layers of dashed lines on or off to achieve not a total erasure of extant wall material, but a blurring of property ownership lines across multiple houses and lots. This establishes a new way of identifying property extents and limits in the drawing method, whereby the gaps between existing houses become as hierarchically significant (or indeed, insignificant) as the internal spaces of the homes themselves. As such, a gap between two buildings might be left as a gap or fashioned into a room in an experimental process akin to the isolated Porous Room studies, where suburban possibilities can be explored spatially without being tethered to traditional ownership boundaries or normative adaptive-reuse practice.

Mapped in this manner, built and unbuilt elements are rendered equivalent, and space is conceptualised and defined in an alternative way to traditional representation methods. Devoid of architectural or occupational information, one is presented with gridlines on which to snap various layers of program, landscape, form, and material. As with Porous Rooms, this allows design investigations that have the singular ambition of testing the logic of fit whilst minimising the limitations that customary aesthetic or programmatic biases can present. Perhaps most significantly, the linear construct of the drawing means that either existing or new allotment titling can be reinstated without degrading the conceptual system that has been established. This is important if one assumes that the abstract drawing is to eventually return from an experimental realm to more normative architectural and suburban design results. Thought of in this way, certain existing walls sitting variously on the dashed grid might become party walls between occupancies based on an appropriate fit for an intended new outcome. As a physical strategy, the diagram ignores the existing property titles whilst simultaneously enabling their return, if desired. The drawing is in equal measures subversive yet stabilising.

Whilst the Grid Block exercise strategically reduces suburban elements into an abstracted lattice of raw site and building elements, it does not otherwise assume a tabula rasa as the drawing might mistakenly suggest. It has been argued in Chapter 1 that much of the character of an established suburb rests with its mature landscape and as such, this must be accommodated in the grid as a subset of the overall system. Whilst in an overall sense the arrangement of mature trees and bushes across an entire block will be randomised, they can be seen to follow a grid pattern described as 'unknown but understandable': unknown since a single allotment may have no mature landscape or a lot, but ultimately understandable at a block scale as mature landscape elements generally fill the voids between buildings. Again, using geomatic data, existing mature trees and bushes can be plotted using the centre of their canopies, and where relationships can be drawn based on alignments or adjacencies between elements, these can be given a grid line that is dashed to represent the fact they are only somewhat knowable (Figure 18.5). As is the case with the locations of the external house walls, it is important to reiterate that the dashed lines of the diagram are indicators only of *predictability* (or lack thereof) within the grid system, and not of *significance*. Having identified trees as an integral part of the system, they act spatially to suggest moments across the diagram where relationships might be established between built and unbuilt space.

With the diagram complete, it can be compared to the suburban block that informed it and the two read as a complementary pair (Figure 18.6). Where the actual block can prove difficult to reconsider en masse as the individual nuances of each house and each lot take hold, in abstracted diagrammatic grid form it becomes more supple as the relationships between key components become less congested and more elemental. What the diagram suggests is a mechanism by which current and future assemblage processes might operate, and whilst

18.5
Unknown but understandable grid: trees.

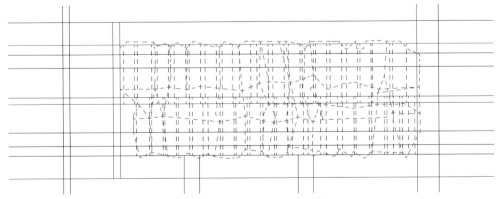

unknown but understandable grid: **Trees**

18.6
An aerial view of the study area.
Source: Base GeoTIFF image courtesy of the City of Burnside.

this exercise has been undertaken for an inner suburb of Adelaide, its specificity is not its focus, nor even its significance. The methodology inherent in the drawing, whereby the complex established suburb is abstracted to its simplified elemental form, allows for the technique to be used as a discovery tool in any neighbourhood consisting of a similar kit of parts.

Bluefield exercise 4: The Block Apartment

Purpose of the exercise: To speculate on the spatial and organisational capacity of an established neighbourhood block in a way that might otherwise be difficult to imagine.

The Block Apartment combines the Porous Rooms and Grid Block studies to temporarily reimagine a suburban block as a single united housing entity without the traditional suburban divisions of space and ownership. The exercise contemplates potential housing outcomes if the existing individual houses are thought of merely as components of larger apartment blocks rather than the self-contained dwellings they currently are. As a design exercise, it transitions from representational grid work to the more tangible realm of traditional architectural representation of program. Its starting point is the overlay of existing external walls onto the 'house width' gridlines previously established in the Grid Block exercise. Where key internal walls of the existing houses are definable, as is often the case with the hallways of cottages and bungalows, these are drawn, creating an array of walls perpendicular to the street (Figure 18.7). In places where the housing is repetitive and with a simple floor plan arrangement, this part of the exercise will be relatively straightforward. For areas with more varied housing, more complex plans, or steep topography, the reader will need to use their discretion in distilling the neighbourhood block to its simplest form.

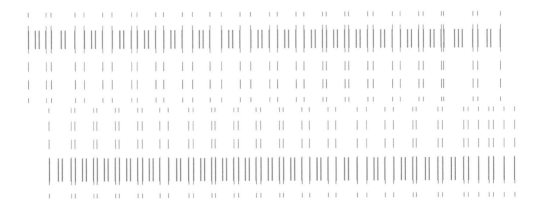

18.7
Existing external walls (and predictable internal walls) mapped on to the house widths grid established in the Grid Block exercise.

At this stage of the exercise, no distinction is made between the houses and the spaces between them, with the two states of solid and void treated as interchangeable and of equal value. The existing houses, liberated from the drawing embellishments usually provided in site or floor plans, read as a continuous bar code across the block, as the walls running perpendicular to the street frontage are emphasised while all others are ignored. This creates a focus not just on the key external and internal walls of each house as they relate to movement from the public street to the private backyard, but on the spaces *between* houses. The diagram thereby treats both these built and unbuilt spaces uniformly, with building and open space rendered equivalent.

Having established the rhythm of rooms across the block, the diagram is ready to be used as a test of dwelling capacity and diversity. Keeping with the theme of abstraction, this is achieved not by designing a tailored approach to the block, but by overlaying case study housing not usually seen in a low-rise suburban setting. The purpose of deliberately clashing incongruous housing forms is twofold: when overlaid at the same scale, these transplanted projects allow the spatial capacity of the neighbourhood to be understood in a new light while demonstrating the variety of housing types an existing field of suburban housing might accommodate if thought of differently. Additionally, the overlay process enables a much faster way of working without getting lost in the nuances of a tailored intervention. Importantly, this process allows the logic of such a reimagining exercise to be ignored; such a proposition is unlikely to ever be realised, yet the process can still deliver meaningful insights.

Being a fanciful exercise allows one to look deliberately outside the local context for international precedents that are distinctly 'other' but have the potential to reveal the untapped housing potential of suburbia. This collaging activity enables the borrowed apartment prototypes to become the source material and reverses the order of thinking that would otherwise occur if one was to develop contextually driven housing from the ground-up. In this way, the emphasis of the investigation is shifted away from the traditional (and often restrictive) adaptive reuse principles of a single property and towards a broader (and more liberating) exploration of the more varied housing models the settlement pattern could theoretically support. As an extension of Grid Block, this is an exercise in studying the capacity of the existing suburbs, again divorced from any pre-emptive restrictive logic to underpin *why* one might develop in this manner or *how* it might conceivably be achieved.

By way of example, four urban housing projects can be applied to the same neighbourhood block explored in Grid Block, with each chosen for the diversity of housing they provide and their seemingly incongruous fit with the prevailing conditions:

1. Aires Mateus and Associates: Housing for the Elderly (Alcácer do Sal, Portugal)
    *   Described as part hotel, part hospital,[3] communal gathering areas of living, dining, and socialising are located on the ground level of the facility. The living quarters, arranged over the top two floors, use a generous corridor space to provide storage on one side, thereby freeing space in the apartments themselves. Arranged as a private hospital room would be, with one bedroom and a private bathroom, each unit has access to its own small balcony and is physically detached from its neighbouring units for acoustic privacy. The result is a housing facility that couples aged-care efficiency with sociable collective living.

2. Kazuyo Sejima and Associates: Kitagata Apartment Building (Gifu, Japan)
    *   Commonly known as the Gifu Apartments, 107 dwelling units are provided over ten storeys. Arranged as a series of connective 2.4m wide x 7.2m deep rooms (7'10½" x 23'7½"), together the rooms form 30 different apartment types ranging from 49–80m^2 (527–861 sq ft). Connected by a 1m (3'3") deep ablutions zone on one side and a 1.4m (4'7") wide shared corridor on the other, room modules are offered in either single or double heights which when combined, allow for housing types to be arrayed both horizontally and vertically. The result is a choice of housing configurations and spatial and formal variety as the building's height increases to provide double height spaces to approximately half of the dwellings.[4]

3. Mateo Arquitectura: 26 Housing Units (Amsterdam, The Netherlands)
    *   Part of West 8's master planned Borneo-Sporenburg housing development, Mateo Arquitectura's patio housing scheme maximises accommodation by playing to West 8's design rules of building hard to the site edge to maximise density whilst taking advantage of the outward views of surrounding water. Exterior space is replaced with internalised courtyards to provide light, ventilation, and private open space. Dwellings are arranged over three storeys and are of 11 different housing types ranging from three to five rooms from 110–180m^2

Backgrounding design studies: a 'designerly' way of seeing

(1,184–1,937 sq ft). Spatially, the complex is arranged as two strips of 11 back-to-back townhouses with street frontages, with a third strip of four houses running perpendicular to bookend the peninsular.[5]

4. Steven Holl: Void Space / Hinged Space Housing (Fukuoka, Japan).
   - With an ambition to provide a variety of apartment choice, flexibility, and divisibility via the incorporation of moveable internal partitions and joinery, Holl's Nexus World housing is arranged over four floors. Due to the proportions of the lot, access to natural sunlight precluded a single massive building block. Holl's response was twofold: a finger shaped plan to allow light and ventilation laterally into the building across its width, and cross-over apartments[6] so that at least part of each apartment has access to direct sunlight.[7]

Each case study is incorporated into the neighbourhood block in a way that maintains the distinct design principles that underpin their idiosyncratic plan arrangements. Reduced in the first instance to only their essential wall forms, each is mapped to scale over the existing infrastructure of existing walls to test transferability. This is done using the simple measures of size and spatial fit (Figure 18.8). In doing so, it forces the apartment footprints of the case studies to be massaged to the wall arrangements of the existing houses.

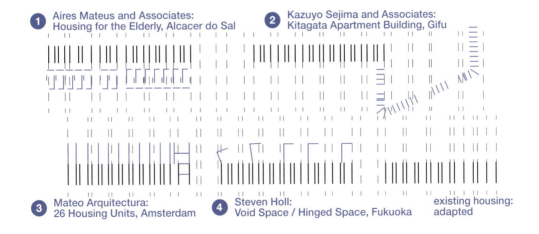

18.8
Four case studies mapped onto existing conditions.

With the Alcácer do Sol housing for the elderly (scheme 1 in the diagram), the existing housing is reconfigured, while the 'borrowed' case study dwelling units are located behind, separated by a connective walkway. The retained cottages here become additional dwellings in the likeness of the case study accommodation, along with common dining and recreation spaces. In the cases of the Gifu (2), Amsterdam (3), and Fukuoka (4) buildings, the existing houses are subsumed by and integrated with the case study apartments, demonstrating the ease with which the original housing forms can be moulded to new apartment configurations. When viewed in its entirety, and with the tree canopy overlaid on the tree grid, the established block reads as a housing hypothesis – an *idea* for a variety of potential housing types rather than a fully designed precinct (Figure 18.9).

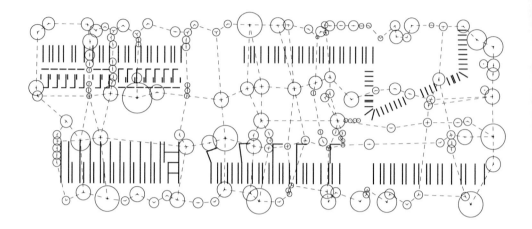

18.9
A housing hypothesis using existing house stock and located in and around the existing mature tree canopy.

The task remains, then, to shift this abstraction exercise towards programmed architectural space. This begins with a return to the Porous Rooms study and the assumption that the existing houses are in their most degraded or porous (and thereby most flexible) form. A set of design parameters can then be established to deploy Porous Rooms strategically across the block with some form of unifying logic:

1. All rooms of the existing houses must retain their corners, as doing so:
   - enables the opening of one room to another simply with a lintel, as described in Chapter 17;
   - permits the reinstatement of walls by blocking these new openings later if required, thereby increasing flexibility;
   - retains ceilings where desired, further establishing the economic and cultural value of retention; and
   - spatially identifies the lineage of the existing room and house, thereby evoking memories of past use and the evolving character of the place.
2. The front wall of front rooms remains intact, as doing so:
   - retains the cottage's identity and contribution to streetscape, deemed important in undertaking this early design testing of character-shaping, which is discussed in Chapter 3; and
   - maintains the local material palette and established fine grain of the area.
3. All walls of rear rooms are available for change, as this:
   - maximises spatial opportunities.

4. Hallways are deliberately not drawn, but are formed of the spaces between left-hand and right-hand sided rooms, as doing so:
   - blurs the legibility of the traditional territorial boundaries of the individual house; and
   - renders the hallway spaces as hierarchically equivalent to the spaces between houses, thereby allowing them to be considered as undefined and potentially usable space.

Overlaid on the grid, the porous rooms read as remnants of the established settlement pattern of the individual houses (Figure 18.10), but viewed in isolation with the tree grid, they take on the generative framework of a larger unified housing system amongst a varied landscape field (Figure 18.11).

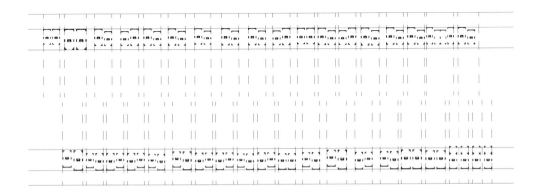

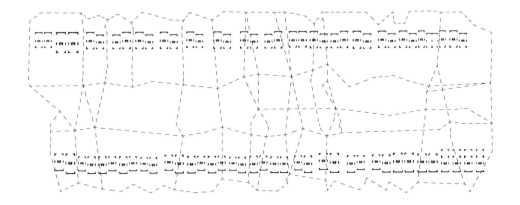

18.10 and 18.11
An existing housing system forming a generative framework.

Viewed across the entire block, what becomes apparent in the Block Apartment exercise is that density, which is most often discussed purely in terms of housing numbers and building scale, and is avoided altogether in many established neighbourhoods, is only one component of what older suburbs might theoretically be capable of supporting. A far more interesting and potentially useful outcome of the exercise is the ability to see the types of unanticipated housing forms that traditional blocks could accommodate if diversity rather than density was the guiding principle. When the floor plans of incongruous case studies are morphed with the reconfigured plans of the prevailing housing stock, one might discover that, conceptually, an established suburban settlement pattern adapts equally well to a space enclosing strip building as it does cross-over apartments, townhouses, or units for ageing people (Figure 18.12).

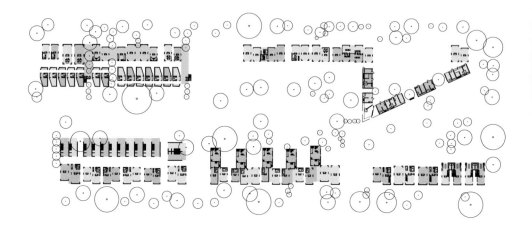

18.12
Floorplans of the 'borrowed' case studies mapped onto the reconfigured plans of the established neighbourhood housing.

When observed in its current form, a traditional neighbourhood block reads as somewhat impenetrable, compact, and tightly packed, despite the fact it is formed of multiple single-family home allotments of generous proportions. However, when re-presented as a hybrid of existing housing and disparate housing prototypes, the spatial capacity of the block can be seen differently. To illustrate this, a final piece of notable urban infrastructure can be collaged into the scheme: New York's High Line – a transformative elevated urban park that provides valuable open green space coupled with economic generation for the neighbourhoods through which it snakes along its 23 city blocks. Its utility in this collaging activity is its ability to serve as a benchmark for the types and sizes of landscape spaces that one neighbourhood block might house. Here, stages one and two of the High Line, accounting for approximately 1.6 hectares of landscape (4 acres), have been collaged across the site in multiple configurations. Such an exercise is a test not just of capacity or fit, but of the quality of external spaces that might be achieved. In retaining only those building elements that constitute the original base housing (removing the 'commonly accepted anomalies' discussed in Chapter 4), a landscape band around 50–60m wide (164–197') is released in the centre of the block, within which the High Line might be dissected and strategically arrayed (Figure 18.13).

Backgrounding design studies: a 'designerly' way of seeing

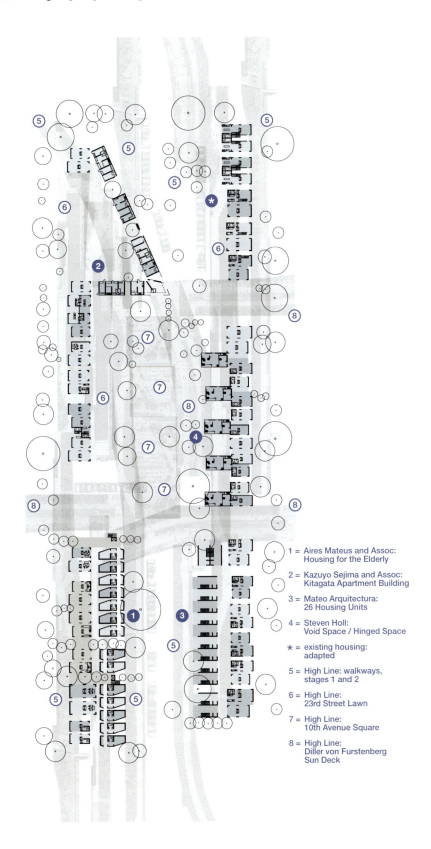

18.13
The block apartment.

In this final Block Apartment scheme, open spaces are reimagined as being formed of multiple High Line landscaped and urban forms:

- Stage 1 and 2 walkways and garden beds (identified as 5 in the diagram): generally measuring around 8m wide (26') and providing a variety of landscape, seating, walking, and viewing options, these have been collaged variously between and around buildings.
- The 23rd Street Lawn (6): measuring 8 x 80m (26 x 262'), used as a gathering space and supplemented with raised decking for seating, this is collaged into the study area three times.
- The 10th Avenue Square (7): the largest single space in the High Line at approximately 20 x 20m (65½ x 65½'), this terraced gathering place is incorporated four times.
- The Diller von Furstenberg sun deck (8): a 16 x 75m long strip (52½ x 246') consisting of a walkway and garden bed down one side and band of sun lounges, path, and a water element for feet cooling in spring and summer down the other, this is cut up and collaged into the study area four times.

Observed in this collaging of well-known pieces of urban infrastructure into an established neighbourhood setting, is the spatial capacity the suburbs have when existing building matter is pared back to the original housing structures and then accreted back to a more fully occupied proposition. Although the results of the exercise will vary with the size and nature of the existing housing stock, the lot sizes, and the size and nature of the imported building and landscape case studies, what is evident in this example is:

- the quite considerable size of the block relative to the sites of the collaged case studies;
- the potential malleability of the existing housing stock when it is used as the spatial basis for the borrowed housing types;
- the equivalence of size between the retained housing and the seemingly incompatible urban housing of other places and eras;
- the transferability of alternative housing systems to that existing housing stock; and
- the resultant housing choice, household diversity, and increase in housing numbers that might be realised through such an architectural and urban rethinking.

Significantly, both the quantity and potential quality of open space that might be sustained by such an older neighbourhood has become evident, and importantly this has occurred whilst mapping and retaining the existing mature landscape across the block.

As an architectural process, The Block Apartment begins with the proposition that the differences between an internationally recognised contemporary apartment block and the settlement pattern of more anonymous neighbourhood housing might not be significant when viewed across a broader territory, and comparisons might yield clues for new housing types. The consequence then of having achieved speculative territorial schemes having first explored room-scale tactics, is that one can then work back across scales reflectively as a logical extension of the task. This is the objective of the resulting outward communication studies that follow in the next chapter.

Notes

1 Nigel Cross, *Designerly Ways of Knowing*. London: Springer, 2006.
2 Carsten Nicolai, *Grid index*. Berlin, Germany: Gestalten, 2009.
3 Aurora Fernández Per, Javier Mozas, and Javier Arpa, *Density is Home*. a+t density series. Vitoria-Gasteiz, Spain: a+t Architecture Publishers, 2011, 130.
4 Christian Schittich, ed., *In Detail: High-density Housing: Concepts, Planning, Construction*, In Detail (Basel: Birkhäuser, Edition Detail, 2004), 82.
5 Oliver Heckmann and Friederike Schneider, eds., *Floor Plan Manual: Housing*, 4th ed. (Basel: Birkhäuser, 2011), 324.
6 'Cross-over' or 'through' apartments are those arranged over more than one level and overlapped with other apartments above and/or below such that each apartment has access to two façades for light and ventilation.
7 Heckmann and Schneider, *Floor Plan Manual: Housing*, 164.

19 Generative design studies for bluefield housing

Outward communication studies

Witnessed in the Porous Rooms, Grid Block, and The Block Apartment design experiments is a range of schematic options to understand established housing differently, and to test how it might support change. This may be realised by making houses smaller or larger, and by either increasing or maintaining current density levels. They are exercises in creating a diversity of housing choice through adaptation, as opposed to simply replacing single dwellings with more compact and more numerous homes. Underlying these methods of analysis is an assumption that one might operate across traditional land titles into broader territories. Under these conditions it becomes plausible that some dwellings could combine into bigger houses with multiple kitchens, bathrooms, utilities, and circulation spaces – a scenario that might see members of the same family or a friendship group purchase adjacent properties together and live semi- or wholly-collectively. As such, neighbourhood housing might not only go down in size but grow up, as suburbs accommodate not just smaller houses in greater numbers, but larger, more varied homes. Depending on the design devices employed, major organisational change, such as spreading ownership laterally across lots, might result from relatively minor physical change, as seen in the collaging exercise of The Block Apartment (Chapter 18).

A mechanism is required, then, to take the observations found in these internal design studies and reconcile them as usable external strategies that

286

DOI: 10.4324/9781003293736-25
This chapter has been made available under a CC-BY-NC-ND license.

Bluefield exercise 5: Seven Design Tactics

others can deploy as a generative design tool. This is the focus of Seven Design Tactics.

Bluefield exercise 5: Seven Design Tactics

Purpose of the exercise: To extend the preceding bluefield housing backgrounding exercises into a suite of generative spatial tactics that are used to test new housing ideas for an established neighbourhood block.

Seven Design Tactics is a set of location-specific parameters that can be used to speculate on new forms of infill housing across a neighbourhood block. They can be used in workshops or design studios to create speculative housing designs that are then analysed and organised into patterns such as the Suburban Operations catalogue presented in Chapter 4. These Operations were created with this method after using the Tactics (and the Algebraic Siting Strategies that follow) in two undergraduate architecture design studios at the University of South Australia. The same housing grid created in Grid Block (Chapter 18) is used, thereby representing 'typical' neighbourhood conditions for the purposes of the user's study. As with the previous studies, the reader will need to create their own underlying spatial definitions based on local conditions, including any allowances for topography. These local nuances will likely result in tactics that are different to (or at least variations of) the tactics described here. In direct terms, Grid Block is used to establish the foundational armature of the block; The Block Apartment explores the types of unexpected housing typologies this grid can theoretically support; the Design Tactics analyse these outcomes to identify the key spaces of infill opportunity; the Tactics are then used by others to develop infill designs; and the Suburban Operations are the types of development patterns that can summarise these infill forms.

The number of Design Tactics will likely vary with different neighbourhood blocks in different cities. Seven are described here for the inner-suburban Australian block in question:

1. Between zones (Figure 19.1):
   - Presenting a dispersed series of small spaces laterally across the site, these are the areas that encourage connection between houses and over traditional lot divisions. They are premised on the idea that dwelling might extend across collective space rather than be contained within existing ownership divisions.

19.1
Between zones.

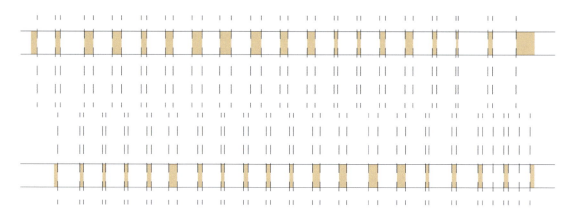

2. Lateral titling (Figure 19.2):
   - An imaginary datum running through the existing houses separates the street-facing rooms from those at the rear. This lateral division line reconfigures land titling parallel to the traditional street frontage in lieu of running perpendicular to it. This opens space behind dwellings for new uses.

19.2
Lateral titling.

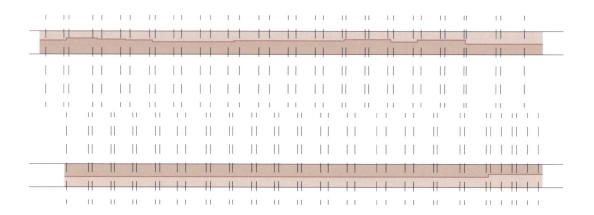

3. Active front yards (Figure 19.3):
   - Reconsidering titling arrangements parallel to the street requires front yards to return to their traditional more highly activated state. This requires focus on existing mature landscape at the street edge of lots, the established streetscape pattern, and how a more active and social street presence might be developed.

Generative design studies for bluefield housing

19.3
Active front yards.

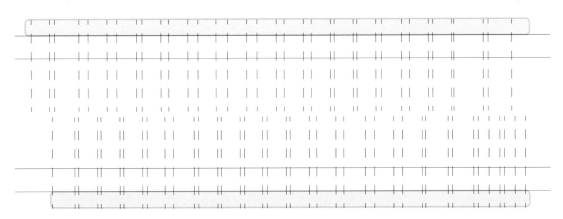

4. Malleable back zone (Figure 19.4):
   - This is the zone of land around 3m or 10' deep at the back of older Australian houses, where small lean-to extensions are located; this tactic can be amended for other housing types, as necessary. Gathered as a pair of linear strips across the width of the suburban block where the original lean-tos once existed, the zone at the rear of the houses allows the opening of the back walls to light, ventilation, and access, and creates opportunities for internal lateral streets or walkways. The term 'malleable' refers to the fact that this zone may be landscaped, built on, or a combination of the two. Useful rear additions, where identifiable, can be incorporated into designs in the Back Zone.

19.4
Malleable back zone.

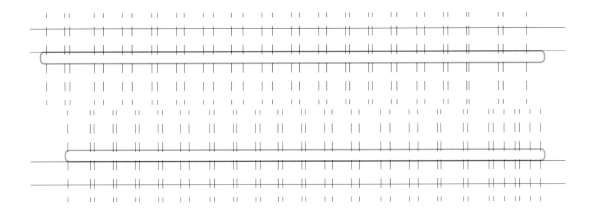

5. Strategic spatial exchange (Figure 19.5):
   - This is a transfer of accommodation from the Back Zone into the base form of the existing housing. The loss of building matter at the rear of the houses, even if individually small, creates an accommodation deficit when the house is reduced to its main rooms. The tactic of

Generative design studies for bluefield housing

exchange encourages this lost accommodation to be folded into the remaining parts of existing house through building up or out, or via internal alterations. The loss of building elements in the rear allows the gain of something else such as landscape or construction that supports new accommodation models.

19.5
Strategic spatial exchange.

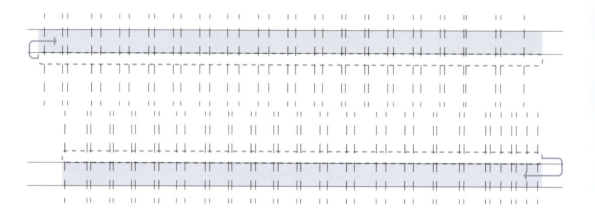

6. Binding central zone (Figure 19.6):
   - This is the backyard area between the rear walls of existing houses that often provides a large territory with which to work. In older Australian suburbs this can commonly measure between 50 to 60m from rear wall to rear wall (around 165 to 200'). When considered as a single land mass it becomes a substantial zone for the retention of mature landscape and tree corridors, and for the strategic gain of building matter, new landscape, inner paths, and car parking where necessary.

19.6
Binding central zone.

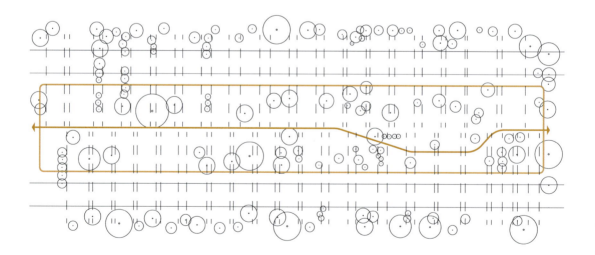

7. Strategic loss (Figure 19.7):
   - A: minor – the deliberate loss of one dwelling to achieve other gains as part of a broader spatial strategy.
   - B: major – the deliberate loss of two or more dwellings that may or may not be immediately adjacent or behind each other, for strategic advantage.

19.7 Strategic loss.

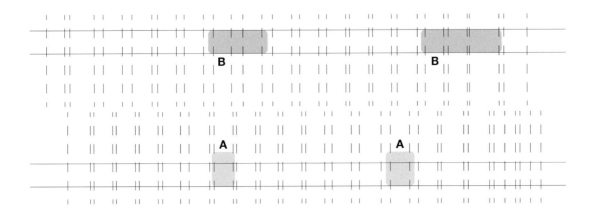

Seven Design Tactics is generative. The way each tactic is expressed is deliberately open and abstract. One might imagine, for example, applying 'lateral titling' in combination with 'between zones' to create new outcomes. This thinking could be applied to any one tactic at any scale to design experimentally. Importantly, these tactics, tailored with local neighbourhood research and presented logically, can be experimented with by others. Indeed, an argument can be made that for the tactics to be written or adapted for a neighbourhood and be truly generative, they *must* be tested by others as a means of escaping the individual's tropes that might just as easily inhibit possibilities as enable them. Inasmuch as they set up principles and frameworks that offer a more speculative approach to traditional zoning policy, the tactics offer a way of exploring housing options and of speaking differently: of compelling us to find the suburban eccentricity that is already there and transforming what we think we already know.

When combined, as in Figure 19.8, the tactics and the manner of their abstract drawing imply a form of mat building readable as a simplified graphic landscape. Enabling the conceptual detachment of rear additions, and all other accrued occupational extensions, and reducing building matter to the base form of the original housing, means that these remnant structures can strategically be joined together sideways quite readily, as each room retains access to light and ventilation at the rear. Insofar as the existing gaps between buildings currently operate as easements between buildings, they might become connective and filled with elements such as kitchens, bathrooms, or entrances to form another way of doing a mat building. This thinking is a liberation of the singular way of looking at older neighbourhood housing, in that it reinvents the traditional mode of accretive growth that appears behind single houses and reimagines

19.8
Seven design tactics.

this laterally: backyard growth replaced by side yard growth where the newfound central land mass behind the existing housing stock becomes new ground for housing and landscape investigations.

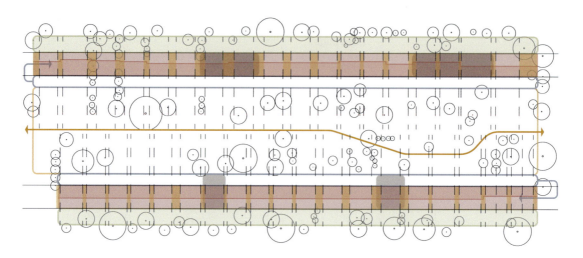

Bluefield exercise 6: Algebraic Siting Strategies

Purpose of the exercise: To quickly generate hypothetical yet realistic neighbourhood blocks as sites of design investigation in which the Seven Design Tactics can be explored.

Because Seven Design Tactics can be tailored to local conditions, they can be applied to real sites. However, to undertake broader city- or neighbourhood-wide investigations of housing options outside of a narrow focus site, a mechanism is required for defining a *hypothetical* study area – one that allows for speculation unencumbered from the specifics of an actual place. This means creating an imagined site that is specific-enough to be representative of prevailing suburban conditions, yet sufficiently generic as to represent an expanded suburban territory where the new ideas may be deployed. A deliberate distancing from the idiosyncratic matter of an actual place can free the practitioner, researcher, or student to speculate on housing possibilities that might otherwise never be considered. It allows one to remain at a critical arm's length from the subject matter to move beyond any preconceived limits the place may be seen to have. 'Limits' here include aesthetic, historic, political, cultural, commercial, or physical traits; issues that are critical to resolve but can serve as early impediments that shut down any discussion of change before it can be explored.

This requires a codified way of describing local suburban conditions so those undertaking housing studies can commence their work quickly while producing useful design data. If the morphological properties of neighbourhood houses and their sites can be shown to be of a type, one can create representative settlement patterns by presupposing the types of houses in play and their spatial relationships to each other. Figure 19.9 shows an example of the types of Australian cottages used in the design studies of Part 3. Based on a detailed analysis of inner-suburban housing in Adelaide, the diagrams amalgamate site and housing data that represent large areas of the city's older suburbs. Common minimum dimensions are displayed, meaning the diagrams show some of the most restricted conditions likely to be experienced, with real sites and houses likely to be at least the same size or larger. Resembling similar older neighbourhoods across the country, these diagrams can be made to represent other places with only minor tweaking based on local spatial and building data. As with the other design studies of this book, the reader can adapt the methodology to local conditions to establish their own set of neighbourhood housing metrics. Seen in the diagrams are the houses (H), side walkways (W), and carriage lanes (C), each with their typical dimensions. The term 'carriage lane' is used strategically to underline the fact that these housing typologies predate cars, with the current-day driveways originally designed for horse and carriage. The reader may choose to use the more explicit 'driveway', particularly for post-war car centric suburbs.

19.9
Example site and housing morphology diagrams for two lot types: with a carriage lane and walkway (top) and with two walkways (bottom).

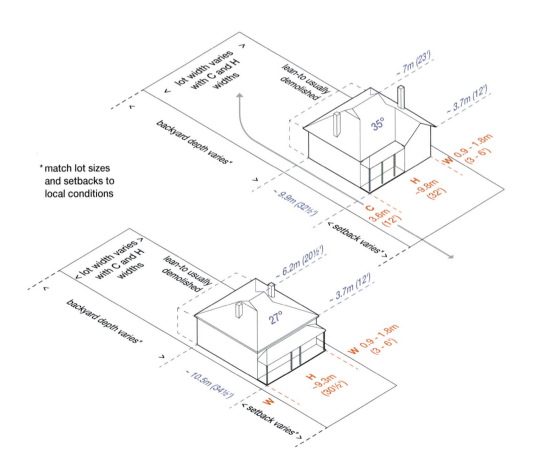

With this typical data diagrammed, the user can create an imaginary yet representative neighbourhood block. This is done by creating any combination of houses, walkways, and carriage lanes at their discretion, while working to given front and rear setbacks. Overall site dimensions do not need to be stated, as they will be determined by the choices and combinations of houses (H), carriage lanes (C), and walkways (W) in an exercise of Algebraic Siting Strategies.

The user can consider what might be possible, for example, if they imagine two houses with two adjacent walkways between them (in algebraic terms, H + W + W + H) or two houses where one has a walkway immediately adjacent the carriage lane of the other house (H + W + C + H). Furthermore, using the identified standard widths of the morphology study, consideration can be given to the spatial effects of (for example) having two walkways of 1.8m each between houses (6'), compared with one walkway of 0.9m and one of 1.2m (3' and 4'). Under this logic, one can imagine various siting arrangements that position the houses as close together as 1.8m or 6' (that is, two adjacent 0.9m / 3' walkways) or as far apart as 7.2m or 24' (that is, two adjacent 3.6m / 12' wide carriage lanes). By deliberately ignoring existing title boundaries, other than as the means by which to consider how wide an existing walkway or carriage lane might be, the user can instantly consider the suburban block as a system of housing parts rather than as a collection of individual properties.

Using the Algebraic Siting Strategies method, a multitude of imagined yet plausible siting permutations can be established as a suburban context with which to experiment, such as:

(W + H + W) + (W + H + W)

(W + H + C) + (W + H + W)

(W + H + C) + (C + H + W)

(C + H + W) + (W + H + W)

(C + H + W) + (W + H + C)

(C + H + W) + (C + H + W)

(W + H + W) + (W + H + W) + (C + H + W)

(C + H + W) + (W + H + W) + (W + H + W)

(C + H + W) + (C + H + W) + (W + H + C) … etc

Once established and understood as a tool to generate imaginary places that replicate the real conditions of established suburbs, Algebraic Siting Strategies can also be used as a descriptive tool to simplify and explain an existing local context to others. Figure 19.10 shows an example, where a pair of villas in the Sydney suburb of Hornsby can have their settlement morphology described using the formula (W+H+C) + (W+H+C). In this way, the tangibility of the algebraic method is made visible as an abstractive device to not only conceive of imaginary suburban conditions for experimentation, but to describe their real antecedents.

Generative design studies for bluefield housing

19.10
A pair of houses in Sydney, which can be described algebraically as (W+H+C) + (W+H+C).

With a site of investigation established, exploratory work can be done with dexterity, working at the scale of the entire block. Design agility is deemed important, as it is aligned with the notion of experimenting in broad terms without getting subsumed into the nuances of character requirements or heavily contextualised design. Agility can be achieved by initially restricting the exercise to only designing through physical models to experiment intuitively with formal and scalar relationships. This can then be followed by more detailed exercises that incorporate the Seven Design Tactics to offer more nuanced outcomes. As a set, the following exercises – which are written as a set of instructions – are well suited to weekly experiments by groups of three or four students in a design studio or participants in a workshop setting.

Task 1: volume

Goal: To explore formal and spatial possibilities based on suburban morphology rather than program or site specifics (Figure 19.11).

Method: Physical models and model photographs with drawing/diagrammatic overlays.

Lots: Use any combination of identified housing typologies and the Algebraic Siting Strategies to create nine to twelve adjacent lots that together form a representative field of neighbourhood housing.

Description: For this exercise, construct simple massing models of the houses at a scale of 1:200. Arrange them on a flat surface set apart, at scale, using the side and rear distances described in the morphology diagrams. In the spaces between, model building forms that instinctively feel like an appropriate fit. How 'fit' is determined is for the individual to argue. Do not get engrossed in function or number of storeys or the number of buildings on one site. Think instead of massing across the created field using volume, form, mass, and scale. The field of lots that are created is also at your

Generative design studies for bluefield housing

discretion. For example, you might choose to arrange them back-to-back: five lots wide x two lots deep, with an empty allotment for a nine-lot study, or six lots wide x two deep for a twelve-lot study. Alternatively, you might choose a linear arrangement of nine or twelve lots wide or create any combination of side-by-side and back-to-back arrangements. There is no right or wrong choice. Not fixing the houses to a base means that multiple arrangements can be made, photographed, rearranged, and worked with again.

Consider open space between the existing houses and the new insertions you will create. How much space do you instinctively feel is appropriate and what are the types of dimensions you feel are suitable? What do you consider is the minimum width and breadth of an open space in this field and why? Consider also that you are working with established suburbs with established landscape. How might mature trees become a significant component of amenity? Google Earth is a good resource here for scanning an established suburb and getting a sense of the mature landscape conditions in neighbourhoods such as the one you are creating for this exercise.

19.11
3D design testing by undergraduate architecture students using an imagined site created with the Algebraic Siting Strategies and typical house and lot morphologies.
Students: Christopher Hill, Janai Lemar, Timothy Podobny, and Claebon Sandell, University of South Australia.

Formal + Spatial Exploration

Continuous building form from street front to behind existing villas/cottages

"Meteorite" form between multiple villas/cottages

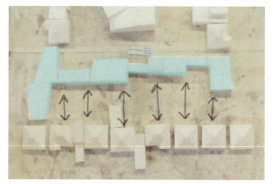
Continous street-to-street linear form. Connecting to existing buildings?

Task 2: diversity

Goal: To explore the possibilities of dwelling diversity by designing dwellings for 1, 4, and 6+ people over multiple sites.

Method: Physical models (can be reworked from Task 1), digital overlays, and drawings focusing on three of the Design Tactics.

Description: Having undertaken preliminary investigations around volume, form and 'fit', consider now how dwelling diversity might be introduced to a suburban field. Use modes of communication best suited to the task. Again, working with either nine or twelve lots, design dwelling arrangements that are formed of existing houses coupled with new additions, alterations, and suburban insertions:

- Design dwellings for 1 person, 4 people, and 6+ people.
- In determining the make-up of your occupants, consider the demographic issues outlined in Chapter 1 and the varied forms of suburban living described in Chapters 2 and 9.
- Determine what you think is an appropriate mix of functions, rooms, or program.
- As with Task 1, consider appropriate open spaces between the houses and your new insertions and the types of open space qualities you feel are needed and can be supported by your ideas.

Design tactics: For this task, test the first three of the Seven Design Tactics.

1. Between Zones
2. Lateral Titling
3. Active Front Yards

Comment on the tactics' efficacy: what do they enable or restrict, and how useful (or otherwise) are they as a generative design tool? How might they be enhanced, adapted, or replaced by a different tactic?

Task 3: flexibility and mixed-use

Goal: To explore the possibilities of flexibility and mixed-use by designing for dwellings, businesses, civic functions, and public space over multiple sites.

Method: As per Task 2, now adding the remaining Design Tactics to the methodology.

Description: Consider now how a mix of uses might be introduced to your suburban field, designing dwellings and mixed-use arrangements that are formed of existing houses coupled with new additions, alterations, and suburban insertions:

- Design dwellings that might suit a variety of household structures.
- Experiment with complementary mixes of commercial and civic programs.

- Consider how a building (new or existing) might be flexible enough to support multiple uses either over time or at the same time.
- Consider both private and public/shared open space within the overall scheme.

Note that the expectation is not to design something that is all things for all people, nor is it to provide resolved designs; the considerations listed here are prompts to aid your thinking around the types of activities a modified neighbourhood block might support.

Design tactics: In addition to deploying the first three Design Tactics, add the remaining four to the investigation:

4. Malleable Back Zone.
5. Strategic Spatial Exchange.
6. Binding Central Zone.
7. Strategic Loss.

As with the previous task, comment on the new tactics' efficacy and limits.

Task 4: intensification

Goal: To explore the possibilities of densification by designing for dwellings and/ or businesses and/or civic functions and/or public space over two adjacent sites. This may require a shift from the programming methods used in the preceding tasks, as what makes sense on nine or twelve lots might not work on two. Consider designing dwellings that might be adaptable to small-scale commercial or civic activities, rather than trying to design a full mixed-use development on a mini two-lot scale.

Density target: At least 34 dw/ha or 14 dw/acre (net).

Calculate and report how many people per hectare or acre being accommodated, based on your described household structures.

Method: Physical models, digital media, and drawings (plans, elevations, sections) utilising any combination of the Seven Design Tactics.

Description: Having undertaken preliminary investigations around volume, form and 'fit' (exercise 1), dwelling diversity (exercise 2), flexibility and mixed-use (exercise 3), consider now how a mix of uses or an increase in dwelling density might be introduced to a suburban field when the number of available allotments is substantially reduced.

This exercise should be reflective, meaning that it should be informed and driven by what has been discovered in the prior tasks. It should also be generative, as it sets the groundwork for the types of detailed double lot design studies shown in Chapter 11.

Two important functions are served by the algebraic production technique and its coupling with the design tactics. In the first instance, the established housing, defined by local patterns and simplified to their common metrics, can be quickly assembled into what participants recognise to be a very familiar suburban setting. When undertaken at the University of South Australia, students reported that the assembling of their neighbourhood fictions heightened their awareness of prevailing suburban patterns that they had previously not noticed or recognised as so ubiquitous. For others, it enabled them to think anew about housing with which they felt completely familiar but had not critically engaged with. For students new to the city, the exercise was a short-cut to understanding local conditions in a tangible and reflexive way. Second, the exercises work to decouple the assemblage of housing in an established suburb from the types of precinct-specific traits that dominate so much NIMBY/YIMBY debate, thereby enabling intensification studies to be undertaken with the heat taken out of the argument.

Divorced from a real site and the architectural nuances of the housing, participants can speculate on new housing forms freely and hypothetically before homing in on more detailed lot studies. As this shift in scale occurs, where the intricacies of program and architectural intervention demand resolution, the design studies can become more normative while still being informed by the social, spatial, and landscape aspirations of the speculative work. This returns the housing discussion to one of audience, which is the topic of the following and final chapter.

20 Housing for whom?

Lessons from the Town Hall floor

Discussing change through narrative arcs

Looking to find its place in older neighbourhoods with established character, bluefield housing will always face the challenge of having to argue why it should be allowed to disrupt the status quo, even if the housing change it will bring about is both physically and numerically small by other infill housing standards. But even minor change is change, and it requires the bluefield advocate to create a story of why the change is important, and of how it forms part of a continuum. The purpose of analysing the heritage of a place and its character of activity, as discussed in Chapter 3, is not to say to those who do not want neighbourhood change that "you're wrong". Rather, it is about extending the narrative arc of that location's history into the future such that they can acknowledge their moment in time. It is an exercise in describing the early physical characteristics of neighbourhood housing to understand how different contemporary use is and how we can project that future use will be different again. Where mews, coach housing, and carriage lanes for example, once related directly to the traditions of English housing in general and the use of the horse and carriage in daily life at the turn of the twentieth century, they have morphed into new uses on lots that now accommodate cars. And household structures predominated by large families, traditional and predictable roles, and short retirement lives, have since become diverse in their make-up, more varied in the way they operate, and with occupants living into much older ages. Meanwhile, the ratio of income required to comfortably

300

DOI: 10.4324/9781003293736-26
This chapter has been made available under a CC-BY-NC-ND license.

afford rent or mortgage payments has risen sharply, dramatically increasing the number of people affected by housing stress. Seen as a whole, these observable and understandable narratives of neighbourhood and social change add a different dimension to local preservation conversations and help to tilt the argument away from how neighbourhoods should be protected from change toward one of "how can we expect it not to?". Such observations can diffuse tense discussions by making a simple observation: the original custodians of a neighbourhood could not possibly have predicted what its physical, use, or societal characteristics would become today any more than we can predict the future beyond our own understanding of the place in its current time. What is given, however, is that we can anticipate that our housing future will be different.

Housing for whom? The power of personification

Housing advocates accustomed to engaging in NIMBY/YIMBY debates will often describe situations where existing residents oppose housing intensification in their neighbourhood while also proclaiming their social credentials – social media is replete with descriptions of 'lefty NIMBY' oppositionists who intellectually understand the need for more diverse and numerous housing yet oppose it being provided in their neighbourhood. Opposition is often grounded in arguments around the housing proposal being too big or having too many residents. This book has argued that the low-rise bluefield housing model, innately tied to single-family neighbourhood housing through its reworking rather than replacement, is a mechanism to deliver more housing with the heat taken out of the scale and fit argument. However, adding housing in small numbers and dispersed arrangements, it will only ever be an adjunct to desperately needed larger housing developments, and even with the issues of building scale, traffic, and neighbourhood fit accounted for, the model will regularly have to be justified on the grounds of whom it is housing.

Re-emphasising the infill debate from 'what' to 'for whom', requires scenario planning that helps an audience personify the residents, while also helping to understand why the housing scheme is designed the way it is. Many NIMBY activists and lawmakers will lean on issues such as car parking and street traffic to explain why an area should not be intensified and while these are important issues, they are not equivalent to the provision of safe, secure, and more affordable housing for people who otherwise struggle to access it. Establishing an understanding of the needs of vulnerable older people, for example, makes it harder for negative infill tropes such as car parking to be weaponised against densification. Similarly, describing life events that can translate demographic change into relatable life stories, dramatically shifts the housing debate. An increasingly relevant example is the 'grey divorce', where older women put off leaving their partners until their children reach independence, often due to abuse or control by their partners coupled with a financial reliance on them. Additionally, there are the increasingly common sharing narratives described in

Chapter 2 and observed as scenarios for the design studies of Part 3: parents moving in with their children, children with their parents, and multigenerations of related and unrelated people living together for financial and social gain. When the 'why' of new housing is successfully described through scenarios and personification, the 'how' may have already passed its first hurdle.

Co-design

An increasingly used mechanism for engaging audiences with an issue is to bring them along in the process through co-design. Although now common and broadly understood, this is still an evolving field of practice that can take many forms, from facilitated workshops and round-table discussions that encourage open debate, to tailored exercises that ensure every participant has an equal voice. Such was the case with the Cohousing for Ageing Well (CHAW) project, where the four single lot design studies of Chapter 10 were first developed.[1] The project aimed to test the types of lots that could accommodate the bluefield model across four local council areas for which the model was a good demographic fit for people wishing to age within their community. A formative co-design workshop served as a collaboration tool with existing residents and council staff to gain two key understandings that would inform the project: resident attitudes to this new form of co-located neighbourhood infill (both positive and negative), and what programmatic and spatial aspects were important to achieve in the home if residents were to downsize into the bluefield model. With a mix of audience members, from residents with strong local knowledge and experience but no understanding of the design and zoning process, to council staff responsible for the delivery of community services and zoning laws, it was important to develop a co-design process where each participant had an equal voice. This is vital when working with large groups where the loudest voices in the room can discourage other participants from speaking up, thereby skewing the information being gathered. For CHAW, a tailored co-design process was designed and facilitated at the University of South Australia by Aaron Davis, a specialist in community engagement processes as they relate to design.

Participants were presented with two draft designs to illustrate to residents how a cohousing arrangement in the bluefield model might be created for 'small' and 'extra-large' sites. These were pinned to walls in large format, allowing multiple people to stand around the designs and talk together. The same designs were also provided in a smaller format on tables, where those who wished to study them privately could do so. Rather than confirming a preconceived hypothesis, the workshop sought the 'lived experiences' of participants, regardless of their level of interest in living in a cohousing development themselves. As such, residents were tasked with individually identifying the degrees of sharing they could imagine living with, and those that would be barriers or outright 'deal breakers'. This enabled those who were very open to shared living and those who were not to share their knowledge of how the cohousing model could be

Housing for whom? Lessons from the Town Hall floor

made to work. Importantly, the workshop was designed such that every participant was able to record their own experiences and their individual responses. This enabled information to be gathered from all participants equally, thereby avoiding the feedback being biased by the most vocal participants.

A true co-design process is not a 'design-by-committee' approach; depending on the nature of the project and the stage at which co-design is undertaken, there is still a role for the designer to facilitate the process using their disciplinary experience and expertise. The CHAW co-design workshop began with a presentation of the preliminary designs for the two example sites, to show how a cohousing development on a single lot might function and be arranged, and to demonstrate that the model required a potentially substantial downsizing from the type of dwelling in which the participants might currently be living. Exercises for the participants were designed in two parts, the first being a spatial budgeting process.

The typical elements of a house (large bedroom, small bedroom, laundry, kitchen, etc) and its garden (large shed, small shed, small garden, large garden, etc) were provided as cut-out blocks, all to scale and categorised in different colours to enable easy identification. Each had a simple label such as 'large lounge, 20m^2 (215 sq ft)'. A base sheet was provided at the same scale, on which the participants could arrange their spatial pieces. This was arranged in 5m^2 (55 sq ft) increments to make it easy to see how much of the spatial budget remained. Spaces were split into private and shared and were coloured grey for built elements and white for garden elements. Space was provided on the

20.1
The spatial budget kit created for the Cohousing for Ageing Well co-design workshop by Aaron Davis.

base sheet for the participants to provide basic demographic information (if they wished) of the council area they lived in, the nature of their existing house, and the makeup of their household (Figure 20.1).

The base sheet allowed 50m^2 (540 sq ft) for a private dwelling, 20m^2 (215 sq ft) for private outdoor space, and another 50m^2 for shared indoor facilities. These budgeted sizes were determined from the two preliminary designs, which suggested that a backyard home of around 50m^2 and a common house of 50 to 70m^2 (540 to 750 sq ft) was likely to provide a good balance when attempting to maximise the number of additional houses created while still maintaining a garden setting compatible with existing neighbourhood conditions and enhanced urban tree canopies.

Exceeding the spatial budgets was not permitted. With more choice in the functional cut-outs than space allowed for their allocation, the exercise challenged participants to prioritise their dwelling inclusions and exclusions, as they imagined downsizing to a much smaller housing footprint. Furthermore, the exercise enabled participants to consider which elements they felt they could

20.2
The spatial budgeting exercise in the Cohousing for Ageing Well co-design workshop, undertaken by residents and council staff as an individual task. The kit contains a base sheet.

forego in their private dwellings by locating them in the shared facilities of a common house (Figure 20.2). Being an individual exercise there was no wright nor wrong approach, and no compromises to be made with other participants. This generated distinctive and genuine responses.

In the second exercise, split into three worksheets, participants reflected on and described the elements of a common house they would be happy to share and not share (and the reasons why), the people they would be happy or unhappy to share with, and the things that would help them feel more comfortable about sharing facilities. The observations from this exercise, which allowed for both private and honest reflection and for shared discussion amongst the group, are described in the Introduction and in Chapter 7. What results from a co-design process such as this is meaningful and considered data unencumbered by feelings of self-consciousness from the participants. It allows the information to be gathered and reviewed so that it can then inform the project with genuine impact, with the result being anonymised housing scenarios that are nonetheless founded in real stories.

Lessons from the Town Hall floor

Presenting the bluefield housing model to various groups over several years, including to lay and professional audiences of residents, practitioners, and decision-makers, has revealed a common trait, regardless of the audience profile: people accept the underlying premise and social promise of the model much more clearly and openly when they can imagine its potential residents. And these imagined residents do not have to be directly relatable. Often, the best discussions of the potential for new neighbourhood housing comes when participants become engaged in the conversation to the point where they offer their own imagined scenarios under which they can see the scheme being of value to others. It has not been uncommon for people with initial reservations about the co-location aspect of bluefield housing to arrive at a point where they come full circle in their resistance, sharing their own familial or friendship scenarios for which the model might work well.

What follows – in no particular order – are some of the lessons learned from taking the bluefield model through various community, government, and industry consultations. The visual collateral of a planning and design presentation, such as those in this book, will never be enough to convince an audience of a housing scheme's merits on their own. They must be supported by a coherent and compelling argument that is clear in its narrative and conviction, but open to challenge and betterment. These observations are no more clever than they are exhaustive or innovative, but are offered as common-sense approaches that can defuse potentially tense discussions while demonstrating an openness to ideas:

- Go into every presentation anticipating that you will learn something new about your work, including how to present it better.

Housing for whom? Lessons from the Town Hall floor

- Tailor what you say to your audience and avoid jargon wherever possible.
- Similarly, tailor what you show. Different people have different visual literacies and drawings that are clear to you may not be clear to others, even when they are professionals within industry or government. Be prepared to rework your visual collateral based on how it was received in a presentation.
- When presenting to industry professionals or policy makers, consider that they too are likely to be working for positive change; you are not their hero but a colleague working towards shared goals.
- When presenting to lay audiences, never make a resident feel bad for living in a single-family home, or for living alone in a large home, or for having extra bedrooms that are not being actively used. Demonising the single-family home demonises its residents. It is insensitive and insulting, and unlikely to ever bring an audience closer to your way of thinking.
- Understand that so-called NIMBYs probably know their neighbourhoods better than you. Give them this respect and let them see that you know and appreciate this.
- At the same time, know your history. Be sure to understand how the neighbourhood came to be and how it is formed now. Starting a presentation or discussion with a summary of your understanding of the place demonstrates to your audience that you are invested in making a positive contribution to it and that the work you are about to show comes from an intelligent and empathetic base.
- Understand the types of poor development that have already occurred in the neighbourhood and acknowledge that residents often have the right to be suspicious of new forms of housing if poor outcomes are all they know. Afterall, the likely reason you are attempting an alternative solution is because you agree with them that there may be a better way. Be prepared to describe and demonstrate why your scheme is not one of the poor schemes with which they may be familiar.
- Understand the types of good development that may not be evident to residents and use these as positive case studies. Where possible, demonstrate that your scheme shares similar traits with those projects and is not without precedent.
- If arguing that neighbourhood change should be allowed to occur with your proposal, ensure you are able to describe the types of change that have already occurred over the life of the place. Chapters 3 and 4 offer clues to the types of thinking that can be applied here when giving a neighbourhood 'permission' to change.
- In presenting historical neighbourhood change, avoid weaponising it. Strip it of emotion and accusation and discuss it neutrally as an evolving neighbourhood continuum.
- Listen before responding. While you may have worked on your scheme for many months or even years, and presented it multiple times to various stakeholders, the audience is seeing it for the first time and in a summarised form. They will inevitably raise questions or concerns that you have already

addressed and resolved. In these situations, it can be tempting to talk over the questioner in your eagerness to resolve the issue. Have patience and respect and be open to even familiar questions and comments adding a new layer of thinking and nuance you have not heard before.

- The more advanced and resolved a scheme is, the more difficult it can be to perceive it changing or being improved. However, be open to ideas and interpretations that you will not have considered. Communication in presentations should be a two-way street and often the best feedback will come from people who are seeing your long-held ideas for the first time. They are responding intuitively to your work and potentially identifying problematic aspects or positive opportunities that are not apparent to you.

- The more you present your work the more you will be able to pre-empt and prepare for audiences' questions and comments. You should therefore hold cards up your sleeve, as not every convincing argument will make it into your presentation. If running a visual presentation, have additional supporting slides located after your final slide and come to these during discussions if necessary. It will give you confidence that you have your full range of material should you need it, while demonstrating to your audience during discussions that you are across a broad range of issues.

- Sometimes discussions turn confrontational, with audience suspicions coming to light. If you do not stand to make a real or even perceived financial or other gain from your proposal, explain your neutrality when necessary: tell your audience why you are doing what you are doing. This is made easier for academics and other housing proponents with no vested interest in the housing outcomes, by explaining that the work is centred on creating a common good rather than a tangible personal gain.

- Maintain your composure. This can be difficult when it feels like the audience is turning on your ideas. If this happens remember that any audience is likely to be a mix of interested and not-so-interested parties, but there is probably at least one person there who will champion your idea, even if they do not speak up at the time. It is not uncommon for open discussion to be negative while private discussions after the presentation are positive.

- If you feel the audience has misunderstood your proposal this is probably your fault; review the presentation to better understand what will be required next time. It may be one drawing, one statistic, or one statement that better explains or clarifies your intentions.

- If challenged with the question of "Why don't you do this sort of thing somewhere else?", respectfully push back on this. Where is this other place? How do we decide which neighbourhoods need to be told to accommodate our necessary additional housing? And how do we solve the issue of housing choice in the suburbs we decide will be immune from change?

- Bring the issues back to the residents in a relatable but non-threatening way: if their neighbourhoods are gentrifying, where will their children be housed? If they themselves are reaching an age where they are thinking about their own housing futures and homes that might be a better fit, do they have alternative housing choices within their community? If they live alone and would like to strengthen their community network, might denser and more socially connected housing be an option? And if not for them, what about for the people they know and love? People can soften or even reverse their opposition to new housing when they can imagine themselves, their family, or friends benefitting from the scenario, even if it is not in the foreseeable future.

- At various stages of a proposal's life important decision makers or gatekeepers will be brought into a discussion that can affect its progress, either negatively or positively. These people may have a narrow but significant focus on the project relative to their area of expertise and their sphere of influence. Examples are planning law, finance, and land titling. They are likely to inherently relate your proposal to their business-as-usual understandings to see if it can fit existing structures. As a result, with good intention they can ask a deceptively simple question to cut through the mass of project material and get to the crux of what they can do to help: "I'm trying to understand what you're trying to achieve here – can you explain it to me?". Always be prepared to precis your body of work in the moment and in only one minute. This will give you around 150 words – choose them wisely and have a single image on hand that can do much of the heavy lifting.

Ultimately, the alternative housing advocate's best argument will be one that demonstrates that neighbourhood change is not being introduced with the new proposal in question – it has been occurring for generations. Respectfully ask your audience the following rhetorical question: how much of your neighbourhood would be recognised by the original residents if they could be brought here today? The older the neighbourhood, the more set in its ways it may be, but the more change it will have not just endured but allowed and encouraged. Ask your audience at which point in history we should draw the developmental line in the sand, as discussed in Chapter 3. Do we take away the cars, carports, and garages and reinstate horses and stables? Do we remove bathroom extensions and relocate toilets back outside? Do we remove all additions to the base house, reverse the modern open plan, and reinstate the home to first principles?

In posing these questions we respectfully ask our audiences to consider which changes to their own housing they would never want to lose. Where an audience becomes oppositional, these questions must be posed without accusation. It may be tempting to label NIMBY arguments as hypocritical, but in many cases the neighbourhood change that has delivered residents improved lifestyle and amenity has happened so gradually that it cannot be easily identified by its beneficiaries. If this point can be made and understood, we are then positioned to state that change has been occurring for generations and the one guarantee of suburbia is that it will continue to change. To suggest, then, that a neighbourhood should be locked in time in this year's version of it, is to do a disservice to its original inhabitants and to those who will come after us. A healthier approach is to therefore recognise that neighbourhoods exist on a continuum and that change can be managed by providing the housing we need with an empathetic and carefully considered approach to neighbourhood fit.

In advocating for new places on that housing continuum, be dogged, but understand that housing change requires kindness coupled with patience. It is a long game and one to be played intelligently, respectfully, and with compassion for those already in the neighbourhood and for those who hope to be.

Note

1 Damian Madigan, *Cohousing for Ageing Well: Design Report*, University of South Australia (Adelaide, 2020).

Index

Note: Endnotes are indicated by the page number followed by "n" and the note number e.g., 12n3 refers to note 3 on page 12. Entries in *italics* denote figures.

access and mobility 118–21, *120*, 124, 148, 153, 220–1, 260–1
accessory dwelling units (ADUs) *see* backyard homes
Additional Dwelling Units (ADU) Ordinance, Chicago 39, 41n24
Adelaide, South Australia xiii, 46, 52–3, *84*, 85, 248, 252n2, 276, 293
aesthetics xiv, 47–9, 51, 56, 60, 68, 78, 92, 95, 98, 134, 269–70, 272, 274, 292
affordability 4–5, 12n2, 12n5, 18, 20, 22–6, 29, 30–1, 35, 37–8, 40, 47–8, 82–3, 87, 89, 91, 98, 101–2, 117–18, 143–4, 148, 211–12, 216n4, 219, 222–3, 225, 228, 233–4, 301
ageing: design for 10, 118–19, 282; in place 9, 38; population 9, 21, *22*, 143
agency 11, 19, 62, 104, 242, 247
age value 49–50, 67
agreements: family 241; resident 11, 125, 166, 169n4, 235, 241–4
Aires Mateus and Associates 278, *279*, *283*
alterations, additions and renovations 4–5, 7–8, 12n3, 20, *21*, 39, *48*, 49–50, *52*, 55, 60, *61*, 62–77, 88–9, 91, 95–7, 117, 121, 125–6, 136–9, 143, 212, 222, 224, 228–33, *230*, 248, 265, 269, 289–91, 297, 308
anticipatory design *see* staged development
apartments xiii, 1–2, 5, 24, 42–4, 47, 85, 113, 119, 165, 172–3, 190, 192, 225, 233, 263, 266, 276–85
attics 39, 61, 124, *125*, 139

Bachmann, Theo 52–6
backyard homes: accessory dwelling unit (ADU) xv, *xvi*, 1, 4, 6–7, 12n3, 31–2, 37–9, 73, 97–8, 105, 214, 222–3, 231–2, 246; carriage house 37, 39; coach house 6, 37, 300; Fonzie flat 37; garden suite 37; granny flat 37, 97, 214, 216n3; in-law apartment 37, 97; junior accessory dwelling unit (JADU) *xvi*, 97, 214, 246; laneway housing xv, 1, 37–9, 140, 143, *198–200*, *202*, *204*, *206*, 207, *208*, 246; mews house 6, 207, 300; secondary suites xv, *xvi*, 1, 38, 47, 62, 97, 139, 214, 221, 245–6; tiny house movement 214, 216n4
banks *see* lenders
basements 39, 44, 61–2, 73, 129n8, 139, 173
bathrooms 3, 22, 61, 65–6, 70, 77, 97, 102, 112, 117, 119–21, *119–20*, 124–5, 135, *180*, 183, 231, 239, 261, 266, 278, 286, 291, 308
battle-axe development *94*
bedroom numbers 4, 22, 118, 101–2, 117–18, 135, 140, 144, 169n3, 222, 249
Bennett, Alysia 28n22, 220
bicycles *see* cycling
bluefield housing: and affordability *see* affordability; and other housing definitions iii, 8–9, 11, 12n1, 89, 246–7; borrowing for 232–4; design exercise 1: Stuff 258–62; design exercise 2: Porous Rooms 60, 70, 125, 262–7, 271, 274, 276, 280–1, 286; design exercise 3:

310

Index

Grid Block 271–9, 286–7; design
exercise 4: Block Apartment 266,
276–87; design exercise 5: Seven
Design Tactics 287–92, 295, 297–8;
design exercise 6: Algebraic Siting
Strategies 287, 292–99; existing
uses of the term 8–10; incentivising
12, 93, 96, 138, 217–27; land titling
for 12, 233–7, 247, 274, 308; patrons
of 228–32; seven principles of
91–102, 218, 221; zoning rules for
169n2, 169n5, 218–21, 245–50
blue rinse 9, 90n11
blue spaces 9, 13n7, 90n11
blue zones 9
Borneo-Sporenburg housing 278
boundaries see land assembly and land
division
Boyd, Robin 62–3
Brand, Stewart 258–9
brownfield iii, 8–9, 11, 42, 85–9, 246
building codes 120, 142
building footprint 117, 134, *174*, 191,
205, 212, 249, 272
built form 2, 97, 212, 249
building height xiii, 134, 248–9, 257
bungalows 47, 60–1, 63–4, 138, 222–3,
262, 276
by-laws 234–5, 241

California Housing Finance Agency's
(CalHFA) 223
California 100 initiative 211
car parking 3, 33, 42–4, 57, 77, 100,
104–7, *107*, 112, 128, 129n10,
134–5, 137, 140–1, 148, 169n5, 215,
219, 235–6, 248–50, 301
carriage house see backyard homes
carriage lanes see driveways
case study approach 133–4, 137, *222*,
255, 277–9
ceilings 122, 124–5, *126*, 139, 266, 280
Certificate of Title see titling
Chapin, Ross 34
character and heritage iii, xiii, xv, *xvi*, 5,
11–12, 20–1, 24, 40, 43, 47–60, 62,
66–7, 73, 76–8, 86, 88–89, 91–2,
95–7, 117, 138–9, 212, 214, 216,
218, 220, 224, 249–50, 263, 266,
270–1, 275, 280, 295, 300
Chicago Bungalow Association 60–1,
222–3
circulation 24, *119, 121*, 123, 260–1,
263, 286
cityLAB, UCLA 7, 37–8, 222, 232
City of Sydney Alternative Housing
Ideas Challenge 25
climate change 101–2, 126–8, *129*
clotheslines see laundry
coach house see backyard homes

co-design 10, 108–9, 302–5
cohousing 3, 11, 33–7, 93, 110, *188*,
190–1, 214, 242, 247, 302–3
cohousing 'lite' 34, 247
Cohousing for Ageing Well project 10,
108, 302, *303–4*
co-located housing iii, 3, 12n1, 92, 94,
104, 114, 144, 223, 234, 246,
249–52, 302
commercial and mixed-use 42, 65, 66,
85–6, 135, 144, 225, 226, 292, 297–8
Commonly Accepted Anomalies 59,
62–77, 89, 136, 282
communes see sharing
Community Housing Fund (UK) 33
community housing providers (CHP) 4,
9, 35–6, 92, 144, 160, 221, 226, 230,
241–2, 244
companion animals see pets
construction spending 83, 225, 230–2
construction types 139
contracts see agreements
corridors see hallways
cottage xiii, 20, 62–5, *63*, 67, *68*, 136–9,
262–3, *266*, 276, 279–80, 293
courtyard housing *2*, 30, 35
COVID-19 pandemic 20, 26, 30, 83,
144, 230
Cox, Philip 63
Cross, Nigel 270
cross-over apartments 173, 279, 282,
285n6
cross-overs 106, 250
Cuff, Dana 11, 28n22, 232–3
culs-de-sac 82
cultural memory 5, 49–50, *96*, 266;
see also nostalgia
cycling 75, 85

Davis, Aaron 302, *303*
dead-ends see culs-de-sac
deemed-to-satisfy (DTS) approval
processes 217–18, 248
deliberative development 33, *35*, 230;
see also intentional communities
Deicke Richards Architects 36
demolition 20, 50, *52*, 63, 95, 101, 127,
217–18, 230–1, *237*
density: definition and calculation
xiv-xv, 27n12, 135, 141, 197; gentle,
hidden, and invisible density 47;
increases xvi, 1–2, 6, 12, 24, 27,
47, 51, 58, 91, 96, 113–14, 118,
138, 197, 207, 212, 245, 255, 298;
population density *84*, 112
Density and Diversity Done Well
Competition, Brisbane 25
Design Guide for Older Women's
Housing, Schored Projects and
Monash University, 222

311

Index

Design Review 250–1, 252n3
design thinking and methods xiii-xiv, 69, 118, 134–42, 251, 255, 262
design toolkits 221–2
Designing With Downsizers project, Sheffield University 34–5
development scorecards 127, 220–1
diagramming 12, 68–9, 77, 216, 222, 255–62, 270–2, 275–7, 293, 295
Di Mari, Anthony 68
divorce *see* grey divorce
DIY (do-it-yourself) 20, 62, 231
downsizing 9–10, 22, 34, 89, 91–2, 123, 144, 165, 302–4
driveways and carriage lanes 45, 64–5, 71–2, 74, *75*, 112, 128, *129*, 135, 137, 182, 250, 293–4, 300
dual-key 65
duplexes *see* infill
Durrett, Charles 33
Dunham-Jones, Ellen 86

Ecoburbia 36–7, 230
EcoDensity initiative, Vancouver 38
Edmonton Infill Design Competition 26
Edmonton Missing Middle Infill Design Competition 25–6
electric vehicles 128, *129*, 224
Elliott, Joseph 53–8
Expanding Housing Options in Neighbourhoods, Toronto 39
extensions *see* alterations and additions

family agreements *see* agreements
fencing *see* privacy
financial institutions *see* lenders
fire protection and fire doors 122, 142, 153, 166, 183, 191, 220, 237, 240
flexibility iii, xv, 26, 53, 60, 121–3, 128, 129n2, 141, 153, 169n3, 182–3, 191, 197, 226, 238–40, 261, 279–80, 297–8
'flipping' houses *see* house flipping
Fonzie flat *see* backyard homes
footpaths *see* infrastructure
form-based codes 68–9
fossil fuels 126, 128, 129n9
Foster, Sheila 40
Fourflex housing proposition 220–1
furniture 52–3, *122*, 123, 256–7, 260–1

garbage *see* rubbish bins and waste
gardens *see* landscape
garden suite *see* backyard homes
gas (natural / liquid petroleum) *see* fossil fuels
ghostboxes 86
granny flats *see* backyard homes
grants 222–4

greenfield iii, 8–9, 11, 42, 81–3, *84*, 85, 88–9, 231, 246
green energy 128, *129*
greenhouse gas (GHG) emissions 126
greyfield iii, 8, 11, 13n6, 23, 42, 86–9, 246
greywater recycling *see* wastewater
grey divorce 32, 301
Groves-Raines, Nicholas 224
guest bedrooms 3, 33, 164, 166, 190, 306
Guterres, António 126

hallways and corridors 24, 125, *126*, 137–8, 258, 262–3, *264*, 276, *277*, 278, 281
Herd, Brian 241
heritage *see* character
heritage protections 66, 95, 138
High Line, New York 110, *111*, 282, *283*, 284
homelessness *see* precarious housing
Home of 2030, London 26
Holl, Steven 279, *283*
homeshare *see* sharing
house flipping 20, 225
household structure 5, 21, *22*, 26, 48, 77, 135, 183, 251, 297–8, 300
housing associations and providers *see* community housing providers (CHP)
housing grants *see* grants
Housing Industry Association (Australia) 231
housing as investment 19–20, 143, 225, 234
housing markets and real estate 4, 12, 20, 24, 30, 65, 82–3, 88, 217–18, 225, 228–30, 234

Iaione, Christian 40
Illinois Property Tax Assessment Freeze 224–5
incentivising *see* bluefield housing: incentivising
infill: duplexes xv, *2*, 5, 22, 25, 38, 45, 53, 87–8, 223, 245; fourplexes *2*, 26, 28n22, 220; housing yield xv, 20, 22–4, 35, 81–2, 93–4, 172, 219, 226, 228, 245–6; minor 1, 20, 27n12, 45, 88, 91, 112; triplexes *2*, 5, 88, 223
Infill Opportunities design research project, Monash University 106, 112, 134–5
informal housing and development 61–2, 218, 221
infrastructure: footpaths 81, 141, 272; fossil fuels 126; furniture and fittings, 260–1; green 81, 87, 216, 282; hard vs soft, 121–2, 240; public 17, 37, 82–3, 85, 110, *111*, 282, *283*, 284;

Index

recreational 81–3; roads 27n2, 42–3, 81–3, 141, 272; water catchment 218

in-law apartments *see* backyard homes

innovation 12, 25–6, 40, 92, 95, 134, 213–16

Innovation in Social Housing project, University of South Australia 123

intensification *see* infill

intentional communities 35–7; *see also* deliberative development

Intergovernmental Panel on Climate Change (IPCC) 102, 126

junior accessory dwelling units (JADUs) *see* backyard homes

Karakusevic, Paul 222

key-worker housing *see* suburbs: working-class

knock-down-rebuild development (KDR) iii, 6, 8, 20, *21*, 45, *46*, 86–9, *87*, 91, 95, 144, 212, 214, 218–9, 221, 225, 228–31

LA ADU Accelerator Program 31–2, 223

Lacaton and Vassal 102

LA Low-Rise Design Challenge xi, 26, 105, 220

land: assembly 26, 69, 105, 137, 143, 211–13, 223, 275–6; division iii, *xvi*, 26, 45–7, 87, 93–5, *108*, 137, 140, 169n2, 172, 214, 217–19, 224, 233–9, 247, 249, 251, 287; size *see* lot size; tax 83, 224–5; titling *see* titling; value 22, 85–6, 101–2, 225, 228–9, 243

landscape: architecture 104; deep root soil zones 3–4, 100, 110, 128, *129*, 233, 249–50, 252n2; gardens, vegetation, and private open space *xvi*, 18, 25, 34, 36–7, *48*, 54, *55*, 57, 59n13, 81–2, 88, 95, 99, *100*, 101, 104, 106–8, 110–15, *120–1*, 128, *129*, 139, *146*, *151*, *158*, *163*, 166, *188*, *198*, 212, 252, 303–4; loss of 20–1, 45–6, 50, 57, 87, 91, 100, 192, 205, 212, 220–1, 233, 235, 245–6, 248–9, 277–8, 284, 296–8; tree canopies and corridors iii, 21, *87*, 88, 91–2, 100, 110, 128, *129*, 207, 214, 218, 250, 252n2, 256–7, 279–80, *280*, 290, 304

Land Management Agreement (LMA) 235, 247, 252n1

laneways 39, 54, 106, *107*, 140, *165–8*, 189, *191–6*, *198–200*, *202*, *204*, *206*, *208*, 212, *236*, 246, 272–3

Lang, Peter 18

laundry: washing lines 11, 100, 104, 107, 109, 123, 219, 239; washing machines 11, 109, 261

lenders 213, 223–4, 232–4, 237

light and ventilation 24, 61, 69, 121–2, 124, 127, *129*, 220, 249, 259, 278–9, 285n6, 289, 291

lintels 61, 125, *126*, 265, 266, 280

Livable Housing Australia (LHA) Design Guide 119, *120*, 148, 260

London, Geoffrey, et al 112

Los Angeles ADU Accelerator Program 31–2, 223

Los Angeles Department of Building and Safety (LADBS) 39, 222

Los Angeles Mayor's Office 26

lot consolidation *see* land assembly

lot size xiv–xv, *xvi*, 3, 7, 39, 46, 81–2, 93–5, 97–8, 137, 142, 169n2, 219, 233, 248, 284, *293*

Luscombe, Guy 91

market housing *see* volume housing

Mateo Arquitectura 278–9, *279*, *283*

McCamant, Kathryn 33

McMansions 57

memories and memorabilia 123, *124*, 260, 280

microclimate 30, 218

missing middle housing iii, xv, 1, *2*, 24–6, 28n22, 39

mixed-use *see* commercial and mixed-use

Monash University 106, 112, 134–5, 222

mortgages 38, *84*, 101, 225–6, 232–3, 300–1; *see also* lenders

multigenerational living 10, 30–2, 34, 38, 92–3, 118, 183, 214, 241, 260, 302

multiplex *2*

Narara Ecovillage 35–6

National Construction Code (Australian) 119, 142

neoliberalism 222

newness value 20, 49–50, 58, 86

New South Wales Missing Middle Open Ideas Design Competition 25

Newton, Peter 86

New Urbanism 78

New York City Mayor's Office 129n9

Nicolai, Carsten 271

NIMBYism / YIMBYism xvi, 2, 6, 45–7, 58, 78, 89, 211–16, 252, 299, 301, 306, 308; *see also* QIMBYism

nostalgia 50–1, 56, 67, 86; *see also* cultural memory

Older Women's Housing Project 35

open space *see* landscape: gardens, vegetation, and private open space

Index

Opportunity Zones, US 225
Opticos Design *2*
overlooking *see* privacy

Parolek, Daniel 24; *see also* Opticos Design
passive design strategies 83, 100, 126–8, *129*, 221
performance-assessed (PA) approval processes 118, 220, 248
personas *see* scenario planning
pets 113–14, 235
photovoltaic (PV) cells and batteries 127–8, *129*
pocket neighbourhoods 33–5
podium bases 24
politics xiii, 2, 6, 8–9, 17–19, 45, 54, 88, 292
population density *see* density
precarious housing and homelessness 31
profit *see* housing markets
property tax *see* land: tax
property value 9, 19, 224–5, 234
privacy 25, 32, 34, 37, 46, 101, 105, 110–11, 114, *115*, 123, 160, 197, 263, 278: fencing 3, 34, 46, 64, 94, 106, 141, 233, 249; overlooking 134, 139, 141, 249; and zoning for 249
public transport 42–3, 82, 105–6, 160, 169n5, 218

QIMBYism 77–8, 89; *see also* NIMBYism / YIMBYism
quality 7, 26, 109, 117, 221, 235, 248, 250–1, 282, 284

race xiii, 6, 17, 20, 26, 45
rainwater tanks *see* water collection and tanks
ramps *see* access and mobility
real estate *see* housing markets
renovations *see* alterations, additions and renovations
renting *xvi*, 4, 6, 19–20, 30–2, 35, 37–9, 53, 58, 92, 101, 117–18, 136, 144, 154, 211, 223, 225–6, 228, 230, 233, 239, 242–3, 300–1
residents agreements *see* agreements
Riismandel, Kyle 45
Riegl, Aloïs 49–50
rubbish bins and waste 3, 44, 54, 82, 100, 104, 106–8, *106*, *109*, 123, 134, 140, 219, 235, 239, 257

scale 95, 97–8, 135, 138–9, 249
scenario planning and personification 12, 214, 301–2
Schneider, Tatjana 123

Schored Projects 222
scorecards *see* development scorecards
secondary suites *see* backyard homes
Sejima, Kazuyo 278, *279*, *283*
setbacks xiii, 5, 17, 24–5, 66, 69, *71–2*, 93–5, 97, 106, *107*, 134, 248–9, 272–3, *293*, 294
sharing *xvi*, 3–4, 9–11, 29–31, 92–3, 101, 107–9, 114–15, 142, 144, 229, 233, 241, 247, 301–2, 305; boarding houses 214; case studies 31–40; communes 33, 214; homeshare 31; share houses 32–3, 36, 214, 241; shared landscape xv, 7–8, 85, 98–100, 109, 112, *115*, 138, *206*, 207; shared living 31, 34–6, 242, 302
Sharing With Friends housing association 36, 242–3
sheds 34, 107–8, *109*, 138, 140, 257, 303
short-term rentals 39, 225–6
sidewalks *see* infrastructure: footpaths
single-family homes xii, xv, 1, *2*, 3–10, 18, 24, 26, *35*, 36, 38, 44, 46, 48, 52, 56–8, 83, 85, 88, 91–8, 105, 144, 218, 231–3, *236*, 237, *238*, 240, 245, 250, 252, 282, 301, 306
site coverage 3–4, 25, *44*, 45–7, 94–7, 134, 138, 212, 231, 248–9, 256
slack space 123, *124*, 260
Small Housing BC, Vancouver 222
speculative development 4, 19, 218, 229–30
staged development 95, *199*, 199–207, 238, *239–40*, 240
stamp duty *see* land: tax
standard plans 39, 99, 221–2, 229, 263
streetscape 3, 5, 12, 44, 88, 95–6, 160, 190, 212, 249–50, 280, 288
StopThePop campaign, Chicago 60
storage xiv, 54, 61, 100, 107–8, 117, 122–5, *123*, *125*, 219, 261, 263, 266, 278
storeys 248–9
Studio Bright 35
subdivision *see* land division
Suburban Operations 68–77, 89, 125, 287
suburbs: middle-class 17, 19, 228; working-class and key worker 17–18, 54, 220
Superbonus 110% tax credit scheme, Italy 224
sustainability: environmental 6, 23, 26, 37–8, 43, 86–7, 95, 98, 100–2, 105, 121, 125–8, *129*, 129n8, 217–18, 220–1, 224; financial 6, 12n5, 24, 26, 29, 32, 37–8, 40, 95, 101–2, 126, 148, 207, 226, 236–8, 302; social 6,

Index

10, 12n5, 24, 26–7, 30, 35, 37–8, 40,
92–3, 98–9, *100*, 101–2, 128, 133–4,
148, *151*, 220, 230, 235–8, 247, 249,
270, 299, 302, 305

taxation incentives 224–5
terrace houses 25, 62, 137
third places 86
Till, Jeremy 58, 123
tiny house movement *see* backyard
homes
titling: community title 233–6, 241, 247;
company title 234; moiety title 234,
244n10; strata title 233–4
topography xiv, 276, 287
townhouses *2*, 5, 85, 119, 279, 282
traffic 82, 218, 272, 301
transit oriented developments (TODs)
and transit corridor developments
42–4
trash *see* rubbish bins and waste
trees *see* landscape
triplexes *see* infill: triplexes

UCLA cityLAB 7, 37–8, 222, 232–3
unit developments 2, 33–4, 45, 113,
160, 233
University of South Australia 287, *296*,
299, 302
urban heat island effect (UHI) 21, 23, 87,
111–12, 214, 216, 250

value *see* land: value; *see also* property
value
VAMPIRE Index 83, *84*, 257
vegetation *see* landscape
ventilation *see* light and ventilation
Victoria, British Columbia xv

Victorian-era housing 47, *51–2*, 53, 56,
58, 62, *63*, 137
villa *51–2*, *63*, 294
volume housing and market housing 4,
19, 83, 119, 228

washing lines *see* laundry
Washington State House Bill 1660 39
wastewater 36, 112
water collection and tanks 36, 54, *55*,
111–12, 127–8, *129*
water loss 21, *87*, 111, 216
water-sensitive design 36, 111–13, *120*,
121, 128, 250
water table and ground water 21, 62,
85–6, 110, 218
West 8 278
Williamson, June 86
Women's Property Initiatives (WPI) 35
working-from-home *2*, 114, 239
Written Family Agreements *see* resident
agreements

yards 4, 6, 20–1, 26, 29, 34, 36–7, 45,
54, *55*, 56–7, 59n11, 65, 73–6, 81,
93, 99, 113, 141, 288, *289*, 291–2,
297
yield *see* infill
YIMBYism *see* NIMBYism
Yoo, Nora 68

zoning 3, 6–8, 12, 25, 36, 38–9, 43–4, 48,
61–2, 66, 68, 83, 94–7, 111, 118, 127,
134–6, 140–1, 169n2, 169n5, 217–22,
227–8, 233, 245–7, 269, 291, 302;
for bluefield housing 248–51; single-
family zoning 5, 18, 58, 83, 88;
see also form-based codes